Program Planning and Evaluation for the Public Manager

Fourth Edition

Ronald D. Sylvia
Emeritus, San Jose State University

Kathleen M. Sylvia
Sober Living by the Sea

WAVELAND

PRESS, INC.

Long Grove, Illinois

For information about this book, contact:
Waveland Press, Inc.
4180 IL Route 83, Suite 101
Long Grove, IL 60047-9580
(847) 634-0081
info@waveland.com
www.waveland.com

10-digit ISBN 1-57766-778-6
13-digit ISBN 978-1-57766-778-0

Printed in the United States of America

7   6   5   4   3   2   1

Contents

PART TWO
Process Evaluation: The "Other" Approach   73

---

four   **Standards-Based Evaluation:**
Matching Operations to Expectations   75

five   **Monitoring and Improving Internal Processes   91**

PART THREE
Measuring Organization Outcomes   113

---

six   **Conducting an Outcome Evaluation   115**

About
the Authors

Ronald D. Sylvia, PhD, is Professor Emeritus of Political Science at San Jose State University. He previously taught at the University of Oklahoma and Old Dominion University in Virginia. He has been an active consultant to governments at all levels. His other books address human resources management in government and leadership through the ages.

Kathleen M. Sylvia, MPA, RN, is Executive Director of Sober Living by the Sea, a leading behavioral health provider located in Newport Beach, California. She has more than 35 years of managerial and executive experience in both the public and private sectors.

Preface

Thirty years ago, when the first edition of this text was written, program evaluation was only just emerging from the shadow of classes in social science research methods. Evaluation methodologies were by-and-large statistically based, and evaluations that were worth doing measured only outcomes. Scientific rigor was the order of the day. Today, program evaluation is taught separately from research methods in most MPA programs. Process (how programs are organized and how work is conducted) is as important as outcomes in determining program appropriateness and effectiveness. Program evaluation has evolved from a method for showing others that program contributions are worthwhile to being an integral part of program management and adaptation.

Furthermore, the fields of health care, social services, education, and law enforcement have established their own standards against which program operations are to be assessed. National accrediting bodies have established systems of rigorous peer review to ensure the quality of program processes and outcomes. These standards, moreover, prescribe both process- and outcome-based methodologies that agencies must undertake to sustain accreditation.

Program evaluation, by extension, has moved from the status of applied research methodology to being an indispensable component of program operations. Agencies often have full-blown offices of evaluation. Even very small agencies have quality assurance committees that meet regularly to ascertain whether program operations comply with professional standards regarding process as well as outcomes.

Ironically, the substance of disciplinary-based evaluations has come full circle as accrediting agencies, particularly those in education, are insisting that program managers demonstrate that they have carefully thought through their mission, have allocated resources appropriately, and that their programs are achieving their intended outcomes. Thus, programs in higher education with the stated goal of imparting the skills of critical thinking and the ability to communicate effectively orally and in writing must be prepared to demonstrate how they impart such knowledge (a process standard); and they are asked to devise measures for determining that their graduates can, in fact, think critically and communicate effectively (outcome standards). In a phrase, agencies are judged on how well they perform the missions they set for themselves.

Another phenomenon that has emerged over the last two decades is the increased use of *nongovernmental organizations* (NGOs) to carry out programs that governments deem worthwhile. These are for the most part not-for-profit charitable organizations that must demonstrate worthwhile ends consistent with the wishes of funding agencies. Furthermore, they must demonstrate success in achieving their stated goals to sustain or expand program funding. (Others are for-profit contractors that are not treated here.)

This book is divided into three highly interdependent sections. Part I treats systems theory and program planning, with an emphasis on organizing to achieve agreed-upon goals. The synthesis of systems and planning is illustrated through the devices of program and project planning and queuing theory. Part II emphasizes organization processes, beginning with standards-based program accreditation. We then illustrate how process intervention is utilized to achieve program adaptations and strategic change. In Part III we consider measuring program outcomes in terms of intended and unintended impacts. Finally, we take up cost-benefit analysis. In this era of shrinking resources, appropriate and efficient utilization of public resources is still the primary concern of legislative bodies. Being a good steward of the public purse, moreover, is an integral part of executive leadership.

Like the first three editions, the fourth edition of this text utilizes concrete case studies to immerse students in the techniques of program evaluation. Many of the original cases have been retained, and several new ones have been added. We have also integrated case materials by developing outcome evaluation exercises based on the materials covered in the planning and process chapters. We have tested this approach in our own classes and find that students more readily can develop indicators and measures when dealing with familiar program materials.

part ONE

Frameworks for Organization Analysis

As our starting point we take the assumption that one needs a framework for examining organizations that is compatible with program evaluation. Experience has taught us that organization charts and communications diagrams are excellent for describing organization structures and for fixing responsibility. They are less useful for tracking how the work is accomplished and are least applicable to assessing organization outcomes. In Part I, therefore, we focus on three fundamentals: systems theory, the theory of planning, and the synthesis of the two in program planning and design.

Chapter 1 introduces the concepts of systems theory upon which the foundation of this book rests. Systems theory examines the organization holistically—that is, all aspects of the operation are considered to be interdependent. One cannot, therefore, affect change in one division without impacting the others. One advantage of systems theory is that it allows us to examine organization outcomes in terms of the inputs that set the system in motion and the internal mechanisms whereby the system operates.

Chapter 2 provides a theoretical discussion of planning. The discussion then turns to the application of planning theory, using an example from the private for-profit sector and one from the public sector. The chapter then presents the various levels of planning, from national economic planning to project organization and design. The chapter concludes with a series of pitfalls and caveats that program planners must heed in order to be successful.

Chapter 3 combines systems concepts and planning into a practical tool for program managers to use in designing their programs and getting

1

them authorized and funded. The chapter introduces the reader to Program Evaluation and Review Technique (PERT), which is a project-planning device imminently suited to designing everything from construction projects to welfare programs. The discussion then turns to project calendars or Gantt charts. Project calendars utilize the same theoretical framework as PERT but are much easier to apply. A project calendar used to obtain funding for an anti-sex-trafficking program in Vietnam illustrates the application.

The chapter concludes with a discussion of queuing theory, a device for diagramming the flow of work through the organization. Queuing theory seeks to understand the flow and sequencing of work through the organization. By identifying crucial steps and decision points, it allows the analyst/decision maker to see how things are done and to make adaptations necessary to improve efficiency.

chapter one

Systems Concepts

Both program planning and program evaluation are heavily influenced by systems theory. Systems theory is a conceptual framework for ordering one's thoughts about an organization or project. The terms *systems approach* and *systems analysis* refer to the applications of systems theory and its accompanying quantitative techniques.[1] A closely related useful framework is **structural functionalism**.[2] This theoretical framework for making cross-cultural/organization comparisons uses two elements of organizations. The first element is *structures*, defined as an established pattern of interaction over time. Some structural examples are hierarchies, social classes, and departmentalization. The second element is *functions*, which are critical organizational activities such as rule making and adjudication, production, and adaptation. In other words, the paradigm of structural functionalism allows the investigator to inquire as to how different organizations interact to perform activities vital to their missions. Systems theory goes even further and offers three distinguishing advantages to program evaluators. First, the systems approach strongly stresses the environment of a program. Second, it permits an analyst to describe the interactions between a program and its environment. Third, and perhaps most importantly, it can be used to analyze internal organization processes and their interactive nature.

This chapter introduces the concepts and general philosophy of systems theory. It provides an introduction to many terms that will be used throughout this book. The chapter begins with a discussion of systems environments and the elements that influence the processes of the organization. Then a description of a basic systems model is presented, including the concepts of goals, inputs, outputs, feedback loops, and the conversion process whereby inputs are transformed into policies and programs. The

3

macro-functions of organizations and the need for functionally specific subsystems are discussed next. The interface of organizations' environments and subsystems then are illustrated with an example from the field of education. The chapter concludes with an executive checklist that summarizes the advantages that a systems framework can provide an organization.

The Systems Model

A simple model (illustrated in figure 1.1) shows the basic elements of a system. A threshold assumption of systems theory is that the system under analysis can be usefully differentiated from its environment. Analysts illustrate the system under study with a solid-line rectangular box. A system may have **subsystems** and may actually be a subsystem of a larger **suprasystem**, as illustrated by the series of boxes in figure 1.1. For example, the system under study might be the college of social sciences at a university; it is represented by the solid line in the figure. The outer box represents the university suprasystem and is depicted with a broken line. The various department subsystems within the college (sociology, psychology, economics, and so forth) also are represented with broken lines.

Figure 1.1   Simple Systems Model

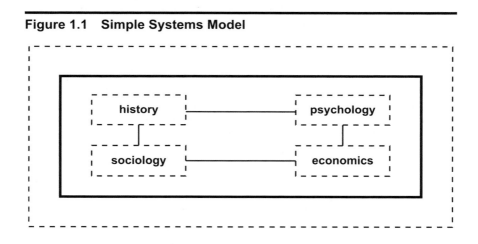

Holism

Systems theory begins with the premise that the system is made up of interdependent subsystems that cannot be acted upon independently without affecting the other subsystems and the organization as a whole. If, for instance, a professor of political science sexually harasses a student, it could result in a legal action that impacts the university as well as the college. Conceivably, a judgment against the university for failing to adequately protect the student could impact the college's abilities to recruit new students and provide classes, and it could also impact the morale of students and faculty.

The San Francisco Bay Area, for another example, can be considered as a complex urban socioeconomic system. When the Loma Prieta earthquake caused a section of the Bay Bridge to collapse, it impacted the total transportation system of the area. It caused traffic jams on various other freeways, traffic backups on surface streets, and overloads of the Bay Area's rapid transit. Slowdowns in the transportation system, moreover, impacted the commerce system as well, because commuters had farther to travel to work, supplies had to be rerouted, and so forth. Governmental systems—local and state law enforcement agencies—also were impacted. Decision-making systems, from local city councils to Congress, were forced into action by the impact of the event in the transportation subsystem.

More recently, the failure of an oil-drilling platform subsystem (the blowout prevention system), combined with some corner-cutting decisions on the part of management, resulted in an explosion and fire that killed eleven people and caused the loss of a multi-million-dollar drilling rig in the near term. In the aftermath the well continued to gush oil into the waters of the Gulf of Mexico for weeks thereafter. The incident triggered a massive containment effort that activated government emergency response systems, principally the US Coast Guard. Other government agencies that became involved included the Environmental Protection Agency, the Department of the Interior, and the US Justice Department— to say nothing of the response of local and state governments and the thousands of private-sector contractors involved with containing the spill.

The suprasystem impacts of the spill immediately imperiled long- and short-term energy policy through the imposition of a ban on additional deep-water drilling while the policy was reviewed for environmental impacts. The spill underwent intense scrutiny from the electronic media with a 24/7 news cycle to fill. Frustrated by the reluctance of British Petroleum (BP) to "enter the docks" of the court of public opinion to answer charges against it, the media offered a forum for every outraged citizen of the Gulf and any political pundit willing to condemn the adequacy of the company's or the government's response. Politically, the Obama administration could not afford to appear indifferent to the suffering of Gulf Coast inhabitants, whether animal or human. It responded by pressuring BP to establish a $20 billion escrow fund to pay current and future claims, even though at the time federal law limited damages in spills to $73 million.[3]

Systems Environments

Systems are in a constant state of interaction with their environments. At a general level, all systems are impacted by the laws, philosophy/culture, and economic conditions of the societies in which they exist. At a more specific level this includes the suprasystems of which the systems are a part, as well as other organizations and social institutions.

Laws

Laws, both in the general sense of all laws and in the specific sense of the laws that authorize a public program, affect program operations. The criminal justice planner, for example, cannot solve the problem of over-crowded prisons simply by executing every fourth prisoner. At times, federal judges have forced lawmakers to choose between releasing a certain percentage of prisoners and building more prisons. The seemingly simple decision to reduce prison overcrowding may set in motion a flurry of activities in various subsystems, like local sheriffs' departments that must house prisoners with relatively short sentences rather than sending them to state prisons. Prison officials and parole boards must develop criteria for early release to minimize the potential threat to society of unrehabilitated criminals.

General laws act as a constraint on evaluation. A program evaluator examining a vocational rehabilitation program, for example, must consider the federal funding criterion requiring that individuals with severe disabilities must constitute half of the people being treated. For rehabilitation programs, the specific law provides both program opportunities and program constraints.

At a more general level, the 1990 Americans with Disabilities Act requires that all publicly accessible facilities, whether governmental or private, provide access to people with disabilities. Elsewhere, the act calls on employers to make "reasonable accommodations" to permit the employment of otherwise qualified persons with disabilities. Similarly, state and federal environmental protection statutes require the filing of environmental impact statements by persons proposing major construction projects. A proposed chemical plant near Chesapeake Bay, for example, must demonstrate that the plant would not damage the ecosystem in and around the bay.

Philosophy/Culture

Philosophy, as used in this book, refers to the public philosophy about specific government actions and may be termed *political culture*. For example, the United States operates under a philosophy that opposes government-operated enterprises, at least in the abstract.[4] For a program planner, this means that programs requiring government interference in the marketplace must be designed with some deception. As a result, items such as transfer payments are often called *insurance programs*. Private companies are often asked to run bankrupt railroads at cost plus a fee, even if the companies were themselves responsible for the bankruptcies, because the public philosophy is less likely to support open nationalization. During the late 1980s, a series of bank failures resulted in short-term takeovers of the failed banks by the Federal Deposit Insurance Corporation (FDIC). The

FDIC quickly liquidated the assets of the banks, in part by packaging and selling outstanding loans to other financial institutions for considerably less than the face value of individual loans. Cultural/legal constraints prevented the FDIC from negotiating settlement loans directly with the borrowers. The difference between the return on the loans and the guarantees to depositors was underwritten by taxpayers.[5] More recently, in the wake of the 9/11 attacks on the World Trade Center, a special fund was created to handle victim claims. The decision expedited the processing of claims and avoided years of litigation. It is also worth noting that the same administrator who handled the 9/11 claims, Kenneth Feinberg, was more recently given the task of paying claims from the Deep Water Horizon incident.[6]

One obvious example of the preference for the private-sector solution is when the Clinton administration undertook a program to streamline government services by applying the principles of private enterprise. This approach manifested the administration's resistance to government-operated enterprises. Like their more conservative predecessors, the Clinton initiatives relied heavily on privatization of services.[7] A second example is the national comprehensive health-care bill, passed in 2010, that never seriously considered a single-payer government option (which was also the case in the failed effort of the Clinton administration). Government-run health care is available only to the elderly, the indigent, public employees, and elected officials.

The current trend is for governments to increase the contracting of services to nongovernmental organizations (NGOs) for the purpose of operating programs such as subsidized day-care services. The logic holds that long-term government costs for employee benefits, especially retirement, are avoided by contracting with NGOs. Furthermore, should it become necessary for financial reasons to discontinue a program, it can be allowed to die without arguments from public-sector unions and all the confusion that would occur if employees exercised their seniority-based bumping rights across departments and programs. There is nothing, of course, to prevent employees of an NGO from forming a union and bargaining for rights and higher wages. That notwithstanding, the use of NGOs does have the impact of reducing the costs of service delivery.

Program planners and evaluators should be diligent in identifying any public values or general philosophical orientations that are likely to restrict program activities or present new opportunities. Those responsible for administering contracts for service must also take care to assure that program evaluation is built into the design of the service and the operating budget of the contracting NGO.

Economic Conditions

Overall economic conditions can directly impact program operations in a number of ways. When the economy goes into recession (defined as two consecutive quarters of negative growth) public managers must anticipate draconian cuts in their budgets. What to cut, when to cut, and how to cut are some of the biggest challenges facing public administrators as they strive as much as possible to preserve the quality of vital services while reducing costs. The primary cost in government services is wages and salaries. When the need to cut becomes greater than a percentage or two, unpleasant choices must be made. Among the options available to managers is furloughing public employees—that is, instructing them to stay home without pay on certain days. For their part, public employee union officials are pressured to make these concessions when the alternative is the layoff of less senior employees. The relative health of the economic system in which programs operate is vital to managers of public systems. Public employees, for example, should not anticipate cost-of-living increases when unemployment is high and the economy is stagnant. Program managers should forgo major expansions in the operations of their subsystems when the suprasystem of which they are a part is undergoing cutbacks from the legislature.

The relationship of government to the economy is by no means unidirectional. Government systems must weigh the impact of their regulatory decisions on the marketplace. Health, safety, and environmental standards add significantly to the cost of manufacturing goods in the United States, which must compete in a worldwide market. Environmental groups and labor unions were among the loudest opponents of the North American Free Trade Agreement (NAFTA) negotiated by the George H. W. Bush and Clinton administrations with Canada and Mexico. The fear was that Mexico would not live up to US environmental and safety standards, which, when combined with lower Mexican wage rates, would prove an irresistible attraction to American industries.[8]

In 2003, California voters recalled a recently re-elected Democratic governor. A number of economic factors as well as government decisions contributed to the recall movement. California state government experienced a budget shortfall in the wake of the dot-com downturn of 2002. The problem can be traced, in large part, to incremental changes in various components of the tax system. Beginning in 1978 with the passage of Proposition 13, which strictly limited increases in property taxes, Californians made a series of incremental subsystem adjustments in tax policy that led to the crisis. In 1988 voters passed Proposition 98, which dictated that regardless of the overall amount of the budget, the percentage of state funds allocated to public schools (grades Kindergarten through 14) could not be less than 49% of the budget. In the previous, relatively good years, the legislature passed a dramatic reduction in car license fees. The license fee was allowed to decrease gradually with the proviso that, if revenues fell short, the fee would increase automatically. In 2001, intermittent interruptions in electrical supplies led the state to sign long-term energy contracts that were well above market value to ensure the continual flow of electricity. The shortage was caused by partial energy deregulation under prior federal-level administrations and by price manipulation on the part of private-sector energy suppliers. Finally, car license taxes tripled in September of 2003. The several billion dollars in revenues helped offset the shortfall, but the increases angered taxpayers, who were experiencing high unemployment and skyrocketing housing costs.

When the economy expanded greatly in the 1990s, decision makers received a windfall of revenues from the capital gains tax on high-income earners (largely the dot-com "nouveau riche"). There was no need for a comprehensive overhaul of the tax system. The 2003 revenue shortfall was insufficient to spur the state's leadership to take a comprehensive look at its system for funding public programs. Indecision and general discontent with the status quo so angered voters that, for the first time in the state's history, enough signatures were secured to force a recall election for governor that took place on October 7, 2003.[9] New governor Arnold Schwarzenegger moved immediately to repeal the increase in car tag fees. He then left it to the legislature as to how to replace the $4 billion in lost revenues on which counties and cities were depending to fund public safety and other vital programs. These problems continued throughout his administration. A complication was the immense economic downturn of 2007. At a more basic structural level, the constitution of the state required that all financial bills must pass by a 2/3 majority, thereby giving inordinate power to the minority of the legislature—the Republican Party. In 2010, by a margin of 55%, voters approved Proposition 25 that reduced the requirement to pass a budget to a simple legislative majority.[10]

Social Institutions

Other social institutions often constrain public programs. For example, program planners seeking to design programs to prevent spouse abuse are constrained by the American concept of the family and the societal support for family units. Previously, the reverence for family preservation inhibited the range of options that counselors could provide to victims. A number of states, however, have come to the realization that treating physical assault as a crime is more effective than treating abuse as a "family matter." Police officers are therefore required, by law, to make an arrest when there is evidence of assault. A number of communities also require their officers to counsel victims on their rights and make referrals to government-run and privately operated centers that may provide shelter, counseling, and legal referrals for victims.[11] In more conservative localities, the program planner cannot consider operating a program that encourages divorce as a solution because this option runs against community values. Thus, the planner's options may be restricted to sheltering victims, counseling them, and trying to provide them with viable alternative economic futures.

Other Organizations

Other organizations often act as competitors for a given agency's resources or clientele. Competitors must be considered in program planning and taken into consideration when evaluating a program. The US Postal Service, for example, began to lose a significant portion of its primary market first to the telegraph, then the telephone. The trend continues in the current era with the advent of e-mail and social networks such as Facebook and Twitter. As if this were not enough, the parcel-post component of the mission is under constant challenge by competitors like United Parcel Service and Federal Express. These private-sector organizations limit postal service options. In the evaluation of programs, on the other hand, organizations that offer similar programs can be used as direct comparisons for the program being evaluated. When such comparisons are made, however, care must be taken to guarantee that the programs are in fact comparable.

Beginning in the 1980s, public policy makers turned to privatization as a means of curbing the rising costs of public programs. These initiatives range from publicly funded not-for-profit family service agencies, to privately operated prisons at the state and local levels, to private contractors hired to implement US foreign policy. In Iraq and Afghanistan, private contractors are engaged to provide security to various agencies and NGOs. They also build infrastructure and train Iraqi and Afghan police and soldiers. In Colombia, private contractors train the military and police in the war on drugs. Locally and internationally, this privatizing does not absolve elected leaders and career civil servants from responsibility for the outcome of the programs in question. Contracting program implementation shifts greater responsibility on agencies regarding regulation of the contractors.

Group Demands and Supports

The demands and preferences of program clientele should be considered carefully in both program evaluation and design. Not only do these demands act as constraints on resources, but often they are used to generate political support for program goals and objectives. The Department of Agriculture, for example, is particularly attuned to the desires of farm groups such as the American Farm Bureau Federation. The federation often acts as an articulate supporter of the Department of Agriculture before legislatures charged with overseeing and funding the agency.[12] At the local level, city planners may find that their well-ordered growth plans are scrutinized by developers wishing to build in one area or another and by preservationist groups and environmentalists who want to limit growth entirely. Also worthy of consideration is the impact of outside interest groups, such as professionals with program expertise, agency employees, legislative staffs, and audit personnel. These groups often have information of value to the evaluator/planner.

Human Resources

The availability of human resources often affects program planning and should affect program evaluation. For example, a health-care delivery system plan for a rural area is limited by the number of medical personnel willing to practice in that area. Paramedics and midwives may be the only viable options. On the other hand, surpluses of social workers permit a welfare agency to hire more workers at less cost and thus consider alternatives that are labor intensive. Evaluators, especially process evaluators, need to be aware of any human-resource problems that may affect program performance. This might include impending layoffs or the advent of union activities.

Technology

The state of technology within the organization and the industry directly affects program planning efforts. To plan effectively, the manager must forecast technological advances and take into consideration their possible effect on the public. Postal service planners, for example, must take into account the rapid expansion of electronic mail. Furthermore, the ability to electronically transfer funds between distant domestic sites and around the world has dramatically reduced the need for certified mail services. It has also greatly complicated the work of banking regulators. Programs that involve solar energy, shale oil, and other new energy forms all depend on the state of technology.[13]

Most recently, the innovations of digital data, especially e-books, has generated experiments in which college students no longer purchase textbooks; instead they utilize digital texts downloaded onto handheld devices such as Kindle, iPad, and Nook.[14] The advent of e-books and the ability to perform online digital research can potentially save students large sums of money. Libraries of the future will require much less shelf space, and librarians will be required to develop sophisticated abilities in the application of electronic searches.

Some legislation, such as the National Environmental Protection Act, requires that administrators consider the possibility of new technologies when planning programs. A program evaluator, too, must be concerned with technology. For example, process evaluators need to know about alternative technologies for processing information or for producing program outputs.

Material Resources

Material resources include physical facilities, energy, and hardware as well as money. In an era when many governments with stable or declining resources are facing increasing demands, the availability of resources is an essential element in program planning and evaluation. Government agencies increasingly must plan to operate programs with fewer material resources. Some government programs are doomed to fail because they have inadequate or even inappropriate resources.

Inputs and Outputs

All organizations, whether public or private, are faced with ever-changing environments. How they organize to interact with external forces may determine their effectiveness and even their survival. Systems theory delineates such relationships by using the concepts of inputs and outputs. Systems theory holds that organizations and programs receive inputs from the environment and provide outputs valued by the environment. Inputs can be broadly categorized as either demands or supports. In program terms, we call them *constraints* and *opportunities*. Each element of the environment may generate constraints or opportunities to a given program. In general, program planning and evaluation require a full inventory of program inputs. More specifically, these inputs form the basis for several types of input-output analysis, including quantitatively based evaluations of program outcomes, cost-benefit analysis, and cost-effectiveness analysis. If the outputs are adequately valued by actors in the environment, the organization can procure sufficient inputs to survive.

Inputs

Inputs can be divided usefully into supports (opportunities) and demands (constraints). For government agencies, support may come in the form of funding for program operations and program authorizations for new initiatives. When an agency approaches the elected decision makers with a proposed new program, whether it is authorized and funded depends on the track record the agency has with the decision makers. The authorization also depends on how well the agency has assessed the need for the initiative, the climate of acceptance in the legislature, and the state of the economy at the time.

Suppose, for example, that a state university assessed the *demand* for higher education in its service region and found that the current system was inadequate to fulfill the demand for advanced training of professionals working in isolated rural areas. Suppose further that the cost of creating additional campuses was prohibitive. University planners might conclude that a program that incorporated a combination of circuit-riding faculty and Internet-based mixed media distance-learning courses (eLearning) centers was the most cost-effective way to meet the demand. Internet connectivity could provide distance learners with library access. The system's designers would do well to carefully educate decision makers in the *suprasystem* and the legislature as to the need. Suprasystem decision makers would include the central administrative authorities responsible for overseeing the statewide university system, and the politically appointed regents who oversee the administrators. Once suprasystem *support* was achieved, these officials could become allies in persuading the legislature to authorize any necessary revisions in the education code and to incorporate funding for the program into its budget. Program planners would be well advised to enlist the support of advocacy groups such as professional associations to assist in educating the legislature as to the value of the program. All public systems face the necessity of ensuring an adequate level of support for their programs.

The California Department of Transportation, for example, has contracted with San Jose State University to provide a Masters of Transportation Management degree to its employees statewide. This is accomplished by interactive classes through a satellite network, real-time video streaming for students who cannot get to a satellite center, and a computer network that allows for group work online and electronic submission of papers. As technology advances and resources shrink, educational administrators seek alternatives to the fixed time, place, and participants in a classroom modality. Internet technology, for example, permits students to access important materials via video streaming to personal computers, and social networking sites like Facebook enable interactive communication between dispersed students working on a group project.

Outputs

There are several categories of program *outputs*. A program may provide goods (missile systems); services (employment counseling); or regulations, adjudication, or support for other programs (recruitment). For outcome evaluation and customer-oriented program planning, the concept of outputs is essential. They may be either direct outputs the program was designed to achieve (e.g., a drug-education program to lower the level of drug abuse) or second-order outputs (e.g., reduced street crime resulting from a successful drug-treatment program).

Many systems theorists need only these concepts to engage in planning or evaluation. For them, a successful program is defined as one that maximizes output based on specified inputs, subject to environmental constraints. Input-output analysis is based on this definition. Such an approach, however, may assume an extremely passive system that is only capable of reacting to changes in its environment. Most theorists prefer a more real-world approach that recognizes the critical role organizations play to affect their environments.

Within-Puts

Proactive systems managers actively assess their environments for constraints and opportunities. This activity is known in systems theory as *within-puts*. Early systems theorists were criticized because they assumed a passive relationship between the system and its environment. The system was assumed to idly await demands from the environment before acting. In the absence of demands, the system was assumed to pursue its current mode of production activities. When a new demand was received, however, it would be converted into new policies or programs that would alter systems outputs in a manner that reflected the new demand. The notion of a passive system is particularly hard to accept in the case of government, with its complex bureaucracies, highly educated professionals, billions of dollars in assets, and the most sophisticated computer decision-support systems in the world.

A more appropriate metric would be to assess organizations on their relative success in strategic planning. Modern systems theorists recognize that effective managers must constantly assess the interface of the system and its environment. Successful for-profit enterprises constantly gather information on customer satisfaction with the goods/services they produce. Furthermore, they actively scan the market for new opportunities. The current quality improvement movement utilizes a systems framework to assess ways of improving the organization's relationships with suppliers (inputs), the operation of production subsystems (the conversion process), and customer service (outputs and demands).[15] More recently, managers of government programs have undertaken proactive management planning modes. This approach can be usefully illustrated by examining the actions of the United States Air Force in the wake of the first Gulf War.

In 1990, under the leadership of Saddam Hussein, Iraq successfully invaded Kuwait and then massed troops on Kuwait's southern border with Saudi Arabia. By so doing, he seriously menaced the petroleum supplies on which much of the industrial world depended, especially Western Europe, Japan, and the United States. The Iraqi threat to the international community threatened long-established trading systems and military alliances as well as the political sovereignty of Iraq's neighbors. The United States, under the leadership of President George H. W. Bush, orchestrated a multilateral military response that constituted one of the largest applications of military force since World War II.[16]

Two aspects of this military success are relative here. First is the rapidity with which the deployment took place. This was made possible by the existence of an adept military transport system. In addition, having anticipated the need for such a deployment, military planners had stored munitions in forward areas (such as Oman) and had entered into cooperative arrangements with the governments of Saudi Arabia, Egypt, Qatar, and other countries. This resulted in runway access and other infrastructure preparations that accommodated the rapid buildup. (Ironically, these contingencies were undertaken in anticipation of a possible attack from Iran rather than Iraq.)

Of perhaps greater interest than its rapid deployment is the fact that the Air Force was not satisfied with its performance. Despite an overwhelming victory, the Air Force reconfigured its structure to enhance its flexibility in light of its Gulf experiences and the end of the cold war. During the cold war, the overriding priority had been offsetting the threat of the Soviet military. The Air Force was organized into a strategic command (long-range bombers and missiles) to deliver nuclear weapons to a tactical command (fighters and fighter bombers) and a supply group known as the Military Air Lift Command. With the collapse of the Soviet threat, the Air Force recognized that future wars probably would not require massive strategic concentrations. The Gulf War emphasized the need for flexible responses using composite wings made up of fighters, bombers, and support aircraft. The Air Force undertook this reconfiguration despite the overwhelming approval and support it received from Congress and the public based on its Gulf War performance.[17]

Military planners continually adapt their tactics to deal with new threat contingencies and the possibilities provided by new technologies. In the wake of September 11, 2001, the United States and its NATO allies invaded Afghanistan. The Taliban regime was quickly toppled by a combination of alliances with local military groups and the judicious use of precision guided weapons.[18] In 2003, the United States and its allies also invaded Iraq in search of suspected weapons of mass destruction with the second goal of regime change. Of course, mission drift from military engagement into nation building in both countries challenged the military in ways that military planners did not anticipate, and previously planned war-fighting contingencies were inadequate to the new mission.

In the wake of ostensible battlefield victory, the occupation forces of the two countries were faced with insurgent movements that used suicide bombers and roadside bombs to attack the post–war regime and US troops. This led to a paradigm shift—first in Iraq and, as of this writing, in Afghanistan—involving the entire mission. First, sufficient troops were placed to meet threats on a piecemeal basis. Specifically, the strategy was changed from one of mass-force desert warfare to a counterinsurgency strategy that seeks to engage local tribal leaders in the fight against insurgents. The approach was supplemented by training and equipping indigenous personnel to carry the fight and provide effective law enforcement. The approach also calls for building democratic institutions and eliminating corruption from program administration.

The strategy seems to have worked in Iraq insofar as local Iraqi groups became willing to eject al-Qaida from their midst. It is too soon to tell whether the nascent democratic structures can work. The counterinsurgency strategy may prove less viable in Afghanistan, where the insurgents are by and large Afghans who also enjoy a base of support just beyond the border in Pakistan.

Feedback

One special type of program input is *feedback*. The environment receives outputs from the program and feeds back information about its reaction to the outputs. Program evaluation is a type of feedback generated about a program. Evaluations can be generated from oversight agencies or legislators, or they can come from within-puts. Program executives may utilize feedback to assess the effectiveness of the program they deliver. Feedback also can be generated by reports, audits, clientele reactions, and the responses of other social institutions.

In simplest terms, positive feedback comes in the form of program support, such as the authorizations for new initiatives, increased funding, and so forth. Negative feedback may take the form of demands for alterations in program goals or structures. Prudent managers engage in systematic feedback monitoring. In the case of private companies, this may involve sophisticated market analyses that include customer satisfaction surveys, market-share analyses, trend projections, and the like.[19] Public managers sometimes do *needs analysis*[20] to see how well they are meeting the needs of the audience targeted by the program. They may also organize focus groups (selected from potential consumers) and undertake in-depth discussions of program performance. Some public agencies organize advisory groups or boards to provide ongoing feedback about the program.

Feedback permits an organization or program to be adaptive. If an acceptable range of outputs is forthcoming (positive feedback), nothing need be done. Negative feedback tells the organization to adjust outputs. All program plans need to contain feedback systems so that program errors and limitations can be corrected. Feedback, moreover, is the sum and substance of program evaluation. Returning to the Afghan example, those responsible for implementing the strategy were given certain review dates, at which time they must report their progress to civilian policy makers.

Goals

The concept of program goals is central to systems theory. Systems are presumed to be pursuing goals. Most general-systems theorists argue that the goal of a system is to survive and to avoid the pressures toward entropy. This statement, however, is of little use to the program evaluator. Both program planning and program evaluation are more normative; programs should exist because they fulfill some worthwhile goal.

At the most general level, organizations develop broad statements of program purposes called *mission statements*. These statements often contain normative declarations to guide the program staff as they organize in pursuit of the mission. The quality movement, for example, emphasizes a strong customer-service orientation that results in mission statements that prescribe the attainment of organization goals (such as profit and market share) through customer service. Mission statements, ideally, are thoughtfully developed and are distributed to all program staff. The human relations school of management advocates maximum participation of all workers in developing the mission statement. This approach is thought to maximize worker commitment, both to the mission itself and to good-faith efforts at bringing the idealized state into being.

Public organizations too may engage in broad participatory efforts in defining their missions. Unlike their private-sector counterparts, however, public organizations are not free to define their missions as they wish. Legislatures normally specify a *legislative intent* as part of the program authorization. The legislative intent normally identifies a social benefit that the legislature wants to achieve through the creation of the program. The Civil

Service Reform Act passed by Congress in 1978, for example, begins by specifying that

> It is the policy of the United States that (1) in order to provide the people of the United States with a competent, honest, and productive federal work force reflective of the Nation's diversity, and to improve the quality of public service, Federal personnel management should be implemented consistent with merit system principles and free from prohibited personnel practices.[21]

The act goes on to specify an additional nine parameters of the congressional intent.[22]

State and local government agencies also must adopt mission statements that are within the parameters of the legislative intent. For example, the neighborhood parks program of San Jose, California, adopted the following mission statement:

> To provide a well-maintained, safe and aesthetically pleasing park system throughout San Jose's neighborhoods and to provide landscape infrastructure maintenance to San Jose's civic grounds.

Due to legislative intent, however, the neighborhood parks program could not unilaterally branch out into other government functions such as street maintenance or law enforcement. Ironically, perhaps, the Parks Department provides a range of recreational activities from youth services to programs for the elderly. So, the program offers a variety of services that would not be readily inferred from the mission statement.

Operationally, the process of goal refinement is taken a step further with the creation of program goals. Program analysts ask: What is this program intended to achieve? What processes are essential to an acceptable program output? How can the organization be designed to streamline processing? Classical program planning and classical program evaluation both require that program goals be expressly stated. A program with a large input-output ratio that does not attain its goals cannot be considered a success.

Inside the System

Some evaluators, especially those retained by an external stakeholder, sometimes ignore what goes on within the system. They ignore the operational details because they are only concerned with the relationship of inputs to outputs and how well the program has achieved its stated intent (goals). However, others agree with the authors of this book that evaluations are most effective when they contain an assessment of how and why the program is operated in a particular manner. By including the "internal workings" of the box, evaluators can provide recommendations to program staff on how the system operates. In fact, in the current era of quality assurance and program compliance, agencies are required to have ongoing program monitoring systems in place.

Internal Subsystems

Every system is composed of a group of interrelated subsystems. For the program to function effectively, each subsystem also must function properly. A decline in productivity in one subsystem impacts the system as a whole. The internal systems can be divided into any number of subsystems and sub-subsystems. For our discussion, we use seven subsystems that are essential to the operation of any program or organization: production, managerial, adaptive, maintenance, support, accountability, and marketing. The interrelationships of these subsystems are illustrated in figure 1.2.

Figure 1.2   Program Subsystems

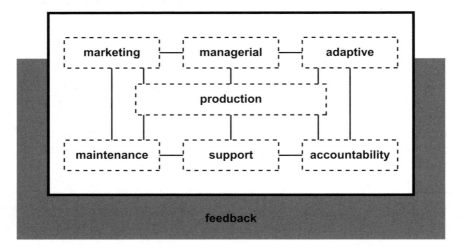

The Production Subsystem

This subsystem is the mainstay of the organization. Production activities are sometimes distinguished from auxiliary activities by the designation *line functions*. Support activities are called *support functions*. The mission of a university, for example, might include the education of students, creation of new knowledge, and service to the community. The production (line function) apparatus for educating students is the offering of classes, laboratories, tutorials, and so forth. The university faculty is organized into academic departments wherein professors individually and collectively teach curricula and engage in research (creation of knowledge), consulting, and other community service activities. These organization components are called the *structure* of the system.

Also essential to these activities are technical operations in support of the mission. These would include the university library for collecting and disseminating information and the computer system for analyzing data.

Some systems theorists use the term *technical system* interchangeably with *production*. Technical system is a convenient way to describe manufacturing organizations in which the production line is in fact a technology system. In a university, however, the primary "technology" for educating students is classroom teaching, which is not normally technology intensive. The same holds true for most service organizations. The principal technology of a mental health clinic, for example, is one-on-one, client-counselor consultations.

Returning to the university example, other operations in support of the education mission include student housing, admissions and records, health clinics, security, and parking operations. When evaluators examine program outputs and processes, the principal indicators of program success are drawn from the production function. Some systems theorists believe that many production subsystem problems can be traced to inadequacies in other subsystems. The growing field of program compliance, therefore, scrutinizes support systems as well as the production function.

The Managerial Subsystem

This subsystem defines the goals for the program and organizes the program around those goals. Chester Barnard, an early managerial theorist, believed that upper management's function was to determine structural arrangements.[23] Once these structural decisions were made, the remainder of the program's decisions could be made by middle- and lower-level managers. Programs can survive with an ineffective managerial subsystem, but they cannot survive long without any managerial subsystem at all. The importance of the managerial subsystem increases in a turbulent environment. When management must constantly adapt a program to changing environmental demands, ineffective management may be fatal to the program. On the other hand, if the environment is stable, programs can flourish with little guidance from top management once decisions have been routinized—that is, clearly defined as *standard operating procedures*. For example, a welfare agency standardizes the criteria for eligibility and the benefits that a particular client is entitled to receive. When in doubt, an eligibility worker can consult the policy and procedure manual as to how to proceed.

The current trend of team-based management alters the dynamic of the management subsystem but not its importance. The advent of computers, too, has reduced the need for layer upon layer of middle managers, who previously were necessary to relay information up and down the chain of command and across departments. Today, virtually anybody in any division can communicate directly with anybody else in the organization. The rush to substitute information-processing technology for paid managers, however, ignores the other vital functions that managers perform, including problem solving, organization memory, the development of subordinates and, most important, leadership.

The Adaptive Subsystem

This subsystem is concerned with anticipating the future and preparing for it. The adaptive subsystem deals with strategic and operational planning. Programs lacking an adaptive subsystem may continue indefinitely, even if no one benefits from their existence other than program employees. Large, complex organizations may create a planning division that takes primary responsibility for strategic planning for the overall program. The importance of good contingency planning is illustrated by examining the US-led invasion of Granada. The invasion, while successful, took longer than anticipated and was not precise in its execution. The suboptimal invasion resulted from inadequate intelligence regarding the topography and road system of the island and the deployment of opposition troops. Notably, the same commanders led the successful coalition to liberate Kuwait from Iraq a short time later.

Structurally, the adaptive subsystem may have several components. Long-range strategic planning may be carried out by agency executives and a centralized planning staff. Program planning is normally the province of senior managers, while operations planning is carried out in conjunction with mid-level managers and first-line supervisors. Furthermore, participation advocates call for the involvement of all workers in ongoing efforts designed to enhance the quality of operations.

The Maintenance Subsystem

This subsystem performs the procedures necessary for program continuation. Routine physical maintenance is one example; maintenance of employee records is another. Without these types of maintenance and the enforcement of job-related rules, programs would soon collapse. In general, program planners and evaluators assume that adequate maintenance subsystems exist. However, this may be an inappropriate assumption for some programs.

A subcomponent of organization maintenance is constancy of purpose—that is, the goals and values of the organization must be reinforced and new members of the organization must be socialized into organizational frames of reference. This component is the responsibility of the managerial subsystem; some refer to it as leadership. Sadly, some public-sector executives assume that agency employees share their views about why the agency exists and the services it should be providing—and they do so at their own risk. Failure to develop and sustain a consensus around the agency's mission can lead to poor morale among workers who doubt the commitment of managers (some of whom may be political appointees) to the mission. In extreme cases, this neglect can lead to open conflicts, seriously undermining managerial initiatives.

The Support Subsystem

This subsystem is often called *pattern maintenance*. Support subsystems procure the inputs the program needs to operate—such as people, materials, and technology. Programs can decline in effectiveness if support subsystems cannot provide the needed inputs. Traditionally, government agencies were thought to have little control over the amount and type of resources they were allocated to meet the demands for the services they delivered. Mass-based procurement systems often limited technology options (e.g., one type of computer). Similarly, the centralization of the human-resources recruitment systems made many managers willing to accept whomever the recruiting system generated.

Clinton-era innovations and reforms in government led to a decentralization of purchasing that allows each agency to tailor its procurement policies to its own specialized needs.[24] Agencies also are being granted greater autonomy over the recruitment of personnel through reforms in the civil service system. The result has been dramatic reductions in the amount of time it takes to procure a new piece of equipment or to replace a retiring worker.

At a more general level, effective management of the support subsystem is part and parcel of the quality movement in both the public and private sectors. Quality advocates encourage organizations to substitute product quality and positive, ongoing relationships for the traditional approaches advocating that an organization be the lowest bidder among competitors. Such systems are more difficult, though not impossible, to implement in the public sector, where bid rigging and undue political influence are potential problems.

The Accountability Subsystem

This subsystem serves as the internal management information system. Simply put, these systems ensure that managers exercise due diligence in managing the public funds entrusted to them. The accountability subsystem generates the reports, audits, and evaluations that must be performed for use by internal management. Program executives must consciously avoid weak accountability subsystems. They also should avoid systems that are so strong that they burden line personnel with reporting requirements to the extent that little time is left for the performance of core program functions; this is known as *suboptimization of goals* (see below). For example, defining productivity solely on the basis of counting heads can cause workers to focus on their numbers rather than on service to clients. In rehabilitation agencies with elaborate reporting systems and production quotas, some personnel may compete for easy "rehabs" and avoid the more difficult cases. While this may be rational for the individual counselor, given the accountability system it is counterproductive for the program that must also serve the severely disabled.

The accountability subsystem is also responsible for generating the evaluation data required by such external actors as the state legislature, the city council, federal compliance officials, licensing agencies, and the overhead agency of which a given program is a part. Continuing the rehabilitation agency example, the organization might be part of a state department of human services that requires ongoing progress reports. The rehabilitation agency must submit annual performance reports to the Rehabilitation Services Administration of the federal government. In addition, the executive director may wish to provide specific members of the state legislature with data on services to their constituencies (which also might be considered a marketing activity).

The Marketing Subsystem

Some programs have marketing subsystems that "sell" the program's outputs to the environment. Other programs are basically passive. Since in the public sector programs can operate without them, marketing subsystems are not counted as an essential subsystem. Some program managers, however, recognize the importance of program marketing, which they undertake in diffuse as well as concentrated forms. Examples of diffuse program-marketing strategies can be found in the precision flying units operated by the various branches of the military. Concentrated marketing efforts targeted at congressional oversight and budgeting committees are the responsibility of legislative liaison offices.

Suboptimization

All the subsystems of a program are interrelated, and each affects the others. The managerial subsystem, for example, provides goals and structure for the production subsystem. In turn, the accountability subsystem provides information for the managerial subsystem. Because all subsystems are interrelated, **suboptimization** may become a problem when one subsystem attempts to maximize its goals without any concern for its impact on other subsystems, thus becoming harmful to the overall system. For example, an accountability subsystem that maximizes reports, audits, and controls would prevent overall optimization because workers would be filling out forms rather than producing program outputs. It is important, therefore, that program executives prioritize agency goals among auxiliary-systems staff as well as among production personnel. A cynical but apt management adage purports that the worst thing an agency can do is to do something very well that should not be done at all.

Applying Systems Theory

The preceding discussion of systems theory is fairly abstract. To illustrate how these concepts can be used in program planning or program evaluation, we will use the example of a school system that decided to substantially shift its mission. The tradition of a basic education at public expense is deeply rooted in the culture of the United States. Over the years, the core curriculum of reading, writing, and arithmetic has been expanded to include science, sociology, history, and so forth. In addition, some profound sociological changes became readily apparent in the 1980s and continue to have an increasing impact on the environment of public schools in the twenty-first century. Women have gone to work in unprecedented numbers. Furthermore, divorce, which was rare prior to World War II, has become commonplace, thus increasing the number of female-headed households. All of this has brought new demands to school systems.

Consider one hypothetical school's adaptation. An urban school district decided to perform a needs assessment to determine what, if any, adaptations in the school's offerings would be appropriate to better serve its clientele. The survey, along with an analysis of school records, determined that the majority of families—both single-parent and dual-parent—were in need of before- and after-school childcare services.

District administrators recognized a need for the accountability subsystem to conduct a systematic impact analysis to determine the space, costs, and human resources that would be necessary to make adaptations for an extended-hours program. Furthermore, if the shift were to be undertaken, a substantial consensus among district teachers would be prerequisite to marketing the proposed program to the school board. A series of meetings with teachers found them to be enthusiastically supportive of the extended-hours program. The teachers' contributions were formidable and to the point. They recognized the potential for tutoring students in academic subjects, and they developed plans for various extracurricular activities to focus the children's energies during the extended hours.

The Parent Teachers Association was enlisted to support the presentation of the proposal to the school board. A sliding scale was developed to charge parents who could afford the service a cost-only fee. Parents who could not afford the program would be provided the service free of charge. While board members were not enthusiastic about additional expenses, they were supportive of the longer school day and were responsive to their clientele—voting parents. The program was funded, with the proviso that an evaluation be undertaken to supply the board with feedback on program impacts.

The administration designed a three-year review of the program. Direct program outputs were measured through a review of student performances on standardized tests in reading and math. The findings revealed some modest improvements in student performance. Notably, longer operating hours did not result in substantial increases in maintenance costs or facilities deterioration. However, heating and cooling costs did go up. District administrators had underestimated the costs of operations, and some adjustments in fee structure were necessary. The program also had some *unanticipated* impacts. Vandalism of school property decreased, as did the level of gang activity in the neighborhoods around the schools. Also significant was a decrease in the district's dropout rate. Because the decrease was slight, the administration determined that a longer-term study was necessary to ascertain whether the decrease was a direct result of the new program or merely a short-term aberration.

Applying Systems to Management: A Checklist

Applying and reapplying systems concepts to the organization is the stuff of executive management. A comprehensive examination of the system and its environment should be undertaken on at least an annual basis. Assessments of managerial initiatives and the effectiveness of various programs within subsystems are ongoing.

Annually, managers should reevaluate the organization's mission in the following contexts outlined below.

1. **Organization mission**, which may be the element of program management that receives the most lip service and the least real attention. At a minimum, the organization must maintain a substantial within-house consensus on the agency's mission and program priorities (see chapter 2 on planning).

2. **Stakeholders** in the environment, who may be:

   a. *Clients*, defined as those who receive direct services from the agency or pay for such services. There also may be *potential* clients, such as when a parks department decides to undertake a senior citizen day-care program.

   b. *Overhead decision makers*, who define the mission and supply funding. These may be members of the city council, the state legislature, or Congress.

   c. *Suppliers and contractors*, whose prices and product quality can greatly influence program quality.

   d. *Program competitors*, which may be other agencies competing for a finite pot of money or could be other agencies or not-for-profit organizations that wish to provide the service in question.

   e. *Program regulatory bodies* that may change the standards against which programs achieve their accreditation, thus impacting the ability of the agency to get state and federal licenses and to collect reimbursements for services rendered.

3. **Technology assessment**, as used here, is not limited to equipment and computers. It also refers to program delivery systems. A counseling-center technology might therefore be therapist-client interactions. A technology shift might occur if a welfare agency or a police department chose to change from a central operating location to employing storefront service centers. Twenty-first-century organizations, moreover, are impacted by available hardware technologies and delivery systems. A rape crisis-counseling center might be highly dependent on telephone hotlines that must be staffed with trained counselors. Psychotherapeutic and drug and alcohol treatment groups that utilize nonassembled group sessions using Internet technology have begun receiving accreditation.

4. Program monitoring, including:

a. *External accountability.* Annual reports are a fact in modern organizations. Businesses must report to boards of directors and stockholders. Public agencies also are accountable to overhead authorities (see chapter 6 on conducting outcome evaluations and chapter 7 on evaluation designs).

b. *Internal accountability.* Providing useful, decision-oriented data on operating systems facilities' program compliance can flag problems before they become crises and allows for timely program adaptations (see chapter 4 on process evaluation and chapter 5 on program adaptations).

All the foregoing procedures are enhanced by the application of systems thinking. Viewing the organization holistically is indispensable to executive leadership, even though it is rarely considered by rank-and-file employees caught up in the press of program operations. Recognizing the inextricable linkage of organization subsystems is equally important.

Notes

[1] See Michael Reed and Michael Hughes (eds.), *Rethinking Organization: New Directions in Organization Theory and Analysis* (Newbury Park, CA: Sage, 1992); see also Paul Colomy, *The Dynamics of Social Systems* (Newbury Park, CA: Sage, 1992); and C. I. Haberstroh, "Organizational Design and Systems Analysis," in *Handbook of Organizations*, ed. J. Marsh, (Chicago: Rand McNally, 1965), pp. 1171–1212.

[2] For a complete foundation in development of the field see: Paul S. Adler, *The Oxford Handbook of Sociology and Organization Studies*: Classical Foundations (New York: Oxford University Press, 2010). See also Robert K. Merton, *Social Theory and Social Structure* (New York: The Free Press, 1968 [1949]).

[3] For what is being done in the aftermath of the spill (as of this writing), visit: http://www.restorethegulf.gov/

[4] In *The End of Liberalism The Second Republic of the United States* (40th Anniversary Ed.) (New York: Norton, 2010), Theodore Lowi contends that the United States operates under the public philosophy of interest-group liberalism. On the other hand, Daniel J. Elazar, in *American Federalism: A View from the States* (New York: Harper Collins, 1984), identifies three separate political cultures in the United States: the traditional culture, the moral culture, and a culture based on individualism.

[5] See Pat L. Talley, *The Savings and Loan Crisis: An Annotated Bibliography* (Westport, CT: Greenwood Press, 1993). See also Andrew Michta, L. William Seidman, and Georgie Anne Geyer, "Focus on the 90's: Economics at Home, Turmoil Abroad," *M. L. Seidman Memorial Town Hall Lecture Series #26* (Memphis, TN: Rhodes College, 1992). For a readable discussion of the types of practices that led to the collapse, see Michael Binstein, *Trust Me: Charles Keating and the Missing Billions* (New York: Random House, 1993).

[6] "Kenneth R. Feinberg, *New York Times* September 2, 2010. http://topics.nytimes.com/topics/reference/timestopics/people/f/kenneth_r_feinberg/index.html

[7] Al Gore, "National Performance Review: From Red Tape to Results, Creating a Government that Works Better and Costs Less," *Report of the National Performance Review* (New York: Times Books, Random House, 1993).

[8] For a more complete discussion, see Steven Goberman and Michael Walker (eds.), *Assessing NAFTA: A Trinational Analysis* (Vancouver: Fraser Institute, 1993); and Victor Bulmer-

Thomas, Nikki Craske, and Monica Serrano (eds.), *Mexico and the North American Free Trade Agreement: Who Will Benefit?* (New York: St. Martin's Press, 1994). On the environmental implications, see Terry L. Anderson (ed.), *NAFTA and the Environment* (San Francisco: Pacific Research Institute for Public Policy, 1993).

[9] "Arnold Schwarzenegger." *New York Times* May 27, 2010. http://topics.nytimes.com/top/reference/timestopics/people/s/arnold_schwarzenegger/index.html?scp=1&sq=california%20recall%20&st=cse

[10] Deborah Bowen, *Statement of Vote: November 2, 2010, General Election,* Statewide Ballot Measures (revised January 6, 2011). https://www.sos.ca.gov/elections/sov/2010-general/complete-sov.pdf

[11] For a more complete discussion see Mary Ann Dutton, *Empowering and Healing the Battered Woman: A Model for Assessment and Intervention* (New York: Springer Publishing, 2000); Michael Steinman (ed.), *Woman Battering: Policy Responses* (Cincinnati, OH: Anderson Publishing, 1991); Helen Eigenberg, *Woman Battering in the United States* (Long Grove, IL: Waveland Press, 2001).

[12] See Robert P. Howard, *James R. Howard and the Farm Bureau* (Ames: Iowa State University, 1983).

[13] For information on technology assessment, see William Johnson, *Public Administration: Partnerships in Public Service,* 4th ed. (Long Grove, IL: Waveland Press, 2009), p. 193.

[14] Steven Kolowich, "Students Face New Textbook Picks: Rent vs. Buy, Print vs. Book." *USA Today,* August 31, 2010. http://www.usatoday.com/news/education/2010-08-31-ihe-textbooks-digital_N.htm

[15] For a review of quality efforts, see Alexander Hiam, *Does Quality Work?: A Review of Relevant Studies* (New York: Conference Board, 1993); see also David K. Carr, *Excellence in Government: Total Quality Management in the 1990s* (Arlington, VA: Coopers and Lybrand, 1993).

[16] See James F. Dunnigan, *From Shield to Storm: High-tech Weapons, Military Strategy, and Coalition Warfare in the Persian Gulf* (New York: W. Morrow, 1993).

[17] See Michael J. Mazarr, Don M. Snider, and James A. Blackwell, Jr., *Desert Storm: The Gulf War and What We Learned* (Boulder, CO: Westview Press, 1993); see also Les Aspin and William Dickinson, *Defense for a New Era: Lesson of the Persian Gulf War* (Washington, DC: Brassey's, 1992).

[18] For a critical assessment of the limits of such tactics see William R. Hawkins, "What Not to Learn from Afghanistan," *Parameters* (Summer 2003), pp. 24–32. http://carlisle-www.army.mil/USAWC/Parameters/02summer/hawkins.htm

[19] See Terry G. Vavar, *Customer Satisfaction Measurement Simplified: A Step-by-Step Guide for ISO 9001: 2000 Certification* (Milwaukee, WI: ASQ Quality Press, 2001); and Earl L. Bailey (ed.), *Creating Customer Satisfaction* (New York: Conference Board, 1990).

[20] For a detailed how-to treatment of needs analysis see David Ryse et al. (eds.), *Needs Assessment. Pocket Guides to Social Work Research Methods.* (New York: Oxford University Press, 2009).

[21] Section 3 of *Public Law 95–454,* 95th Congress: An Act to Reform the Civil Service Laws, reprinted in Frank J. Thompson (ed.), *Classics of Public Personnel Policy* (Oak Park, IL: Moore Publishing, 1979), p. 363.

[22] For an amplified discussion of the nine principles and their impact see Ronald D. Sylvia and C. Kenneth Meyer, *Public Personnel Administration,* 2nd ed. (Fort Worth, TX: Harcourt College Publishers, 2002).

[23] Chester Barnard, *The Functions of the Executive: 30th Anniversary Edition* (Cambridge, MA: Harvard University Press, 1971).

[24] Joshua I. Schwartz, Chapter 9, "Regulation and Deregulation in Public Procurement Law Reform in the United States," in *National Performance Review, Final Report.* http://www.ippa.ws/IPPC2/BOOK/Chapter_9.pdf

chapter two

Planning
The Often-Ignored Function

Failing to plan is planning to fail.

If confronted with the above axiom, managers who are overwhelmed by the press of day-to-day events might protest, "It is hard to devise a plan for draining the swamp when you are up to your fanny in alligators." Managers who are firm believers in proactive planning might reply, "You should not go into the swamp without a contingency plan for alligators."

The foregoing example illustrates the division of thought regarding organizational planning. Everyone recognizes the need for self-discipline, but far fewer exercise self-discipline than talk about it. In our view, the importance of planning cannot be overemphasized. The percentage of a manager's time consumed by planning increases as one advances up the hierarchy. Unfortunately, some managers are never quite able to change their perceptions of their roles from responsibility for carrying out the mission to that of accepting responsibility for mission definition. This chapter provides a rudimentary knowledge of the techniques of program planning.

Inclusion of a planning discussion in a text on program evaluation may seem strange to those who believe that planning should be discussed as part and parcel of general public management texts. It is, nevertheless, easier to evaluate a program that is carefully planned than a program that has merely evolved. We also believe that if program evaluation is ever to become an effective tool of management, evaluation findings must be used for clearly planned, systematic program adaptations.[1]

The interrelationship of planning and evaluation is obvious. Program impacts are difficult to measure in the absence of clearly defined goals.

Furthermore, accountability for program successes and failures is difficult to affix in the absence of clear-cut delineations of program responsibility and authority. These responsibility/authority lines, in turn, are the product of program planning. Conversely, an important step in program planning and effective implementation is a periodic evaluation of program progress.

The discussion that follows begins with an overview of the planning function and its generally applicable principles. Various types of planning are then discussed, including long-range planning, the importance of assessing changes in the organization's environment, and the principles of forecasting. The discussion then turns to the formulation of organizational goals and program priorities. Next are the various levels of program planning, from nationwide to program unit. The discussion concludes with some caveats about potential problems faced by planners.[2]

Planning fulfills several important functions for the organization. First, a plan defines the activities expected of organization members. A plan tells the workers where the agency is going and often when it is going there. This allows employees to understand how their individual efforts fit into the agency's overall activities. Large, complex organizations often operate program planning and evaluation units to assist executives in the assessment of the organization's environment and in preparing for interaction with actors and agencies in the environment, such as members of the legislature and federal compliance agencies. State-of-the-art planning systems seek to involve a cross-section of professionals in the planning process. The benefits of such an integrated approach are threefold: (1) The system taps the intellectual abilities of a large number of employees; (2) the practicalities of plan implementation are included in the planning process; and (3) including line professionals increases the likelihood of a good-faith implementation of the changes called for in the plan.[3]

Second, a good plan establishes criteria for managerial decision making. Plans contain goals and objectives for the organization that can be used by line managers in program design and in resource allocation. A threshold consideration is integrating the strategic and operational planning components. It is unrealistic for agency executives to specify where they want the agency to be in three to five years and then expect that changes called for in the plan will be self-executing. Without ongoing references to the plan while allocating resources and work assignments, the plan becomes meaningless. In fact, the planning process represents a significant drain on organization resources that could be better allocated if the plan is a hollow exercise.

Third, a well-constructed plan permits evaluation. As later chapters of this book discuss, evaluation is not possible without comparisons to some standard, even if the standard is limited to the notion that benefits should exceed costs. Some plans even include projected measures of program success. At the most basic level, it is possible to compare program results with plan objectives.

Fourth, planning can filter and organize the flow of information controlling both the quality and quantity of the information gathered. In areas with long histories of quantification, such as health care, law enforcement, and rehabilitation administration, many times more data are gathered than can possibly be used. The result is a communication overload, wherein valuable information may be lost in an ocean of other data. If a plan clearly defines program objectives, and if these program objectives are translated into measurable indicators of program effectiveness, the amount of data needed for control is finite and comparatively limited. The plan also can be used to design the agency's management information system, including data analysis capacity, inventory control, automated record systems, and human resource planning. Effective planning systems integrate and tailor the information that is needed for external accountability while preserving the ad hoc decision information needed by line managers.[4]

Fifth, effective planning can minimize costs by smoothing workload fluctuations. For agencies with cyclical workloads, such as the Census Bureau or a budget office, planning can reallocate nonessential tasks away from peak demand times. For agencies organized around projects (such as NASA), planning can permit smoother transitions between projects. For all agencies, planning around workload fluctuations can coordinate the divisions within an agency and avoid suboptimization (reduced and/or ineffective resource allocation or the imposition of superfluous bureaucratic procedures).

Sixth, planning permits the agency to schedule tasks, personnel, facilities, outside contracts, and monetary resources—especially when using such techniques as project calendars, Program Evaluation Review Technique (PERT), and the Critical Path Method (CPM), which are addressed in chapter 3.

Despite the numerous advantages of careful planning, many public organizations do little of it. Planning is often done only because the law requires it; thus, a great deal of effort may be expended for a plan that gathers dust. The general lack of effective planning has been explained by James March and Herbert Simon in terms of Gresham's law of planning: Just as cheap money drives out good money, the pressures of daily activities drive out the opportunities for planning.[5] Unfortunately for the organization, many problems become crises that prevent planning simply because the organization failed to plan in the first place. Without employee commitment to changes prescribed in the plan, moreover, there is a high probability that the press of daily activities will absorb resources that otherwise would be allocated to effecting change. To prevent goal displacement, implementation should be included as part of the evaluation criteria for managers, and reporting systems should be specified to ensure that activities leading to planned changes are carried out.[6]

Recognizing the Need to Plan

The first step in the planning process is to recognize that planning can make a valuable contribution to program operations. In some cases, legislatures require agencies to plan: The federal government is likely to require that state agencies submit plans before they can receive federal money. Often, however, such "compliance plans" are merely window dressing because detailed program plans rarely are required. Nonetheless, program managers who take planning seriously reduce the day-to-day problems of program management and are better able to effectively implement public policy. By so doing, they can turn a distasteful requirement into dynamic management tool.

Archetypes of Planning

Executives can be usefully classified according to the emphasis they place on the planning function. At one extreme are those who do not recognize a need to plan public programs that we shall call the *muddlers*. One muddler expressed his disdain for planning as follows: "The legislature defines the mission and appropriates funds. Now, as long as you have funds left, somebody is going to come through the door needing services. When you run out of money, you close the door. What's so hard about that?" This approach assumes a constancy of service demand and refuses to acknowledge any responsibility for mission definition on the part of bureaucrats. By allocating resources on a first-come, first-serve basis, moreover, the agency does not make distinctions between less appropriate expenditures and those that are mission essential. For example, a county road repair department might receive a flood of requests at the beginning of the fiscal year for repairs of potholes and other damage to roads throughout the county. The first-come, first-serve approach would probably not take into account the potential spike in requests for critical repairs that typically follow the winter season or spring rains.

At the opposite extreme are the *hyper-planners* who believe that every detail of operations must be brought into alignment with the agreed-upon plan. Some planning-obsessive administrators focus on defining the agency's future, even at the expense of current operations. As one unenthusiastic planning participant noted, "The boss is always, I mean always, calling a meeting to define or redefine this or that aspect of the mission. Sometimes I feel like I am completely out of touch with what's going on in my section because I am always at a planning session." Obviously, a balance must be struck between planning and operational necessities.

Amitai Etzioni suggests an orientation in which the primary emphasis is on day-to-day operations and decisions that are aimed at solving specific problems.[7] Comprehensive planning should be utilized to solve *recurring problems*, or when the decision is *mission critical* or a question of *organization destiny*. This approach assumes that most problems require minor shifts of emphasis to resolve. When a series of adjustments are made and the problem persists, however, a more detailed approach is appropriate.

Thoughtful planning that examines, as much as possible, each aspect and ramification of a decision is essential when organizations are contemplating fundamental shifts. A university, for example, should not lightly undertake a shift to computer-based learning over classroom teaching, nor should the government enact comprehensive health-care reform without carefully examining the alternatives and attempting to anticipate their impacts on the health-care system and the clientele it serves. For example, under the Obama plan every American will be entitled to affordable health-care insurance and its attendant services. Thus, the demand for nonemergency services at hospital emergency rooms should decline. Along with the decline will be a reduction in nonreimbursed treatments, the cost of which has traditionally been passed along to those with health insurance. While the forgoing can only be a good result, a secondary outcome that has not been adequately considered is the impact of increasing numbers of insured patients demanding service from already overburdened doctor's offices and clinics.

Defining the Mission

The mission statement is a fundamental definition of an organization's philosophy and reason for being.[8] It broadly defines the ends that the organization intends to achieve and the operating principles that will guide its activities toward these ends. A sheriff's department, for example, might adopt a mission statement similar to the following:

> Our mission is to provide the citizens of the county with state-of-the-art law enforcement services in a timely and efficient manner; to serve all citizens of our diverse community with the highest degrees of professionalism, integrity, and courtesy; [and] to provide emergency response, patrol and investigative services in a manner designed to protect the innocent, convict the guilty and maximize the safety of our streets and neighborhoods.

The above statement expresses how the officers are expected to conduct themselves as well as what they propose to do. The inclusion of terms such as *timely* and *efficient* expresses a commitment to effective management of the organization as well as a commitment to law enforcement. *Professionalism* implies that the department will allocate funding for updating the knowledge and skills of officers through training. A commitment to *integrity* denotes that officers will adhere to the highest ethical standard of personal honesty. Further, individual officers will obey the law. The commitment to integrity also implies that the organization will socialize its members' standards of conduct and that the department will police itself. The inclusion of *courtesy* in the mission implies a customer service orientation on the part of the deputies and other sheriff's department personnel.

This necessary first step provides the program staff with a theoretical reference point with which to organize their efforts and gauge their success. Moreover, the process of developing the mission statement can build a consensus among workers, inspire organizational loyalty, and develop a sense of *esprit de corps*. The field of organization behavior has long recognized the benefits of developing mission statements as an initial step in bringing about organizational change, enhancing customer service, and increasing profitability in private companies. In our sheriff's department example, developing the mission statement through a series of meetings with selected representatives of various echelons of the organization would serve two purposes. First, an inclusive approach draws on the expertise and creativity of the widest range of program staff. Second, line members have a hand in the process, especially if the working papers of the groups are widely circulated for comment and criticism during the developmental stage. Employees are much more likely to commit to a mission statement they helped to draft.

Rigorously defined mission statements form the basis of value-driven organizations. As organization members define the mission, they should do so around the values that drive the organization. The result may be a code of conduct that can be enumerated into specific values that officers will uphold. For example, the sheriff's department list of values might begin:

> **Value 1:** I will uphold the law and, to the best of my abilities, enforce it equally without regard to the ethnicity, gender, race, or religion of those being served.
>
> **Value 2:** In the performance of my duties I will conduct myself with honesty and integrity and I will not tolerate dishonesty or abuse on the part of my colleagues.

Values lists may be as extensive or as brief as the organization deems fit. What is crucial, however, is that members conduct themselves in line with the stated values.[9] Organizations that are truly intent on being value driven engage in periodic reviews by the personnel of various divisions, in which they are asked to assess how well they are achieving their stated values and what actions they will undertake going forward to bring the values into operation in daily decision making.

Public sector managers may be reluctant to engage in extensive mission statement activities in the belief that defining the mission is the exclusive purview of the legislature. Unfortunately, many legislative authorizations are too vague to be meaningful without some discussion within the agency. Leaving it to the legislature is to neglect the potential contribution that professional subject matter experts can bring to the definition of the mission. Some authorizing legislation, moreover, is quite dated and may not reflect the current realities faced by the agency. Frequently, the legislature expresses a desire for one or another service and establishes an agency to deliver it. Then, over the course of a number of years, the agency's mission evolves as more and more programs are tacked onto existing missions. Eventually, it may be necessary to dramatically cut the agency's programs; this requires a fundamental redefinition of mission and an ordering of program priorities. Once the mission statement is in place, program managers can define program goals and objectives. Prior to setting goals, however, planners should carefully assess the agency's environment and attempt to define such things as demands for service, resource availability, and areas of potential growth or adaptation.[10]

Needs Assessment

Agencies generally achieve the purposes for which they were designed. At times, however, the needs of the agency's constituency change, or program adaptations become necessary in the face of the changing reality in which the agency operates. Fire departments are a good example of a changing reality. Traditional "hook, ladder, and hose" responses to fires in progress have given way to emergency medical response by teams of trained paramedics who may or may not double as firefighters. In addition, fire services now include hazardous materials response teams. Fire departments have also recognized that fire prevention is less costly than firefighting, so they create fire prevention and inspection units within the department, run by persons commonly known as fire marshals.

In the aftermath of 9/11, fire departments along with police and health-care professionals began developing emergency responses for chemical and biological threats to the population, whether caused by terrorists or industrial accidents. Emergency response preparedness also has led to design strategies for responding to natural disasters such as flooding and earthquakes. Needs assessment, therefore, involves identifying the type of emergency for which to prepare and deciding who will respond with what equipment. The process then involves acquiring equipment and training personnel. At an administrative level, identifying funding sources and/or incorporating the costs of the new response capability into the department's budget is also important.[11]

Preparedness planning takes place at several levels. The fire department must coordinate disaster responses with police, who may well be the first responders on the scene. Medical services are also a critical element of many emergencies. For example, suppose a refinery located in a densely populated area experienced a rupture in a gas storage facility. Dealing with the event would require notifying and evacuating nearby residents, especially those living downwind, and transporting victims to medical facilities equipped to cope with the emergency. Suppressing the leak and cleaning up toxic discharge would also be critical. Planning for emergency response scenarios can involve multiple agencies, possibly in adjacent jurisdictions. Unfortunately, the press of day-to-day operations can encroach on the time available for generating "what if" scenarios. This can have tragic consequences, as we learned on September 11, 2001, when New York City police and fire department personnel could not communicate effectively due to incompatible telecommunications equipment.[12]

Needs assessment can result in improved service quality in nonemergency-oriented agencies that may wish to know how well they are meeting the needs of their customers and whether they maximizing their outreach to potential clientele. Parks departments, for example, have evolved from their role as providers of green space to a role of full-service recreational providers to their communities. Progressive departments may offer everything from sports leagues to Tai Chi classes for senior citizens, to after-school programs for preadolescents.

To optimize service delivery, a department might survey its clientele to determine how well it is meeting their needs. The seniors division, for example, might provide exercise classes, sedentary recreational activities such as bridge clubs, hot meals programs and transportation services. By surveying its seniors, the department might discovery a great deal of overlap between consumers of the hot meals program and other activities. It is equally plausible, however, that consumer groups do not overlap. That is, those who participate in the exercise classes do not use the department's transportation service or the hot meals program. This could be due to the group being a somewhat younger age cohort that still drives or it might reflect the fact that these consumers were unaware of other available services. Furthermore, there might be other services that seniors would use if they were made available. Needs assessment, therefore, could let an agency know how well it is performing as well as how to adapt to better serve its clients. In times of scarce resources, moreover, having a well thought-out needs assessment on hand can help a department identify those services that could be cut with the least impact upon clients. Finally, the department might also wish to engage in demographics analysis to determine if a substantially underserved community of seniors exists.

Forecasting the Future

Because planning is a future-oriented activity, it requires managers to forecast future program environments in order to be effective. In general, forecasting has five steps. The first step is to *describe the organization and its current environment*. Managers must ask such questions as: Who are we? What is it that we do? How do we accomplish the mission, and for whom is it done? Program-specific inputs, outputs, and environmental constraints should be identified. Identifying the agency's enemies, as well as friends and potential friends, is a prerequisite to developing an effective plan. Similarly, an organization's self-assessment of current organizational patterns must be done in the context of its environment. For example, failure to recognize the need for more fuel-efficient automobiles put American manufacturers at a competitive disadvantage with foreign automakers.[13] Changes in the environments of public organizations occur even more frequently than in the private sector. For instance, an incoming political administration may move to cut an agency's budget substantially. When this happens, identifying essential elements of the program becomes critical. Moreover, fending off budgetary attacks requires the aid of friends in the environment. Agencies that cannot mobilize environmental resources will sustain greater damage in austere times than agencies that cultivate linkages with actors in the political environment.[14]

A case in point was the 1998 decision of California voters to replace bilingual education programs in public schools with programs of English immersion. Bilingual proponents, including most of the educational establishment and the majority of the state legislature, argued that non-English speakers must be allowed to learn math and science in their native language until they are competent to learn in English. Otherwise, they run the risk of falling so far behind that they will be unable to thrive academically and eventually drop out of high school. Opponents of the immersion system were unable to convince majority voters, and Proposition 227 passed by 61% of the vote. These data include 47% of Hispanic voters, who comprise the majority of non-English speakers entering the California public schools.[15] Once the "will of the people" was expressed, every school district with a bilingual program had to devise a strategy for moving immediately to the immersion approach (or they scrambled to seek exemptions).

The second step in forecasting is to *project changes in technology that affect the agency.* The US Postal Service, for example, has recently fallen upon hard times because it failed to anticipate the impact of e-mail, text messaging, and online bill payment systems on the demand for mail that is physically delivered by postal workers. A US Postal Service forecast should also include projecting future developments in communications technology such as satellites, microwaves, and other methods of transmitting information. The feasibility of different technologies affects both the demand for traditional mail service and the need to adapt to new service demands.

Similarly, universities have long relied on a lecture/discussion method of service delivery developed in the Middle Ages when there were not enough books for everyone; it was therefore necessary for one person to read the book and present the materials to others. As the cost of university education continues to soar, it may be necessary to reconsider service delivery models in light of such new technologies as worldwide information access and the vast availability of textbooks—both traditional and digital. Classroom lectures may be supplemented or supplanted by independent reading and cyberspace discussion groups. Additionally, digitized information greatly reduces the amount of library shelf space necessary to house books. The newfound space can be used for individual and group study areas that are linked into the library's collection, both by library-owned computer workstations and remote wireless devices such as laptop computers.

The third step involves *forecasting changes in agency clientele*. The Department of Agriculture, for example, needs to know that its clientele will be fewer in number but larger in economic concentration. As the population ages, parks departments may find increasing demand for services to seniors that include health and diet classes and daytime eldercare. This would constitute a major shift from the traditional playground and youth sports orientation of many parks departments.

The fourth step in forecasting is to *identify future opportunities and obstacles*. These may be gleaned from steps one through three or may result from a separate forecasting activity. For example, the postal service would consider its high, fixed-labor costs to be an obstacle and would view new information-processing techniques as opportunities (e.g., scanning technologies to replace the tedious necessity of sorting mail by zip codes using the labor-intensive, old-fashioned hand-entry system).

In the fifth step, *any and all program-relevant forecasts should be made*. Defense forecasters in the late 1980s spent a great deal of time trying to determine the extent and speed with which central military authority would decay in the post–Soviet era in Russia. Two wars in the Middle East and a worldwide threat from global terrorism in the wake of 9/11 have caused a dramatic shift in defense planning and mission preparations. Massive conflicts between nation states have taken a back seat to counter-insurgency and nation building. As of this writing, the Middle East is in a state of flux as citizens rise up against the long-standing authoritarian regimes of their countries. Increased political instability in the region poses a threat to world oil supplies. This will no doubt challenge the planners for the development of alternative fuels as well as diplomatic and military planners. Planning in these circumstances must be flexible and focus on contingencies as well as long-term strategic objectives.

Regardless of how carefully an agency forecasts all contingencies, perfect knowledge is generally not possible and, in most cases, is not desirable because of the costs involved. Determining the number of program-relevant forecasts that are worthwhile is a managerial decision that is highly variable. The prudent manager, however, realizes that knowledge is power and that time spent planning may later be saved through timely and effective program adaptations.

Forecasting Methods

The manager can use several forecasting methods. The most common technique is known as **genius forecasting**, in which one person or a group of persons speculate about a program's future environment. Genius forecasting is based on the knowledge, intuition, and hunches of the individual geniuses with considerable experience in the agency. It has the obvious limitation that the forecast is only as good as the geniuses doing the forecasting. Sometimes an agency will use several genius forecasting groups so that major errors can be checked. Since genius forecasts may be vastly different, a mechanism is needed to reconcile divergent forecasts.

One useful way of generating consensus on forecasts is the **Delphi technique**.[16] Under the Delphi procedure, several people forecast the agency's future environment independently of each other. All forecasts are then tabulated and the summaries are fed back, without identification, to the other forecasters. Each forecaster then revises his or her forecast, taking into consideration the logic, reasoning, and forecasts of the other forecasters. With the anonymity of the process, forecasters are in theory free to change their forecasts based on the Delphi feedback. Compilations are again circulated to the forecasters. The process continues until a consensus is reached.[17]

Delphi is less a forecasting technique than a consensus-building technique. It can be used to build consensus on policies, goals, and programs, as well as on forecasts. As a consensus technique it has some limitations. First, the consensus forecast may not be the best forecast because it is limited by the common perceptions of the forecasters. Second, truly creative forecasts may be discouraged in the iterative process. The particular advantage of the Delphi technique is that the group need not be assembled in order to forecast. So, unlike an assembled process, the written view of each individual is assessed on its merits rather than the forcefulness of personality on the part of the advocates.

Trend extrapolation is a common mathematical method of forecasting the future. Trend extrapolation assumes that the future will repeat the past, and that the variables which have caused changes for the agencies in the past will continue to cause changes in the future.[18] For example, based on past usage, the operations division of an agency might wish to forecast the agency's future energy use, or a city manager may wish to forecast demand for sewage treatment. Although the principles of trend extrapolation are simple (they assume that causes of change in the future will be the same as in the past), the mathematics are fairly complex.

Correlation analysis, usually based on **multiple regression technique**, is increasing in popularity for forecasting. For instance, a state welfare department may need to accurately forecast demand for its services for the next year. From past experience they know their caseloads are determined by the number of women in the population between the ages of eighteen and thirty-five (this correlates highly with Temporary Assistance for Needy Families claims), the number of persons aged sixty-five or older, and the number of unemployed. Using past data, the agency can regress welfare claims on the three variables. This will result in what is called a regression equation. When the expected values for the number of women aged eighteen to thirty-five, the number of persons aged sixty-five and over, and the number of unemployed are entered, a predicted number of welfare cases results. Thus, for example, a 1% change in the female population might predict an increase of .025% in welfare costs. Agency executives could use this figure to calculate a change in actual service demands and could thereby develop budgets and allocate personnel accordingly.

Correlation values can be misleading when the economy takes a dramatic downturn such as occurred in 2008. The combination of mass unemployment and draconian budget cuts within agencies triggered the need for major program adaptations by program managers that varied considerably from their forecast models. Demand for services spiked even as budgets were slashed. Such dramatic shifts, however, are the exception rather than the rule; and fear of them should not dissuade program executives from planning. Having a set of consensus priorities in place, moreover, can assist greatly in determining where to cut if it becomes necessary to do so.

Despite the technical aura that permeates most forecasting, knowing what variables to forecast, the appropriate techniques to use, and the value of the completed forecast is an art. The manager should consider a forecast as an input into his or her decision making; thus the forecast should be evaluated as one of many inputs. A series of future scenarios may be more valuable to the planner than one forecast with precise estimates. Software currently exists which allows forecasting that utilizes sophisticated computer models—but such technological options may be prohibitive for small agencies with limited budgets.

Determining Program Goals

Planning cannot be undertaken without clearly defined goals, because program goals become decision criteria as the process evolves. A good set of program goals includes service goals, effectiveness goals, and efficiency goals. Questions relevant to the planner include: What service is to be provided, and to whom is it to be delivered? How will we know if we have delivered an effective program? What are the minimal standards for success? Under what criteria can the program be judged for efficiency? What should a minimally effective program cost? Are there comparable programs that can be used to measure efficiency?

Only occasionally can program goals be found in the legislative intent, for two reasons. First, in many cases the legislature may provide an agency with only a broad, general mandate. The legislature might express a broad-brush intent, such as the eradication of poverty in a given state. Under such circumstances, the agency must devise both the program and the goals. Second, goals may be missing from legislation because the legislature could not agree on the goals. In an incremental political system such as ours, goals often cause conflict, so negotiation is done on programs rather than on goals. This results in programs without clear goals; the agency must supply them.

Goals need to be stated clearly and concisely, with enough information to serve as decision criteria. Returning to our sheriff's department example, the program goals might include the following in descending order of priority:

1. Provide appropriate and timely responses to calls for emergency police services.
2. Design patrol services to enhance emergency response services and to deter crime.
3. Maximize recovery of stolen property through timely and professional investigative services.
4. Provide efficient, secure, and sanitary incarceration facilities.
5. Maintain relations with other law enforcement agencies through expedited booking procedures and cooperative service delivery systems.
6. Engage in effective crime prevention activities (such as neighborhood watch activities, the sheriff's gang unit, and the youth athletic league).

Managers should also be aware that setting program goals for the agency also can also have positive ramifications for job performance. Studies of the relationship between clearly specified goals and job performance generally show improved results. Conversely, when expectations are not clearly expressed and line managers are left to shift for themselves, agencies' priorities can fall by the wayside as subordinates struggle to allocate resources among competing demands from below. When conflicting goals exist, workers try to maximize the clear goals and ignore the ambiguous ones. In essence, a positive second-order consequence of setting program objectives should be improved employee performance.

Setting Priorities

Every program has more than one objective. These include efficiency objectives, responsiveness objectives, and effectiveness objectives, to name a few. In our sheriff's department example, the overriding priority might be emergency response services. Thus, if it became necessary to cut programs due to budget constraints, the sheriff might work his or her way up from the bottom of the stated goals, leaving emergency response services intact. Alternatively, the sheriff might decide to pass the costs of operating the jail on to the cities that use the service. This response would involve charging each city a booking fee per prisoner. The sheriff could thereby recoup some revenues lost in the budget-cutting process. The department might then be able to continue lower-priority services. At a minimum, the fee could protect core services from being cut.[19]

Developing Alternatives

The next stage of the planning process is developing alternative methods to attain the agency's goals. In some program planning circumstances the number of alternatives is severely limited, while in others there are numerous strategic plan alternatives. The ability to develop alternatives is a difficult skill to teach. It requires creative individuals with substantive knowledge of the area and who are not rigidly bound by past methods of doing the job. One way some organizations develop alternatives is through **brainstorming**,[20] a group process whereby individuals spontaneously offer their ideas. Although other group members can embellish those ideas, negative feedback is prohibited since it makes people reluctant to express unconventional ideas and thus limits the alternatives available to the group.

By developing a list of all possible alternatives before accepting or rejecting specific proposals, the agency gains the broadest possible perspective. Only after listing all possibilities should a critical review occur. The Delphi technique also can be used to generate program alternatives. In contrast to brainstorming, the Delphi approach allows participants to explore alternatives in an unassembled fashion, which can prove to be no small matter for agencies that are geographically dispersed.

Evaluating Alternatives

Each of the proposed alternatives must be evaluated in light of the expressed goals. Our sheriff might consider several approaches to emergency response. A computer analysis of crime frequency by geographic location and time of the day would allow the sheriff to intensify patrols in targeted areas during peak crime hours. Alternatively, the sheriff might consider creating several substations near the areas of most frequent activity. A very small department might have its deputies take the vehicles home with them and remain on-call for unanticipated emergencies on a twenty-four hour basis. Similarly, the sheriff might consider carefully tying staffing allocations in the jail to periods of peak use and scheduling the transport of prisoners to long-term detention facilities in such a way as to free up jail space for the peak demand periods. The evaluation process can be a full-fledged, quantitative, systematic analysis of the alternatives or an intuitive, phenomenological evaluation—or some combination of the two. Whether systematically or intuitively developed, alternatives are assessed in the context of such things as agency resources, secondary impacts on other agency programs, clientele acceptance, and political climate.

S.W.O.T. analysis is currently a popular method for assessing organization circumstances. The acronym stands for Strengths, Weaknesses, Opportunities, and Threats.[21] Individuals or teams are assigned the task of researching and reporting on each of the four areas. Their findings can become the starting point for paths to follow in setting agency policies. Organizations can use the technique to identify opportunities and threats and to shore up agency capacity through employee development programs and the recruitment of skilled persons from outside the agency.

Selecting the Optimal Alternative

In classical planning, the analysis continues until the optimal alternative is identified. In the real world, planners rarely seek one best alternative. Data and measurement may be too poor to permit sophisticated analysis. Goals may be conflicting or ambiguously expressed. There may be insufficient time to analyze all the alternatives fully. Finally, political considerations may foreclose some options. For example, closing an assessment center in the district of the chair of the appropriation committee can prove unwise, regardless of the center's value when weighed against other centers. In the normal incremental decision-making process, planners therefore often select a satisfactory alternative—one that appears to be workable—with the knowledge that other problems can be corrected the next time the program is reviewed.[22] Nor should goals be set in stone; plans can be revised and priorities revisited in light of unanticipated events.

Implementing the Plan

Implementation is the phase in which program planning becomes operational. In order to implement, the agency must design an organizational structure; assign personnel to administer the program; schedule the sequence of activities necessary for full implementation; procure needed funds and schedule their allocation; and provide mechanisms for feedback, control, and evaluation. Successful implementation requires two elements. The first element is the unequivocal support of top management. Without managerial commitment, the planning process becomes an exercise in futility, needlessly raising participant expectations and consuming time and energy that could be better spent on regular operations. The second element is a clear assignment of responsibilities for implementing elements of the plan. A careful delineation of implementation responsibilities is critical because planning usually implies change, and those holding a vested interest in the status quo usually resist change. Responsibility designation is also important because change calls for an extra effort by important organizational actors or a de-emphasis of other program components. Only by specifying who will do what and who is answerable to whom can a plan involving change hope to succeed. (See chapter 4 for a complete discussion of responsibility designation.) When these two factors are in place, managers can be assured that they get what they ordered.

Conversely, managers who merely engage in the motions of planning to placate dissenters or to boost morale may find that the process gets away from them as the participants' enthusiasm for change generates alternatives the manager is unwilling to implement. In such cases it is better to do nothing than to stimulate new conflict and discontent.

Earlier we alluded to the necessity of evaluating plans in the context of an agency's environment, particularly the political climate. Politically, an agency may be unable to implement its ideal plan. But having plans ready when the political climate becomes more favorable allows an agency to move at the opportune moment. In the post–Vietnam era, for example, political decision makers were unreceptive to new weapons systems, military pay increases, and the like. However, the climate changed quickly, partly because of the American hostage situation in Iran and Soviet adventurism in Afghanistan. After the fall of the Soviet Union, military priorities again took a back seat to domestic issues throughout the 1990s. Post–9/11, Afghanistan became an American military problem. The subsequent decision to invade Iraq required a rapid deployment of troops on a scale not seen since Vietnam. The speed with which military officials were able to present decision makers with a full range of detailed defense alternatives can be credited to the planning emphasis in the Department of Defense, an example that should not be lost on other agencies.

Evaluating the Plan

Planning outputs, especially the programs that result, should be subjected to the evaluation process. Evaluation provides feedback to management on program performance and allows completion of the final step, revising the plan. Good planning is iterative; thus, feedback from the evaluation process allows managers to alter those program elements that do not move the program toward its goals. Furthermore, goals can be redefined in terms of current program realities or changes in the organization's environment. The techniques of outcome evaluation are discussed in chapter 6.

Revising the Plan

Because planning is a continuous process, as the evaluation results become available they can be used to restructure goals and objectives. Where new needs arise or second-order consequences appear, the planning process should incorporate them. For example, the federal food stamp program had some negative second-order impacts. First, many senior citizens who were otherwise eligible for the program were reluctant to accept the stamps because of the welfare stigma attached to them. Second, the purchasing power of the stamps was tempting to criminals, who engaged in systematic food-stamp fraud or who purchased stamps (no questions asked) from recipients at a discounted rate of value. The stamps could then be redeemed for cash through confederates in the grocery industry. For years, however, Congress refused to alter the program or replace it with simple cash benefits to those eligible.[23] The issuance of ATM-like cards that can be used only to purchase food products has gone a long way toward protecting the dignity of food-aid recipients and denying criminals access to a fungible resource.

Feedback need not be simply an exercise in negativity. Managers should be encouraged to view the feedback process as part of an ongoing effort at program adaptation. When managers know they will get a second shot at a problem, they will be more willing to attempt a creative solution.

The forgoing discussion of rational analytic planning is actually a simplified version of the process. In reality, planned changes, especially for large projects, is highly complex and sometimes requires excruciating attention to detail. An aversion to compulsive detail management is why many managers refused to systematically plan. When change is advantageous and/or inevitable, avoiding the management of the planning process is synonymous with inviting failure, or at the very least creating the necessity of redoing things that were done incorrectly the first time. To illustrate the complexity of planned change, we offer two examples drawn from the private and the public sector. Note the communalities in the two processes. Both examples use some of the elements of S.W.O.T analysis.

For-Profit Drug and Alcohol Treatment

Suppose a private for-profit drug and alcohol treatment company had a five-year growth plan designed to triple the company's size. Ultimately, the goal might be to grow the company sufficiently to take it public—that is, to offer shares in the company on one of the major stock exchanges. The executive team would begin by considering alternative growth strategies. The company might, for example, identify potential new markets and start by building new facilities, hiring staffs, gaining appropriate licenses and accreditation of the facilities, marketing their services, and so forth. Alternatively, they might decide to grow by acquiring already existing operational facilities. These could then be converted to the company's business model to maximize profit. The latter case would take advantage of the established relationships of the purchased facility, such as referral sources, insurance providers, and the community in which the facility operated. Purchasing facilities also avoids the pitfalls sometimes associated with licensing and staffing. The company could then consolidate its gains and aggressively expand service into new markets. Clearly, the latter is more in line with the company's overarching goal of rapid growth.

The second step is to secure financing for the expansions. This requires drafting a detailed business plan that can be presented first to the company's board of directors for approval and then to potential investors to secure financing. At this point, cost-benefit analysis (see chapter 8) is used to illustrate the efficiency and profitability of current operations. A significant return on investment over several years can demonstrate to investors that the company is well managed. Identifying potential acquisitions may be useful in securing financing, but demonstrating hypothetical growth potential is just as important. Potential is illustrated by using needs analysis. In the case of a drug and alcohol treatment facility, addiction statistics that cite consistent need and the ratio of treatment beds to persons in need of treatment can be quite useful.

Throughout this process, the organization must engage in due diligence to demonstrate that benefits to be obtained will exceed the risks involved. When considering the acquisition of a new facility, the organization must undertake a comprehensive review of the target organization's financial records, including operating costs per unit of service (staffing ratios, facilities financing and maintenance costs, and so forth). The current market value of facilities and equipment must also be assessed. Licensing and accreditation standards to which the facility is subject must be reviewed, including the currency of professional licensing of the staff. If the target company has a history of litigation, it must be scrutinized to assess current and potential liability that might be assumed by the acquisition. The market climate in which the target facility operates must also be assessed to determine current and potential competitors and overall growth potential. The impacts of the acquisition on current operations must also be considered regarding resources that can be leveraged (e.g., applying a standardized policy and procedures manual) and the cost of socializing the new staff into the organization culture (who will train them, over what period of time, etc.).

Finally, the purchasers must scrutinize the asking price for the seller's **business goodwill**, an intangible that can only be guessed at. Failure to do so can result in overpayment and subsequently a longer time frame for cost recovery.

Not exercising due diligence in any phase of the acquisition can result in a failure to achieve the overall five-year plan and/or a loss of revenues and profitability. Failure to scrutinize every aspect of the target facility beforehand can lead to charges of negligence. Failure to accurately disclose costs and debt ratios, at the very least, can result in a loss of profit and at worst could lead to charges of fraud. Failure in any of these areas can lead to lawsuits from investors whose attorneys will argue that company management had an obligation to the stakeholders to gather all this information and to make prudent business decisions.

A plan rooted in the acquisition of existing programs would not preclude program adaptability. Through market analysis, the company might identify a need for other behavioral health services in a given area such as eating disorders or programs with treatment models tailored to specific audiences, such as teenagers or women. The company could more readily expand its offerings by converting treatment beds to the targeted audience. Furthermore, the goodwill of the acquired operation should facilitate the licensing process for the new offerings.

A Joint Library Project

In August of 2004, the City of San Jose and San Jose State University opened the Martin Luther King Library, a 450,000 square-foot, nine-level facility that offers a university research collection, a general public lending library, traditional children's programs, and 400 public-access computer terminals. An initial offering of 500 laptop plug-in facilities was exponentially expanded when the entire campus was adapted for wireless access. Other features of the joint venture included centers for studying the life and works of John Steinbeck and Ludwig von Beethoven.

Built on the corner of the university campus, the library provides access to research collection for university students and faculty. An ample city parking garage and nearby bus stops provide ease of access to the larger community. The nation's first collaborative library project required years of political wrangling, needs assessment, cost-benefit analysis, and due diligence planning and implementation.

As fate would have it, the university and the city outgrew their existing library facilities at approximately the same time. University officials and city leaders immediately recognized the cost savings to be achieved by building one instead of two new brick-and-mortar facilities. Locating it on campus was pretty much a nonnegotiable issue, since the 30,000-plus university students and faculty would be the primary users (approximately two-thirds of the total). On the other hand, the university already owned the land, which represented a huge cost savings. In the end, the city committed to 39% of construction costs—approximately $70 million—and the university committed to 61% or $107 million.

Once the determination was made to explore the possibility a committee was formed to begin the planning process. What ensued greatly resembled the drug and alcohol growth and acquisition strategy illustrated above. Early in the process needs assessments were undertaken to determine how best to serve the combined city/university library-using public. The staffs of both libraries were consulted regarding the rapidly evolving integration of electronic technologies into the library information storage and retrieval systems. In the coming era, for example, linear shelf space requirements for professional journals would be greatly reduced as professional publications are stored in electronic format. On the other hand, the demand for meeting facilities and study areas would likely increase.

Of equal importance to layout and design were the more politically sensitive issues of who was to pay for what. Both the City of San Jose and the State of California have the authority to issue bonds (i.e., borrow money) to pay for capital projects. Just as the executives of the drug treatment company had to put together a business plan to present to investors, so too did the city and the university have to devise a plan and sell it to their respective stakeholders. In the city's case, the city council had to be convinced of the wisdom of the project. The city then used funds set aside through its Redevelopment Agency to pay its share of the construction costs.

In the case of the university, the plan had to be sold to a series of constituencies. Initially, the president had to convince a skeptical faculty of the wisdom of combining the libraries. True, potential cost savings were substantial, but many a curmudgeon resisted the idea of children running amok among the stacks of his or her preferred scholarly collection. In the end, however, the faculty senate approved the project. The proposal then had to be submitted to the chancellor of the California State University System (located 400 miles away in Long Beach), then approved by the

Board of Trustees before being included in a bond package for capital projects that had to be approved by two-thirds of voters statewide.

Staffing problems also arose. City and university library staffs had to be integrated. University librarians are members of the faculty, some of whom have teaching as well as bibliographic responsibilities. They also provide the only graduate program in Library Science in the state. They are members of the California Faculty Association that represents the faculty in collective bargaining with the university. Finally, university librarians are covered by the California Public Employee Retirement System (CALPERS). City librarians too are professionals but with somewhat different reference points. Their role is primarily bibliographic (managing the city's collection) and customer service activities that range in constituencies from children to senior citizens. They are members of the Municipal Employees Federation, and the city operates an independent retirement system not covered by CALPERS. Integrating the two staffs required the melding of two cultures. Furthermore, union and retirement considerations involved careful choices that then had to be negotiated with other constituencies. Decisions were also required regarding the integration of organizational authority structures, decisions to be made in a relatively short time frame when compared to day-to-day staffing decisions for various library functions as well as determining who would pay for what portion of the operating costs. In the end, the decision was taken to operate parallel administrative and human resources structures while sharing operational responsibility when necessary and appropriate.[24]

In addition to these issues, other equally important details had to be addressed, such as physical aspects of the project that involved hiring contractors, filing environmental impact statements, and removing an existing building before the new construction could begin. Of course, this had to be done in a manner that would minimize the disruption of educational activities in adjacent buildings. The project management procedures presented in chapter 3 facilitated the construction process.

The Planning Hierarchy

The planning process contains certain constants that transcend the various levels of planning. Nevertheless, the focus of planners varies according to the planning level. In general, plans form a hierarchy. Those plans at the top tend to be general in scope, covering a great many aspects of organizational activities. In some instances macro-level planning cuts across agency lines. The following list constitutes the planning hierarchy.

1. National planning. The most notable attempts at national planning are the failures by former Soviet states to create five-year plans for economic development using state-owned industries and collective farms that were tightly controlled by the central government. Economic optimism and ideological fervor were two of the factors that contributed to these failures. On the other hand, in Japan national economic planning that tightly coordinated the efforts of government agencies, private manufacturing groups, and banking interest is credited with the post–World War II success of the Japanese economy.[25] In modern-day China, the ability to plan manufacturing growth centrally and unfettered by the sticky complications of democracy has outpaced even the Japanese example.[26]

Because five-year plans and official national plans raise the specter of authoritarian socialism, American planners do not refer to their plans as national. For most of its history, the US government has not planned or has at least consciously resisted systematic program planning.[27] The most notable exception to the no-planning dogma was the attempt by Lyndon Johnson's administration to use a budget system known as Program-Planning and Budgeting Systems (PPBS) as a vehicle for planning federal programs. PPBS failed for a number of reasons, including bureaucratic and political resistance, the complexity of the process, and the difficulty of applying the techniques of cost-benefit analysis to programs with intangible benefits, such as welfare and human services.[28]

Opponents of PPBS argued that the system went against the grain of American democratic values, which hold that the proper method for making public policy is the give-and-take of public debate in which policy antagonists work out compromises involving incremental changes in current policies rather than wholesale changes. Planning opponents argue that projecting long-range plans and committing resources for five years or longer has the effect of denying future policy makers the right to debate the issues that arose in the interim.[29] Worth noting is the fact that, despite its lack of utility for national comprehensive planning, the principles of PPBS are alive and well in the Department of Defense and other agencies.[30]

Ideology aside, public agencies, particularly those requiring the development of new technologies, must plan. Weapons systems are generally obsolete before leaving the drawing board. Similarly, the programs of the National Aeronautics and Space Administration (NASA) require planning years in advance. Nontechnology-based agencies also must plan. For example, the Social Security Administration must project expenditures and revenues, and state and federal transportation departments must plan for the development of new highways and the repair and replacement of existing roadways.

Even agencies for which planning is essential may be frustrated by the changing winds of politics. An excellent case in point was the on-again, off-again plans for the deployment of the B-1 bomber. Developed during Republican administrations, then put on hold by the Carter administration, the program finally came online under President Reagan. The political sensitivity of the bomber is reflected in the fact that subcontractors for it were located in over four hundred congressional districts. (Long-range Air Force plans called for 95 B-1 bombers.) One might erroneously conclude from this example that it is impossible to plan in government. To the contrary, the vagaries of politics make it necessary for an agency to generate a variety of contingency plans. The absence of a range of plans can result in outright loss of funding or the diversion of a portion of an agency's resources to competing agencies that possess a variety of contingency plans to present to decision makers.

2. Agency planning. For most public servants, national plans are fairly remote. The first level of planning that affects most administrators directly is the agency-level plan. Agency plans can be either strategic or operational.

3. Strategic planning. A strategic plan is one that maps out methods of obtaining broad agency goals. These goals may concern program jurisdiction, interest group relationships, congressional allies, and so on. A strategic plan considers more than how the agency can best perform the tasks assigned to it. Strategic plans concern the agency's domain. What functions the agency should perform, whom the agency should serve, and how the agency can maximize its resources are all examples of domain-relevant questions. A good strategic plan is also a prerequisite to optimal operational planning.

4. Operational planning. Operational plans focus on program activities that can be managed within the agency. For example, the Old Age, Survivors, and Dependents Insurance Program generates actuarial plans involving different birth rates and death rates and various demographic trends. This plan forecasts problems that will affect the system. Alternative solutions can then be offered to Congress before problems arise.

5. Program planning. One type of operational planning is called program planning, whereby the manager is given a set of goals and possibly some broad program parameters. The manager then must design a system for successful program implementation. Program planning emphasizes organizing, scheduling, budgeting, and controlling. Several techniques exist to improve program planning. Whereas strategic planning is almost always considered an art, many people believe that program planning is a skill.

6. Unit planning. At the lowest level of planning are unit plans. These may be plans for one aspect of a program or for a single unit of the organization. Although the distinction between program plans and unit plans is somewhat artificial, unit plans tend to be short-range and limited. They are also stated as objectives to implement the goals defined in the planning process. In our sheriff's department example, those responsible for crime prevention activities might set for themselves the objective of obtaining merchant support for the department's youth athletic activities. They also might specify a set number of neighborhood watch meetings for the upcoming year. Because lower-order, operational plans have greater detail and are more useful to the line manager, they are emphasized in this text.

Obstacles and Pitfalls

Regardless of the planning level, there are a number of obstacles and pitfalls of which planners must be aware.

Difficulty in Attaining Consensus on Objectives

Oftentimes politics makes strange bedfellows, such as when George W. Bush worked closely with Senator Edward Kennedy to bring into being the program known as No Child Left Behind.[31] Both sides wished to use the "carrot and stick" of federal funding to require schools to improve the performance of all their students, as measured by standardized testing. The subsequent falling out occurred because the Bush administration refused to fund efforts to help failing schools achieve program ends, as liberals wanted.

This example illustrates a common problem. People can often agree to support a program's end result while disagreeing on methods and resource allocations for achieving it. Achieving program consensus is often obstructed by differing prospectuses. Conflict is almost always present because actors in the policy process view problems differently. As Rufus Miles, a former Bureau of the Budget official, wryly stated, "Where one stands depends on where one sits."[32] In the case of No Child Left Behind, politicians saw themselves demanding results from frequently underperforming schools. On the other hand, local educators on the front lines of program delivery found themselves looking at another unfunded mandate from the federal government that demanded them to spend time and resources documenting performance without additional resources for correcting identified problems.

Regardless of the vagaries of their political environments, reaching a consensus on goals within the agency is essential to effective program administration. Taking the time to reach a consensus, moreover, can pay great dividends when the self-same legislative body that could not agree on program goals requests an evaluation of how well the agency has carried out its mandate.

Oversimplifying Problems

Because top-level planners cannot consider all the nuances of an agency's programs, they may ignore many of the details and gloss over the complexities of implementation. Simplification enables them to plan, but it also weakens the planning process. One way to minimize the possibility of oversimplification is to expand the planning group to include a broad spectrum of organization personnel.

Time Constraints

Planning suffers from both the lack of time to devote to it (the "alligator" problem) and the lack of time to conduct analyses of alternative programs. As a result, planning may be avoided or done with such haste that little analysis is possible. Effective planning requires a commitment of sufficient resources. When the planning process is rushed, moreover, managers may not gather enough information to consider the second-order implications of their decisions. As noted earlier, comprehensive planning and information-gathering efforts are not appropriate to every decision a manager makes. Knowing when to make an ad hoc decision and when to activate a more comprehensive analysis is a mark of effective management.

Information Constraints

Because good information, especially in regard to forecasts, often is not available to the planner, what information *is* available becomes more important. When decisions must be made, timely information takes precedence over quality information. One reason the Government Accountability Office (GAO), the accountability arm of the Congress, has so much influence on decision making is that its inputs are always timely, and suggested corrective measures are presented to the agency prior to public disclosure before the committee. This order of proceeding allows agencies to come before the committee with solutions already underway.

Of course, agencies frequently take issue with the quality of the GAO analyses. Here again, time constraints play a role. Managers who must make decisions absent complete information should take extra care to monitor and evaluate the consequences of their decisions. For example, efforts to reform and reduce the welfare system should include provisions for unanticipated downturns in the economy which, if they occurred, would overload the proposed downsized system.

Cognitive Nearsightedness

Decision makers show a preference for quick, short-term results over often superior long-term solutions. This happens in part because agencies tend to be responding to crises and in part because of the expected short tenure of many decision makers (next year it's someone else's problem). Politicians, moreover, need successes to enhance their chances for reelection. Similarly, private-sector executives tend to favor short-term profits over long-term market share because shareholders will not invest where there is not an adequate short-term return on their investments. A governmental example of this shortsightedness is the Old Age, Survivors, and Dependents Insurance Program. Until recently, when faced with a revenue shortfall, decision makers opted to increase social security taxes and solve the immediate problem, but this turned out to be inadequate. A bipartisan commission subsequently recommended increasing the age for benefit eligibility, bringing Medicare costs under control and reforming the tax code.[33]

Political Constraints

Agency decisions must conform to political realities even when politics conflict with rational planning decisions. Clientele, congress, and elected executives are all capable of limiting the options available to the agency. The Army Corps of Engineers, for example, has often been charged with altering its cost-benefit analyses to fit political realities. On the other hand, Congress may require a specific program and even instruct the agency on how the program is to be administered. The Environmental Protection Agency's plans for air quality, for example, are restrained more by congressional action than by technological feasibility.

The politics of decision making in one arena, moreover, may spill over into another. The Federal Base Closing Commission, for example, impacted higher education in California when it decided to close Fort Ord in Monterey. The president's chief of staff was formerly the congressional representative of the district in which Fort Ord is located. In order to compensate the community for the loss of jobs due to the base closing, it was decided to donate a portion of the land at Fort Ord for a college campus.

State-level education planners had previously determined that an additional campus would be necessary to accommodate forecasted population growth in the county and adjacent areas. An extension site began offering some courses in Salinas some miles east of Monterey. The target population to be served was identified largely as first-generation college students of Latino heritage who would need vocational skills to be competitive for the projected growth in information industries that were expected to move into the area. The new California State University at Monterey, however, identified its clientele as statewide and planned to offer programs to attract persons interested in the arts, oceanography, and Pacific Rim issues. The California State University System lacked sufficient resources to support both the Salinas and Monterey locations; the plans for Salinas were abandoned. Despite their best efforts, therefore, university planners were overridden by political decision makers.

Means versus Ends

Planning should also be concerned with how ends are to be achieved. Not only must the ends be laudable but also the means must be acceptable. An agency must administer a program that treats its clientele humanely, keeps adequate financial records, and considers the expertise of its employees. When ends are established by law, variations in means often become the important variable. In general, planning de-emphasizes means, but it need not do so if the plan contains a process evaluation component (see chapter 5).

Values of Planners

Planners are no different from other decision makers. Despite the norms of objectivity in the planning profession, the planner's values may well influence the outcome of a plan. Michael Vasu's study of the planning profession revealed that planners commonly hold values different from those of the general population. Where managers fail to specify goals and objectives clearly, planners may substitute their own.[34] A redevelopment agency, for example, might define a convention center, a sports arena, and national hotel chains as ideal downtown renovations. The city council, however, should be concerned with the impacts of the proposed changes on low-income residents whose neighborhoods would be torn down to make room for the renovations.

In some instances, however, value-free planning is not always desirable. **Advocacy planning** has gained recent popularity among those who wish to ensure that varied interests are represented in the planning process. An advocacy planner, for example, might be called on to design a military retirement system that maximizes benefits for enlisted personnel or to critique all proposed alternatives from the perspective of enlisted personnel.

The foregoing caveats are presented to divert the novice planner from some of the pitfalls common to the planning process. They are not intended to denigrate the value of planning, which is an activity we believe to be intrinsically worthwhile. Chapters 1 and 2 are designed to provide a foundation in systems thinking and planning. Chapter 3 illustrates how these two elements can be combined to design and implement start-up programs and adaptations in ongoing operations.

Notes

[1] For a group of readings on the nexus between planning and evaluation, see Carol H. Weiss (ed.), *Organization for Policy Analysis: Helping Government Think* (Newbury Park, CA: Sage, 1992); see also Joseph S. Wholey, Harry P. Hatry, and Kathryn E. Newcomer (eds.), *Handbook of Practical Program Evaluation: Essential Texts for Nonprofit and Public Leadership and Management*, 3rd ed. (San Francisco: Jossey-Bass, 2010).

[2] On the principles of planning, see John Bryson, *Strategic Planning for Public and Nonprofit Organizations: A Guide to Strengthening and Sustaining Organizational Achievement*, 3rd ed. (San Francisco: Jossey-Bass, 2004); and Peter Schwartz, *The Art of the Long View* (New York: Doubleday/Currency, 1991).

[3] For a discussion of the benefits of participation see Edward Lawler III, *Organizing for High Performance: Employee Involvement, TQM, Re-engineering, and Knowledge Management in the Fortune 1000* (San Francisco: Jossey-Bass, 2001).

[4] See for example, Ken Laudon and Jane Laudon, *Management Information Systems*, 11th ed. (Upper Saddle River, NJ: Prentice-Hall, 2009).

[5] James G. March and Herbert A. Simon, *Organizations* (New York: Wiley, 1958), pp. 173–211.

[6] See for example, William Bridges, *Managing Transitions: Making the Most of Change*, 3rd ed. (Philadelphia: Da Capo Lifelong Books, 2009); see also F. Beckhart and R. T. Harris, *Organization Transition: Managing and Actions* (Reading, MA: Addison-Wesley, 1977).

[7] Amitai Etzioni, "Mixed Scanning: A 'Third' Approach to Decision-Making," *Public Administration Review* (December 1967): 385–92.

[8] For some examples see Jeffrey Abrahams, *The Mission Statement Book: 301 Corporate Mission Statements from America's Top Companies*, 3rd ed. (Berkeley, CA: Ten Speed Press, 2004). See also John W. Graham and Wendy C. Havlick, *Mission Statements: A Guide to the Corporate and Nonprofit Sectors* (New York: Garland, 1994); and Timothy R. V. Foster, *101 Great Mission Statements: How the World's Leading Companies Run Their Businesses* (London: Kogan Page, 1993).

[9] Randolph A. Pohlman, Gareth S. Gardiner, and Ellen Heffes, *Value Driven Management: How to Create and Maximize Value over Time for Organizational Success* (West Babylon, NY: AMACON, 2000).

[10] See Michael Barzelay, *The New Public Management: Improving Research and Policy Dialogue* (Berkeley: University of California Press, 2001).

[11] See for example, George Haddow, Jane Bullock, and Damon P. Coppala, *Introduction to Emergency Management,* 3rd ed. (Burlington, MA: Butterworth-Heineman, 2007).

[12] The attack on the Twin Towers is a classic example of planning failure. The City of New York located its emergency response center in the Twin Towers in the mid-1990s, even though the towers had previously been the target of a terrorist attack in 1993. Thus, when the towers were hit, the Office of Emergency Services was temporarily knocked out.

[13] For W. Edward Deming's prescriptions for changing the imbalance between the United States and other nations, see W. Edward Deming, *Out of the Crisis* (Cambridge: Massachusetts Institute of Technology, Center for Advanced Engineering Study, 1986).

[14] See Louis Fisher, *The Politics of Shared Power: Congress and the Executive* (Washington, DC: Congressional Quarterly Press, 1981).

[15] To review the arguments associated with Proposition 227, see "English Language in Public Schools Initiative Statute" at http://primary98.ss.ca.gov/VoterGuide/Propositions/227.htm

[16] See Andre L. Delbecq, Andrew H. Van de Ven, and David H. Gustafson, *Group Techniques for Program Planning: A Guide to Nominal Group and Delphi Processes* (Glenview, IL: Scott, Foresman, 1975).

[17] The Delphi technique takes its name from the practice of ancient Greek city-states of consulting the oracle at the temple at Delphi to foretell the future.

[18] See James R. Morris and John P. Daley, *Introduction to Financial Models for Management and Planning* (Chapman & Hall/CRC Press Online, CRC Financial Series, 2009). http://www.crcpress.com

[19] If, however, booking fees are set prohibitively high, municipalities may forego jailing persons who are driving under the influence or who have multiple traffic warrants in order to save funds for booking felons. Evaluators call this a *negative second-order outcome*.

[20] See, for example, Andrew B. Van Gundy, *Techniques of Structured Problem Solving* (New York: Van Nostrand Reinhold, 1981).

[21] See Harvard Business School, *SWOT Analysis I* (Cambridge, MA: Harvard Business School Press, 2005).

[22] The term for this is *satisfice*, developed by Herbert Simon in *Administrative Behavior* (New York: Free Press, 1966).

[23] For a statement of why the food stamp program should be expanded, see Julie Kosterlitz, "Beefing Up Food Stamps," *National Journal*, 125(5) (November 1992): 18–22.

[24] The agreement was reduced to a sixty-five page document: "Agreement for Ownership and Operating of Joint Library Building and Grant of Easement by and Between City of San Jose and Trustees of the California State University on Behalf of San Jose State University," http://www.sjlibrary.org/about/locations/king/operating_agreement.pdf

[25] For a discussion of Japanese planning, see Toyohiro Kono, *Strategy and Structure of Japanese Enterprises* (Armonk, NY: M. E. Sharpe, 1984). See also Michele L. Bechtell, *The Management Compass: Steering the Corporation Using Hoshin Planning* (New York: American Management Association, 1995).

[26] Yanrui Wu, *China's Economic Growth: A Miracle with Chinese Characteristics*. Routledge Studies on the Chinese Economy (Florence, KY: Routledge, 2003).

[27] The states have been more prone to planning than the national government. See Jonathan Rauch, "Economy: Stateside Strategizing," *National Journal*, 21(21) (May 1989): 1294–98.

[28] For a more complete discussion, see Stanley B. Bother, "Four Years of PPBS," *Public Administration Review* (July/August 1970): 423–31.

[29] Aaron Wildavsky, *The New Politics of the Budgetary Process* (Glenview, IL: Scott, Foresman, 1988).

[30] See Donald Axelrod, *Budgeting for Modern Government* (New York: St. Martin's Press, 1988), pp. 282–94.

[31] Patrick J. McGuinn, *No Child Left Behind and the Transformation of Federal Education Policy, 1965–2005: Studies in Government and Public Policy* (Lawrence: University Press of Kansas, 2006).

[32] Rufus Miles, "The Origin and Meaning of Miles' Law," *Public Administration Review* (September/October 1978): 399–403.

[33] Erskine Bowles and Alan Simpson (Co-Chairs), *The Moment of Truth: The Final Report of the National Commission on Fiscal Responsibility and Reform* (with Additional Member Comments—Federal Deficit, Social Security, Medicare, Entitlements) (Washington, DC: US Government Printing Office, 2011).

[34] Michael L. Vasu, *Politics and Planning* (Chapel Hill: University of North Carolina Press, 1979).

chapter three

Getting the Program Authorized and Funded

No matter what the political/economic climate may be, the first two priorities of any program leaders should be getting the program authorized and properly funded. Furthermore, managers of existing programs are sometimes asked by legislators to reprise their program's original intent and assess agency performance in light thereof. These priorities are even more important for nongovernmental organizations that live or die by how well they are able to win and maintain support from funding sources.

This chapter illustrates how the principles of program planning and those of systems thinking can combine to achieve authorization of the program and funding levels that are appropriate for achieving program goals. Systematic tracing of interrelated activities can be used to define problems and to plan programs or adaptations in response to the analysis. The discussion begins with project planning and then turns to queuing theory, which allows program managers to identify and adapt an organization's operating systems.

One of the more formalized operational planning strategies is known as **PERT/CPM (Program Evaluation and Review Technique/Critical Path Method)**. PERT/CPM came into use as a system of project management for projects with definite start-up and termination dates. **Project calendars**, or Gantt Charts, contain many of the same properties as PERT/CPM.[1] Computer technology has made them so easy to use that they have virtually replaced PERT charts among project planners. Both are treated in this chapter. PERT/CPM gained widespread recognition as the system used by NASA to manage the human space-flight programs as well as other projects. It also is useful for social-program planning as well as engineering projects. The linearity of PERT/CPM, along with its clear-cut timetable, makes it appropriate for making new social programs operational and for carrying out the thousand-and-one special projects that must be completed in addition to the regular mission of the agency. Project calendars have the added advantage of allowing the user to easily link sequential variables and to track project costs.

Using PERT/CPM for Program Planning

PERT is one of several forms of network analysis that is used in program planning. A variety of embellishments have been made on the basic version of PERT, but the fundamental concepts remain the same. PERT/CPM utilizes the rational planning process discussed in chapter 2. The end state of the project is defined first. Planners then assess the alternatives for achieving the end in terms of their feasibility, costs, and so forth. NASA, for example, chose to advance its space exploration activities after the moon landings by developing a space shuttle system. Once the shuttle decision was made, the PERT/CPM method became a useful tool for making the plan a reality.

Setting Up a PERT Chart

Ross Clayton of the University of Southern California developed a step-by-step process for setting up a PERT chart.[2] Although this is not the only method, it is a concise, well-structured procedure.

1. The project manager clearly specifies the project's final objective. What will the last event in the PERT chart be? In setting up other portions of the chart, it often helps to think backward from the final event.

2. The project manager should establish a set of working assumptions: How long will the project last? What will the budget be? Specifying the working assumptions means that all participants will be working on the same problem.

3. The project manager develops the subsystem structure of the program. What will be the major paths? What are the key components of the program? These paths can then be further divided into subpaths.

4. The project manager assembles the people responsible for each path into a program-management team. Each path manager may have his or her own mini-program team.

5. The program management team decides how detailed the PERT chart should be, what cost or time guidelines apply, and what the common planning format will be.

6. The project manager, in conjunction with the path manager(s), develops the PERT diagram for each path.

7. The project team combines the PERT paths into a PERT chart for the overall program.

8. The project manager circulates the PERT chart to the management team and, based on their feedback, revises the events and activities to form the completed PERT chart.

Designing the PERT Chart

The examples of PERT charts in this book employ two kinds of symbols: circles or squares, and arrows. The *circles* or *squares* are called *events*. *Arrows* represent *activities*. Every activity on a PERT chart must begin and end with an event. It is an axiom of PERT design that everything that is begun in the diagram must be finished and designated by a discreet event. Events mark time by designating the beginning and end of an activity. Thus, if the first event represented the initiation of the project planning process, the first circle in figure 3.1 would read "project plan initiated." This event would be followed by an arrow that represents the project planning phase. The arrow would be followed by another circle that reads "project plan completed."

Suppose the program planners determined that the planning phase would take 12 weeks, as indicated above the arrow in figure 3.1.

Figure 3.1 A PERT Application

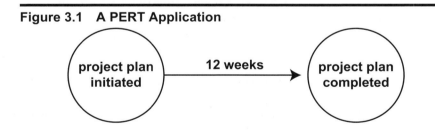

The time estimates for a project activity are determined by using the following formula:

$$\text{expected time} = \frac{\text{optimistic} + 4\,(\text{most likely}) + \text{pessimistic}}{6}$$

Let's further suppose that our project planners wished to determine the amount of time it would take to complete the project planning process. They draw on their program expertise and experience with previous projects to arrive at the three numbers that are used in the time calculations: the optimistic time, the most likely time, and the pessimistic time. PERT uses a standard formula to calculate times that assumes a total of 6 possible time frames. The optimistic, pessimistic, and most likely estimates are weighted to indicate their relative likelihood. The optimistic and pessimistic times are each given a weight of 1; the most likely time is given a weight of 4. Suppose that our experts believe that if everything fell into place and there were no disagreements among the planners, the project planning activity might take no more than 6 weeks. They know, however, that people's schedules do not always match, and other projects can come up that would interfere with the project in question. In a worst-case scenario, the planners believe that this phase could take as long 18 weeks. Based on their past experience, however, their most likely estimate is a 12-week time frame. The PERT formula provides a calculation to estimate a most likely time frame:

$$\frac{6 + 4(12) + 18}{6} = 12 \text{ weeks}$$

The fact that the answer reflects the most likely time is a function of the symmetry of our estimates (the distances between 6 and 12 and between 12 and 18 are the same). The answer would change if different numbered time estimates were used. Some PERT charts retain the three estimates; others just list the expected times. In this chapter, to simplify the illustrations, we will use only the single estimate of the most probable time.

PERT charts are intended to enhance the careful management of time and resources toward an end. They are therefore linear; that is, before an activity on a given PERT line can be initiated, all activities preceding it on the line must have been completed. Each activity in the sequence is completed before the next one can begin. PERT planners consider this principle to be so central that they engage in what is called *backwards planning*. The project team defines the end state, then divides it into its major subsystem components, then reasons each backwards from the end state. Suppose the end state in question was a one-story stucco home built on a slab of concrete (without a basement). All construction activities would be preceded by plan design, plan approval by the planning commission, and the hiring of contractors. These activities are not reflected in the PERT application in figure 3.1. The major subsystems would be the structural system, the electrical system, the plumbing system, and so forth. On the plumbing system line, the last activity would be the installation of the functional plumbing, such as sinks, toilets, and so on. The immediately previous step would be an inspection, preceded by the running of trunk lines (sewer and water) from the subfoundation plumbing hookups to various locations throughout the structure. The installation of the electrical system and the cooling and heating systems similarly would be backwards planned.

PERT is popular in the construction industry because the sequencing of events crosses functional lines—that is, the plumbing ditches to the sewer lines must be dug and the subfoundation plumbing laid out and inspected before the concrete for the slab can be poured.[3] Similarly, as the carpenters construct the frame, their activities must be coordinated with the plumbers and electricians, who must complete their work and have it inspected before the drywall is put up. The project planner, therefore, lays out the various components of the job and calculates the times necessary for completion, making certain to account for linearity (installing the sub-plumbing before pouring the concrete, and so on). During the building phase, the project manager uses the PERT chart (or "the PERT") to coordinate the work of various subcontractors and inspectors.

The linearity of all activities on a PERT chart mandate that they flow in one direction. Backward loops are not permitted because they are inconsistent with the sequential logic. For example, in our construction project an activity arrow could not run from completion of the electrical installation backwards to the start of drywalling. The drywalling activity, although on a different line, would have to be represented as commencing after the electrical work is completed.

To illustrate the application of the PERT/CPM approach to social programs, we have outlined the development of a victim-witness service center in a Western city that we call New Town.

A PERT Application: The Case of New Town

New Town is a medium-sized city with a population of 150,000. It began as a suburb of a major industrial center of 2,000,000. While it began as a bedroom community, over the years New Town has grown in the diversity of its economy and its population. With growth came such problems as urban sprawl and the demand for schools. Both its population size and its proximity to a large industrial city have resulted in an increase in crime. Because it exists in a separate county from the industrial city, it is not serviced by that city's court system, jail, and other municipal services. Until very recently, crimes had to be processed in the county seat located in Centerville, some thirty miles from New Town. The distance caused a variety of complications that included transporting the accused to the court house. Getting witnesses to court proved even a greater challenge because witnesses frequently lacked transportation, had to take extra time off from work, and sometimes had to arrange and pay for child care. To cope with these challenges county voters approved the construction of a new courthouse and jail facility in New Town.

A separate but related problem for authorities is persuading citizens to come forward and testify against criminals. Witnesses may refuse to get involved for a number of reasons. These may include a distrust of authority, or insensitive officials who do not distinguish between criminals and witnesses during their investigations and, as a result, are tough and aggressive toward all present at the crime scene. The problem is compounded when officers harbor prejudices against members of minority groups. When minorities are victims of or witnesses to crimes committed by other members of the same minority group, these victims and/or witnesses may be reluctant to assist white police officers who treat them as if they were the criminals. Persuading them that the peacekeeping mechanisms of society can and will act in their best interest is a particularly difficult task. Breaking down these barriers is a necessary first step in improving authority–community relations before these persons ever would consider using the services of a victim/witness center or, for that matter, assisting in the prosecution of criminals.

There are additional logistical problems of participating in the criminal justice process. Citizens also find the repeated delays in the process a source of frustration. All too frequently, the defense or prosecution will postpone the trial date several times. Each delay makes it necessary for victims or witnesses to take another day off work, secure transportation to the courthouse, and/or arrange for child care. Sophisticated defense attorneys may even use delaying tactics until they determine that all the witnesses are not present, at which time the attorneys will demand that the trial process begin immediately in accord with the client's right to a speedy and just trial. If prosecution witnesses are not present, the judge is likely to dismiss the case.

In conjunction with the presiding judge, the district attorney decided to convince the county board of supervisors that in addition to the new court house, New Town needed a center to service the needs of victims and witnesses. The board, however, demanded to see a concrete proposal that specified program elements and costs before approving the center.

The deadline for authorizing the program would arrive in three months. The district attorney joined forces with the presiding judge and New Town's chief of police to (1) develop a plan for a fundable victim/witness service center and police–community relations program before the start of a budget hearing in 90 days, and to (2) work together for the enactment of the plan.

The end state to be achieved is a joint victim/witness service center program that is to be developed over a three-month planning period and presented to the council for approval. The goal is to have the program operational six months (24 weeks) after council approval. The planning team begins by addressing the subsystems of the three complementary program components—services to victims and witnesses, police training, and the court liaison.

The Victim/Witness Service Center

The mission of the victim/witness service center is to provide services to victims and witnesses that encourage them to testify. The center is also supposed to coordinate court dates with the schedules of the various parties and develop a training package to make police officers sensitive to the needs of victims and witnesses. The subcomponents include:

1. Staffing the center
2. Building or acquiring and renovating a facility
3. Providing transportation services to victims and witnesses
4. Providing child-care services for children of victims and witnesses
5. Developing a court liaison system
6. Providing police with sensitivity training

Using the backwards planning logic, the final event would be an operational victim/witness service center. Suppose the planner decided that the child-care, transportation, and police training activities could be contracted out. The liaison functions would be handled in-house, and an existing facility would be renovated to provide adequate office space for the program. One step back would be a sequence of events indicating child-care and transportation contracts awarded, facilities operational, and liaison established. Each of these activities would, of course, also have starting points. And, before anything else, the program would have to be authorized and staffed. Figure 3.2 on the following page illustrates the components of the proposed center.

This figure illustrates several other PERT concepts. First, one must link together events even when no activity is undertaken. Thus, broken lines connect *staffing completed* to *court liaison system initiated, training contract advertised, child-care contract advertised*, and *transport contract advertised*. Solid lines indicate time- and resource-consuming activities.

The *critical path* is identified by calculating the time required to complete all the activities along each line to determine which line requires the most time. In this illustration the facilities renovation line is the most time consuming. The critical path need not be the most germane or the highest priority of the program; nevertheless, unless the facilities in the above example are renovated on time, the program cannot start on time. In calculating the times for each of our paths, the 4 weeks allocated to staffing is calculated into each of the other lines. Thus, the training path requires 16 weeks: 4 weeks for staffing, 4 weeks to let the training contract, and 8 weeks to operationalize the training.

It will be necessary to develop the judicial liaison component. Support of the judges is essential to program success, particularly in sanctioning uncooperative attorneys and ensuring the timely beginning of trials.

Altering PERT Charts

All events not on the critical path contain slack. This means that more than enough time is allotted for completing these events, which allows for possible delays without setting back the entire project. To determine slack time for each event, first calculate the total expected time for each event. Then, working backwards from the final event, calculate the latest allowable time for a task to be completed and still have the project finished without delay. The difference between the two figures is slack time. For the

Figure 3.2   A PERT Chart for a Victim/Witness Service Center

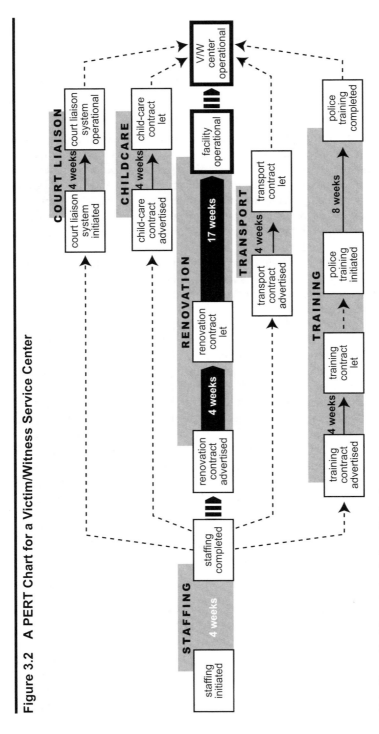

Note: Heavy black bars designate the critical path.

PERT chart in figure 3.2 the critical path would include the staffing time, letting the renovation contract, and completing the renovations (4 weeks + 4 weeks + 17 weeks). The total is 25 weeks. Slack occurs along other paths, such as in the training schedule, which would include the staffing time, contract letting, and the actual training (4 weeks + 4 weeks + 8 weeks). The slack time is calculated as follows:

> 25 weeks (critical path)
> −16 weeks (training path)
> 9 weeks (slack time)

Knowing the exact amount of slack available for each activity can be beneficial because resources from slack can sometimes be transferred to other project activities that are in danger of falling behind. In many cases, however, resources contained along one path are specialized and therefore are not easily transferable. Transfers also are made more difficult when components of a project are geographically dispersed.

Often, somewhere between the initiation and the completion of a task, something unexpected happens that makes it necessary to alter the PERT chart. In the project in figure 3.2, for example, a delay in finishing the renovations for the victim/witness service facility could result from a construction workers' strike against the prime contractor.

Monitoring a Project with the PERT Chart

The PERT chart is often used to monitor the status of a project and flag any potential problems. Many sophisticated computer programs exist to monitor PERT. For a small project, the easiest way to use PERT is first to translate the PERT chart into a schedule that lists the dates that events are to begin and are to be completed. As events are completed, the event circles or squares in the PERT chart are filled in. This permits the manager to quickly see the status of any event. More sophisticated charts are drawn so that the length of each activity line fits a time scale. In this manner all the events to be completed on the same day fall along a vertical line. With such charts, a movable string or line is placed on the chart at the current date. This permits the manager to see at a glance if all paths are on schedule and to locate any problems quickly.

Using Project Calendars

Closely related to PERT/CPM is the project calendar or Gantt chart. Named for its developer, H. L. Gantt, the system was developed to manage military logistics during World War I. The process whereby project calendars are developed is very similar to that of PERT (the end state is defined, then program staff break it down into its component parts and utilize backwards planning).[4] The growing popularity of the project calendar over PERT can be attributed to fact that it is less cumbersome to develop and, more importantly, computer software is available that facilitates the project planning process and the display of the project's component parts.

Project calendars illustrate the inclusive dates of the proposed program across the top of the page. They also use a series of bars in lieu of the start-and-stop circles or squares used in PERT. As the various project components are defined, planners specify a start date and stop date for each activity and link the two dates together using a bar. The process is repeated for each project and its subcomponents until all elements are displayed on the calendar. Subcomponents are linked by an arrow when one is a prerequisite for another.

Figure 3.3 displays a project calendar for the victim/witness service center discussed earlier. The left-hand column of the calendar displays the various projects and their subcomponents. Each of these is followed by a block displaying the estimated duration of time for completion. Across the top is a display of the calendar. Below the calendar are the bars representing the various starting and finishing points of each program component. If one of the computer software packages is used, planners need only specify the start date of an activity and the amount of time that they believe it will take. The software extends a bar from the starting date of the event to its expected end.

In figure 3.3, for example, planners anticipate that four weeks will be necessary to staff the victim/witness service center (row 1 in the project calendar). The program staff of the center will take care of facilities renovations (row 4) and the letting of contracts for transportation, day care (rows 2 and 3), and so forth. The relationship is demonstrated by setting the start-up dates of the appropriate activities to occur after staffing is complete. More direct linear linkages, such as letting the renovations contract and completing the work, are indicated by linking arrows. The same is true of the training contract and its delivery. Subcomponents that are independent of staffing, such as public relations and judicial liaisons, are not linked; instead they occur in parallel time.

The project calendar also contains other interesting subtleties.

- First, each major initiative (listed flush left in bold under the "Task Name" column heading) is distinguishable from its group of subcomponents (the indented entries listed beneath each project heading). For example, the project has the subcomponents of staffing the center, the renovation project, and so forth. Also, each major project (such as the center in our example) is indicated by a 120-day bar that has small hooks on the ends. The subcomponents are noted with regular calendar bars.

- Second, the current date is displayed in the calendar by the perpendicular line that runs across project components. Project managers can use the line to determine which of the components are to have been completed, which are on track, and so forth.

Figure 3.3 A Project Calendar for a Victim/Witness Service Center

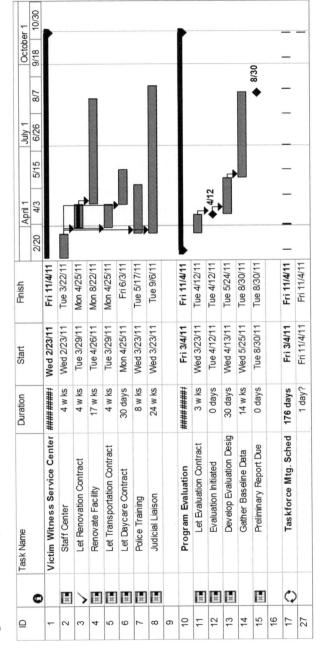

ID		Task Name	Duration	Start	Finish
1		**Victim Witness Service Center**	########	**Wed 2/23/11**	**Fri 11/4/11**
2		Staff Center	4 w ks	Wed 2/23/11	Tue 3/22/11
3		Let Renovation Contract	4 w ks	Tue 3/29/11	Mon 4/25/11
4		Renovate Facility	17 w ks	Tue 4/26/11	Mon 8/22/11
5		Let Transportation Contract	4 w ks	Tue 3/29/11	Mon 4/25/11
6		Let Daycare Contract	30 days	Mon 4/25/11	Fri 6/3/11
7		Police Training	8 w ks	Wed 3/23/11	Tue 5/17/11
8		Judicial Liaison	24 w ks	Wed 3/23/11	Tue 9/6/11
9					
10		**Program Evaluation**	########	**Fri 3/4/11**	**Fri 11/4/11**
11		Let Evaluation Contract	3 w ks	Wed 3/23/11	Tue 4/12/11
12		Evaluation Initiated	0 days	Tue 4/12/11	Tue 4/12/11
13		Develop Evaluation Desig	30 days	Wed 4/13/11	Tue 5/24/11
14		Gather Baseline Data	14 w ks	Wed 5/25/11	Tue 8/30/11
15		Preliminary Report Due	0 days	Tue 8/30/11	Tue 8/30/11
16					
17		**Taskforce Mtg. Sched**	**176 days**	**Fri 3/4/11**	**Fri 11/4/11**
27			1 day?	Fri 11/4/11	Fri 11/4/11

- Third, it is simple to identify recurring events in a calendar. For example, the task force is to meet every two weeks for the duration. These meetings are identified with hatch marks. (See row 17 in figure 3.3, which includes a ⟨⟩ symbol to indicate a recurring event.)
- In Figure 3.3 we also identify an evaluation component for the program that begins with the letting of the evaluation contract and ends with the submission of the preliminary report. The start of the evaluation and the report are identified with milestones in the form of diamonds in the chart. (Evaluation is discussed in detail in chapters 4 through 6.)

Whether employing PERT or project calendars, analysts should bear in mind that the estimates are only as good as the judgments of the project planners who make them. As a consequence, decision makers should view time and cost estimates with skepticism. The methodologies work best when a consensus to act has been achieved, and the planning devices are then used to determine the best and most efficient way to proceed with implementation. The methodologies are less useful when employed as a justification for undertaking the project. In the latter instance program planners should be questioned closely to determine whether the most conservative estimates were applied. When time and costs are optimistically estimated, they can lead to projects that are not completed on time and/or incur cost overruns that require supplemental appropriations. On the other hand, when properly applied, the methods can bring rationality and considerable cost savings to programs.

Other interesting features of the project calendar that are beyond the scope of this chapter include the ability to attach cost sheets to the calendar and to assign specific responsibilities to individuals or work groups. Interested persons should consult the software documentation associated with Microsoft Project.

"Find a Need and Fill It."[5]
An NGO Example

On a worldwide scale, there are many more problems than there is funding to deal with them. Programs designed to eliminate or at least ameliorate the problems of poverty, disease, illiteracy, and human trafficking are just a few of the problems vying for limited resources. Governments and foundations announce requests for proposals (RFPs). These are broadly stated to allow a variety of worthy programs to apply. Though broadly stated, RFPs are specific as to grant eligibility requirements (who may apply) and so forth. RFPs also specify application formats and specific content requirements. Applicants who ignore these requirements do so at their peril.

What follows is a template for those thinking of submitting a grant application. The process is illustrated with a successful grant application to fight human trafficking in the Mekong Delta of Vietnam. Note that the inclusion of a solid evaluation plan enhances one's chances of securing funding.

The most common error that applicants make is not reading the RFP carefully with an eye to addressing each of the requirements. A typical RFP requires that applicants write a program description that illustrates exactly how the proposed project relates to the specifications of the RFP. There is simply no point in applying for funds for a project (regardless of its merits) that falls outside the parameters of the RFP.

The program statement should clearly describe the problem to be addressed and the impacts that the proposed program will have on it. In this example the request for funding was to counter human sex trafficking in the Mekong Delta of Vietnam. The applicants therefore detailed how the proximity of the border with Cambodia made the girls of the border areas particularly susceptible to being conscripted into that country's sex trade. The traffickers lure the unsophisticated peasants, children as young as 12, with promises of lucrative jobs in casinos and restaurants, or they are simply kidnapped.

The largest component of the program was to work with schools to identify at-risk students and provide support to keep them in school. Girls who graduate from high school are more likely to find employment to support themselves and assist their families, unlike dropouts who are prime targets for traffickers. The funding request pointed out that the extreme poverty of the region made it difficult for parents to pay even the minimal education costs of tuition, uniforms, and books required by the government. Parents with more than one child often must make difficult choices about which of their children they can afford to send to school. Because they live in a male-centric society, poverty-stricken Vietnamese parents will opt to send the male children to school in preference to their female siblings. In households with only girls, parents may opt to send the younger girls to school, keeping older girls home to provide day care for very young children; or the older girls may be required to work in the fields or sell lottery tickets to help the family make ends meet. One scholarship girl, for example, was abandoned by her parents and, along with her profoundly retarded brother, was forced to live with an aunt who could barely support her own children by selling vegetables from a street cart. As a result, the child in question was at first required to sell lottery tickets after school and bear the responsibility for most of the household chores before and after school. Eventually, she was made to work long hours in a fish processing plant for a wage of twenty-five cents per hour. Little wonder, then, that families such as this fall prey to the traffickers' promises of well-paying jobs in Cambodia and offers of modest advanced payments to the family.

A problematic feature of Vietnamese society is the fact that once a person has left school for two years, they cannot return to regular daytime classes. All that is available to them is evening school. In the Mekong Delta attendance requires traveling some distance after dark over roads that are little more than footpaths that can become impassable during the rainy season. Furthermore, by law one cannot engage in employment below the age of sixteen. The project therefore devised vocational training to prepare girls for legitimate work in the export garment industry, culinary schools, and cosmetology.

A final program component and the one most directly involved with the human trafficking problem was to provide services to the victims who manage to escape or who are ultimately rejected by the sex traffickers due to disease or age. They arrive back in Vietnam with major psychological and health issues but without identity papers, money, or social support networks. The problem is compounded by the absence of any government-sponsored social welfare programs. These girls can only return to their families—if they are accepted. Without schooling or job skills, moreover, the girls frequently rely on their skills as prostitutes to survive.

The funding request thus spoke to three service elements: prevention, reintegration, and vocational training. Program funding was to come from the United States Agency for International Development (USAID) and from private foundations and individual donors. USAID was asked for a grant to provide scholarships to keep recipients in school through high school. Program staff were to work with local school officials to identify and reach the girls who are most in need. The program would further provide academic tutoring after school and during summer sessions. To ensure tutor quality, the program proposed using school teachers to be paid at their regular salary rate. The project began with three hundred scholarships the first year, expanding to six hundred by the third year. A second prevention component was to be community education regarding the hazards of trafficking, to be accomplished through community meetings and by working with local women's committees.

The reintegration element was to be privately funded and would consist of four components. The first was a program liaison with local police authorities, who were often given responsibility by the government for returnees because no other housing was available. Building a strong, trusting relationship with local officials would also help in getting out the prevention message. The second component was the establishment of a shelter to provide housing for a transition back into society. The program staff also was to provide a third component—a combination of assessment, counseling, and advocacy for the girls. Among other things, the staff was to serve as a buffer between the girls and various government officials to secure identity papers, health-care services, and so forth. The final program component was to develop a vocational training program for the girls so that they would learn how to earn a living. The entire program is represented in figure 3.4.

The vocational training was to be funded by private contributions. Program staff were to develop relations with potential employers to tailor the training to their needs. Staff also worked with women's committees to set up training in garment sewing in remote areas of the delta. Finally,

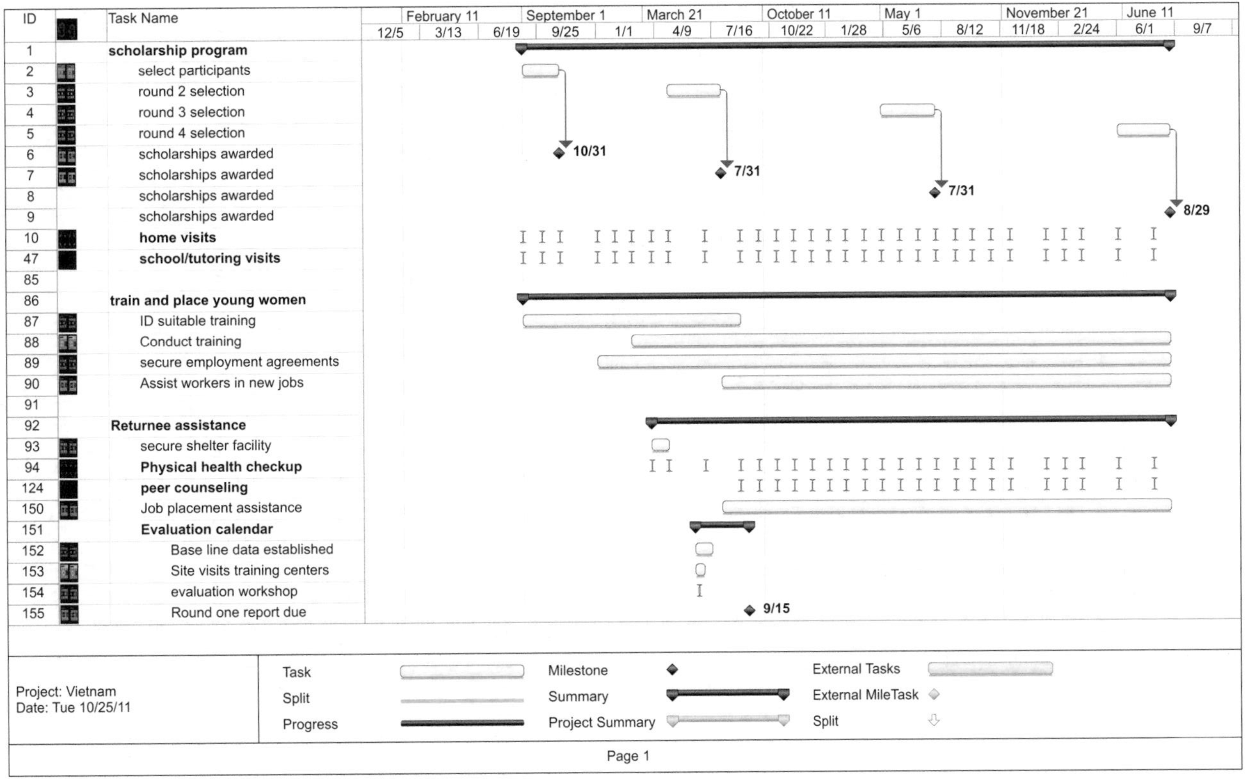

Figure 3.4   Project Calendar for a Program to Counter Sex Trafficking in the Mekong Delta

training in culinary skills and cosmetology were provided by professionals. American and Vietnamese-based chefs agreed to provide training, and cosmeticians in local shops also agreed to work with the project.

Providing potential funders with a precise outline of the program, complete with progress milestones and a plan for evaluation of outcomes, can go far to demonstrate the organization's competence to carry out the program successfully.

Another element of successful proposals like this one is a detailed budget that precisely identifies the cost of each program element. Additionally, funding agencies like to see an outline of the proposed organization structure. Finally, the proposal should specify who exactly is going to carry out the program. This component should include a narrative of the qualifications of program officers and detailed résumés of their education and experience.

The authors are happy to report that the program in question did receive a USAID grant as well as private funding. It has been successfully operating in the Mekong Delta for five years. The returnee assistance component has been so successful that the program has been invited to open a second shelter in northern Vietnam along its border with China.[6]

Queuing Theory

As noted in the planning chapter, comprehensive organization planning is expensive and should not be undertaken lightly. Queuing theory, on the other hand, allows managers to analyze their operations with an eye towards illustrating responsibility for program outcomes and identifying decision points in the process. The example of queuing theory in figure 3.5 uses darker squares to identify starting points or designate events, lighter rectangles with rounded corners to indicate operations, and black diamonds to designate points at which decisions are made. Lines in the queue chart trace the interrelationships between steps in the process. Unlike PERT and GANTT charts, which are strictly linear and sequential, queue charts may indicate an iteration after a decision point. An insurance claims manager, for example, might exercise the authority to send the claim forward for payment, return it to a claims agent for more information or adjustments in the estimate, or to refer the matter to the legal department. By carefully applying queuing technique, managers can track the various components of their operations. The example in figure 3.5 illustrates an application of queuing theory to the admissions process of a graduate program.

The first step in the process is the student's decision to apply to the program. The applicant would first seek application instructions from the catalog of the university. There he or she would learn that the program requires applicants to submit the following items:

1. A formal application submitted directly to the graduate school, either online or as a paper application.

Figure 3.5   A Queuing Theory Flow Chart

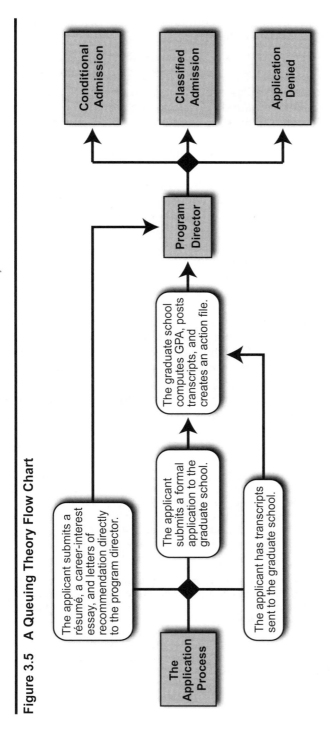

2. Official transcripts from all undergraduate schools attended, to be submitted directly to the graduate school.

3. A résumé, a career-interest essay, and letters of recommendation to be submitted directly to the program director/graduate advisor.

Of course, as with most things there are deadlines to be met. So, if a student has not provided all the required information on a timely basis, he or she will not be considered for admission. In figure 3.5, the decision points are at the graduate school, where students' grades are assessed to determine whether they meet the admissions standards of the program. Once minimum standards are met, the application is referred to the program director, and the faculty review the combination of all the factors, grades, experience, personal history, and career-interest essay, as well as letters of recommendation. The applicant is then notified of the admission decision.

Whether one is seeking a better understanding of existing processes (as in the case of queuing theory) or designing a new program or project (as with PERT and GANTT) the application of systems thinking and rational planning can enhance the decision-making process. However, as we noted at the outset, the techniques are only as good as the information fed into them. If a manager begins with "fuzzy facts" about the nature of the problem under analysis, he or she will very likely come up short of the mark in the ensuing system that is designed. These techniques work best in the hands of pragmatic managers who seek decisions based on the best possible information that will lead to quality results (i.e., programs that come to fruition on time and at or under budget). Knowing what the program is supposed to achieve and how it is organized to do so are the fundamental first steps in program evaluation, to which we now turn.

Notes

[1] See Michael C. Thomsett, *The Little Black Book of Project Management* (New York: AMACON, 2009). See also Harold Kerzner, *Project Management: A Systems Approach to Planning, Scheduling, and Controlling* (Hoboken, NJ: John Wiley and Sons, 2009).

[2] Ross Clayton, "Techniques of Network Analysis for Managers," in Michael J. White, Ross Clayton, Robert Myrtle, Gilbert Siegel, and Aaron Rose (eds.), *Managing Public Systems: Analytic Techniques for Public Administration* (North Scituate, MA: Duxbury Press, 1980).

[3] See R. L. Peurifoy and W. B. Ledbetter, *Construction Planning, Equipment and Methods* (New York: McGraw-Hill, 1985).

[4] See Henry L. Gantt, *Gantt on Management: Guidelines for Today's Executive* (New York: American Management Association, 1961). See also Nathan Goldfarb and William K. Kaiser (eds.), *Gantt Charts and Statistical Quality Control: The Dissemination of New Business Techniques* (Hempstead, NY: Hofstra University, 1964).

[5] This motto, credited to Ruth Stafford Peale, is a prescription for success that applies just as well to the world of not-for-profit enterprises as to the intended audience of would-be capitalists.

[6] A complete description of the program and all its activities can be found on the website of the sponsoring NGO Pacific Links at http://pacificlinks.org

TWO

Process Evaluation
The "Other" Approach

As noted in the introduction, evaluation research grew out of the field of social science research with its concerns for research designs rooted in theory, meticulous hypotheses formulation, and rigorous research methodologies to measure exactly what is intended in a manner that can be replicated by others. Proceeding in this manner, evaluators could assure program stakeholders that the data measured whether in fact a program is achieving its desired ends.

Process evaluations, or assessments of how agencies organized themselves to achieve their ends, were acknowledged as the "other" method but were rarely taught in public administration research classes. This occurred because processes are not readily amenable to standard social science measurement techniques. In addition, process evaluations often require levels of involvement between the evaluator(s) and program staff that are inconsistent with the canons of scientific objectivity.

What was true for the classroom, however, was often irrelevant to the working lives of public administrators, who are routinely called upon to demonstrate that how they are organized to deliver services, the credentials of their staffs, and the types of services they provide all meet the highest professional standards. Furthermore, agencies must demonstrate that systems are in place to monitor program compliance and adapt the system as necessary on an ongoing basis. This phenomenon, known as **accreditation**, has come to be an indispensable component for agencies seeking funding renewal and/or eligibility payment by third-party payers, both public and private.

Accreditation/process program assessment is most recognizable in the field of education, where professional organizations create quasi-independent bodies to establish standards and monitor compliance with them. Similarly, hospitals and clinics that provide health care and behavioral health programs that provide mental health or drug and alcohol treatment are subject to accreditation standards as a condition of obtaining governmental operating licenses and as a precondition by third-party payers such as insurance companies. Standards-based accreditation, moreover, is spreading into the field of law enforcement, where local police departments undertake rigorous self-examination in order to obtain accreditation by the Commission on Accreditation of Law Enforcement Agencies (CALEA). Armed with this external validation of program quality, they can approach city councils for funding renewal or additional funds to correct deficiencies in their service delivery modes. Police agencies that do not already meet the standards can justify requests for training and or personnel and equipment funding in order to upgrade the professionalism of their departments.

A second form of process evaluation can dovetail with accreditation or take place independently. This involves intervention in organization processes. The first step is assessing operations against program goals or stated standards. In the second step, program adaptations are developed to correct deficiencies or alter program direction. The approach also involves post-intervention assessment of the impact of the action on the agency. This may involve application of accreditation standards, measures of program outcomes, or both. In chapter 4 we discuss standards-based program assessments using examples taken from higher education and law enforcement. In chapter 5 we present a four-step model of program intervention and planned change using a behavioral health example.

four

Standards-Based Evaluation
Matching Operations to Expectations

In chapter 1 we discussed the various internal operations within an organization as a group of interrelated subsystems. When combined, they constitute the operations of the entire organization as a system. We also noted that organizations should be examined in their entirety (holistically), since whatever occurs in one subsystem impacts the entire organization. Of particular importance is the interrelationship of the organization to its environment. Program evaluation came about as a method for demonstrating to legislatures and other external authorities that a program was operating in the manner prescribed by the legislature and was achieving its ends in an effective and efficient manner. Chapter 2 emphasized planning, particularly strategic planning. Much more so than their private counterparts, public agencies are responsible for how they perform as well as what they achieve. Evaluation texts often divide evaluation approaches into *summative* evaluations that measure program outcomes and *formative* strategies that assess organization processes.[1] In this text we categorize the types of evaluations as either *outcome* or *process* oriented.

This chapter, however, illustrates that the distinction is not as cogent as it once was. Currently, public programs must demonstrate that they have defined specific missions for themselves that comply with outcomes intended by the legislature. They must also specify how program structure and content are organized to service the mission. Additionally, public programs must demonstrate that they organize themselves to maximize program transparency and accountability. The "nuts-and-bolts" discussion of process evaluation appears in chapter 5. Outcome evaluations are examined in chapters 6 and 7. This chapter, however, deals with the interrelationships of program standards, accountability, and evaluation.

Public social service and health service agencies are responsible for meeting a variety of external quality standards prescribed by professional associations. The standards are designed to ensure that program staffs are professionally qualified, that treatment modalities are consistent with minimal professional practices, and that they function in a manner beneficial to clients. This is in addition to efficiency standards imposed by the legislature or politically appointed administrators. A state-operated children's psychiatric facility, for example, would have to perform its mission in compliance with the mandates of the state legislature and the rules and operating procedures of the state department of mental health. In addition, the agency would have to meet quality standards prescribed by professional accrediting associations to be eligible for federal reimbursements for clients who are wards of the state. The standards are also a precondition for payment by private insurance companies.

The object of all these rules and regulations is to ensure a consistent quality of service that meets generally accepted standards of quality prescribed by the various disciplines represented in the organization. In this chapter we examine the concepts of professional standards, standards-based accreditation, and compliance audits. We are particularly interested in presenting how agencies engage in internal process evaluations to demonstrate compliance with externally imposed quality standards, as well as the achievement outcomes defined in a program's mission statement.

Standards-Based Organizational Assessment

An old vaudevillian asks, "How you doin'?" His partner replies, "As compared to what?" How well an agency is doing depends a great deal on who wants to know and the standard of comparison that is used to judge performance. Evaluators use the term **standards** to encompass a variety of criteria against which agency operations can usefully be judged.[2] Standards may be historical, comparative, industry-based, or engineered. These perspectives may overlap and be used in conjunction with each other, depending on the audience for whom an evaluation is to be conducted. The criteria that standards encompass commonly include appropriateness of activities for serving the agency's clientele and their impact on the problem at hand. Other standards might deal with the timeliness, quality, and quantity of services delivered and how the program monitors itself for standards compliance.[3] Professional associations develop standards for their members and elaborate processes whereby they can gain the imprimatur *accredited*.

Accreditation certifies that the program has demonstrated that the "how" and "what" of the program meets accreditation standards. Accreditation, moreover, is granted for a specific number of years (e.g., 5 or 7 years), after which it must again undergo a review. More and more, however, compliance standards prescribe that a program undergo self-assessment on a routine basis rather than when an accreditation visit is imminent. Normally, programs that do not comply with standards are given a period of time to adjust before losing their accreditation. Losing accreditation can be perilous for programs that are a subset of a larger mission, such as a degree program within a university. When budget cuts are required administrators will favor programs demonstrating that they have met professional standards over those that do not.

Accreditation is a double-edged sword. Overhead administrators and elected officials can use accrediting reports to judge the performance of their subordinates. Conversely, program managers can use deficiencies in accreditation reports to wring funds from their superiors for such things as additional staff and library resources. In some cases, they can make the case for salary increases for themselves when accrediting teams assert that salaries are far below professional standards. The argument goes that quality programs require excellent professionals who cannot be recruited to programs offering substandard compensation packages.

Program Accreditation

Accrediting standards are illustrated using examples from higher education and law enforcement. Masters Degree Programs in Public Administration are accredited by the National Association of Schools of Public Affairs and Administration (NASPAA). NASPAA began as a vehicle for program administrators to meet and exchange ideas on curriculum content, program delivery, faculty development, program autonomy and so forth. Eventually, it developed a Committee on Program Accreditation (COPRA) to move the discipline towards excellence. This working group, in turn, developed a set of quality standards against which programs could judge themselves. In 1986, NASPAA became the official accrediting arm of the Council on Postsecondary Accreditation (COPA) as an accrediting organization for master's degree programs. NASPAA has developed nine (9) standards against which programs are assessed. Five of the nine standards are presented on the following pages.[4]

Standard 1 emphasizes the indispensability of demonstrating that the program is organized and operated to achieve its defined mission. This is a combination of both a compliance standard and an engineered standard. It is an industry standard because it is required of all programs. It is engineered because each program must tailor its own mission to the audience it serves and the specific competencies of its faculty.

NASPAA Standard 1–Managing the Program Strategically

1.1 *Mission Statement*. The program will have a statement of mission that guides performance expectations and their evaluation, including

- Its purpose and public service values, given the program's particular emphasis on public affairs, administration, and policy;

- The population of students, employers and professionals the program intends to service; and

- The contributions it intends to produce to advance the knowledge, research, and practice of public affairs, administration, and policy.

1.2 *Performance Expectations*. The program will establish observable program goals, objectives, and outcomes, including expectations for student learning, consistent with its mission

1.3 *Program Evaluation*. The program will collect, apply, and report information about its performance and its operations to guide the evolution of the program's mission and design and its continuous improvement with respect to standards two through seven.

NAASPA allows for flexibility in program emphasis; one size does not fit all. Some schools of public affairs emphasize the training of persons who will play a leadership role in defining public policy. Others might want to focus on executive development; yet another may have a focus on training city managers. Explicit in the standard is the expectation that programs will emphasize appropriate public service values—that is, values of professional management in a democratic context. In addition, part of the standard sets the expectation that program faculty members will contribute to the creation of knowledge, research, and practices of the field. The program may specify original theory-based research, research aimed at improving the delivery of services, and/or the consulting and training for public agencies. How program faculty meet this standard may vary with their defined mission, but the accrediting agency will hold them accountable for demonstrating whatever they specify.

As evidenced by subset 1.2 (Performance Expectations), of particular concern To NASPAA is that specific learning outcomes, as defined in the mission, be evident in student competencies. For example, it is not sufficient for students to have taken a class in the principles of management. The program must also be able to demonstrate that the students understand and can apply these principles on completion of the class. Some programs include a culminating experience requirement. This can take the form of a comprehensive examination of student understanding of knowledge, principles, and practices included in the program. Others require that students complete a piece of original research in which they demonstrate their ability to apply skills gained in the program to a practical problem or that tests administrative theory. Still others require that the student provide a portfolio of the work they have completed in the course of their studies.

Standard 1.3 (Program Evaluation) stipulates that every accredited program must be able to demonstrate that it has in place mechanisms for measuring student outcomes and that curriculum content remains consistent with the mission statement. Furthermore, the program must demonstrate that during each accrediting cycle it has systematically engaged in ongoing reviews of such things as course content, student learning outcomes, and so forth. This requirement is manifested in compliance with standards two through seven. The aim of this book is to equip students with the basic skills necessary for meeting this sort of standard.

NASPAA Standard 2–Matching Governance with the Mission

2.1. *Administrative Capacity.* The program will have an administrative infrastructure appropriate for its mission, goals, and objectives in all delivery modalities employed.

2.2. *Faculty Governance.* An adequate faculty nucleus—at least five (5) full-time faculty members or their equivalent—will exercise substantial determining influence for governance and implementation of the program.

This standard, perhaps more than any other, relates to organization processes. MPA programs must clearly specify the processes that will be followed to achieve the mission and must provide documentation of those processes (e.g., curriculum components; student advising and evaluation; and recruiting, promotion, and evaluation of faculty).

Faculty Governance (standard 2.2) refers to program jurisdiction and autonomy. The standard does not prescribe a specific structure. The reality is that MPA programs may be freestanding or may be a subcomponent of a larger department or school. Very large programs are housed in specialized schools. All undergo accreditation; therefore, this standard is interpreted broadly by COPRA. The governance standard is designed to assure that the program faculty per se has substantial control of the program. Otherwise, university administrators might create a degree in name only in order to recruit students. It is hoped that substantial autonomy in the hands of subject-matter experts will lead to sound program decisions consistent with the highest standards of the discipline.

An apocryphal story tells how retired General Dwight Eisenhower addressed the faculty of Columbia University on the occasion of his appointment as university president. As the general assured the faculty they had the full support of the university, one professor whispered to his

---

NASPAA Standard 3–Matching Operations with the Mission: Faculty Performance

3.1 *Faculty Qualifications.* The program's faculty members will be academically or professionally qualified to pursue the program's mission.

3.2 *Faculty Diversity.* The program will promote diversity and a climate of inclusiveness through its recruitment and retention of faculty members.

3.3 *Research Scholarship and Service.* Program faculty members will produce scholarship and engage in professional and community service activities outside of the university appropriate to the program's mission, stage of their careers, and the expectations of their university.

---

neighbor, "The general doesn't understand that we *are* the university." Likewise, MPA programs are their faculties. Understanding this truth, NAASPA standard 3 requires a well-qualified faculty as a condition of accreditation (subset 3.1).

American society is a complex mix of ethnicities and religions all of whom have a reasonable expectation of inclusion in public service. The public workforce, moreover, is increasingly female at all levels. Aspiring public managers and executives must be prepared to deal with both the problems and the opportunities that emerge from a diverse workforce. NAASPA, therefore, requires that the curricula of MPA programs directly address diversity issues and that programs will promote diversity in faculty recruitment and subsequent development (subset 3.2). Diversity can further be addressed by bringing in a well-rounded group of speakers and adjunct faculty hires.

As noted in the earlier discussion of the mission statement, faculties are expected to engage in the development of theory and knowledge about public policy and administration. They also are expected to engage in such public service activities as consulting, training, service on boards and commissions and so forth (subset 3.3).

Taken in their entirety, the subsets of standard 4 insist that students be a central focus of the program. For example, subset 4.2 asks programs to match their admission practices to their stated mission. If for example, the mission of the program is to develop executive skills, it would be reasonable to require a specified number of years in management and leadership in government service as a condition of admission. On the other hand, if the mission is to train students for entry-level professional positions, priority could be given to new college graduates over more experienced applicants. Accordingly, subset 4.3 expects a well-developed internship program aimed at new graduates. Furthermore, a site-visit accreditation team would in all likelihood want to interview students and faculty regarding advising practices, job placement strategies, and so forth.

NASPAA Standard 4–Matching Operations with the Mission: Serving Students

4.1 *Student Recruitment.* The program will have student recruitment practices appropriate for its mission.

4.2 *Student Admissions.* The program will have and apply well-defined admissions criteria appropriate for its mission.

4.3 *Support for Students.* The program will ensure the availability of support services, such as curriculum advising, internship placement and supervision, career counseling, and job placement assistance to enable students to progress in careers in public affairs, administration, and policy.

4.4 *Student Diversity.* The program will promote diversity and a climate of inclusiveness through its recruitment and admissions practices and student support services.

The diversity expectations for faculty reflected in standard 3, subset 3.2, extend to students as well in subset 4.4 of standard 4. A quality program is distinguished by providing a climate of inclusion as well as assuring diversity in recruitment and admissions. Reviewing admissions data to assure services to the population in the university's catchment area is a first step. For example, an MPA program in Santa Clara County, California, would seek to recruit and admit members of the large Hispanic and Asian American communities. If either of these communities was underrepresented, special outreach efforts might be made to ensure that qualified persons in these communities were applying to and then attending the program. If a routine review of the student database revealed that a particular subset of students were not graduating in proportion to their admissions (e.g., Hispanic females), a special inquiry could be made as to the reasons; special efforts to mentor the group would be an appropriate adaptation.

Standard 5 (on the following page), the curriculum content standard, is an example of an industry standard reflecting the fact that a substantial consensus exists on a common set of knowledge and skills necessary to manage the people's business. NASPAA is careful to specify that there are no specifically required classes. Nevertheless, programs seeking accreditation must demonstrate how the common curriculum (those classes required for all students) provides the prescribed content.

The titles of classes are less important than their content, which must address the five skills included in subset 5.1. Management and leadership skills are central to preparing students for a public sector career. A program that emphasizes the dynamics of the public policy process would fulfill the second skill criterion, but not the first. Classes in the techniques of management, organization behavior and dynamics, budgeting, and leader-

---

NASPAA Standard 5–Matching Operations with the Mission: Student Learning

5.1 *Universal /Required Competencies.* As the basis for its curriculum, the program will adopt a set of required competencies related to its mission and (to) public service values. The required competencies will include five domains: the ability to:

- Lead and manage in the public governance;
- Participate in and contribute to the public policy process;
- Analyze, synthesize, think critically, solve problems, and make decisions;
- Articulate and apply a public service perspective; and
- Communicate and interact productively with a diverse changing workforce and citizenry.

5.2 *Mission-Specific Required Competencies.* The program will identify core competencies in other domains that are necessary and appropriate to implement its mission.

5.3 *Mission-Specific Elective Competencies.* The program will define its objectives and competencies for optional concentrations and specializations.

5.4 *Professional Competencies.* The program will ensure that students learn to apply their education, such as through experiential exercise and interactions with practitioners across the broad range of public affairs, administration, and policy professional and sectors.

---

ship would do so. Offering human resource management as an elective is acceptable—but having that class contain all the instruction relevant to diversity would not be acceptable because it is not required of everyone.

Subset 5.2 deals with the inclusion of competencies relevant to the defined mission of the organization. A program located in Pittsburg, Pennsylvania, that defined its mission as preparing students for careers in agencies located in the Three Rivers catchment area should contain content specific to the region as well as general management principles. The same criterion extends to elective competencies as in subset 5.3. For example, a program that defined its mission as preparing students for careers in policy analysis might do well to provide electives in quantitative analysis as well as specific policy area expertise (e.g., environmental studies, public health, and so forth).

Subset 5.4 speaks to the instilling of professional competencies. This can be accomplished by a case-study approach wherein students apply their problem-solving skills in a classroom setting. This can be supplemented by internships for those without substantial experience. In addition, the curriculum could involve students in real-world projects for agencies. Some programs require a culminating experience in which students apply their skills to a specific policy issue or the resolution of a specific problem with the guidance of a faculty member. (It is worth noting that in the state of California, all professional graduate degree programs in public universities must provide a defined culminating experience as a requirement specified by law.)

Standards Application

The foregoing standards are the criteria against which programs seeking accreditation are judged. The process evaluation component involves illustrating to the satisfaction of NASPAA that the program is in compliance. This is achieved through detailed written documentation that is preliminarily reviewed by COPRA for compliance. A site visitation by external evaluators is conducted to answer any questions that COPRA may have regarding program compliance with one or another standard. The site-visit team also engages in specific content review to determine the degree to which the program does what it is says it does. Prior to the submission of documentation, however, the program must undertake a rigorous self-assessment that can take a year or more and may involve a number of data-gathering activities, discussed below.

Curriculum Review

Core faculty should periodically review course syllabi and other content materials (a) to determine if the class, as currently taught, fulfills the mission and meets the NASPAA content standards, and (b) to identify any unanticipated overlaps and duplication between the content of various classes in the curriculum.

A Stakeholder Survey

The program faculty identify the organizations and populations impacted by program activities. For example, the faculty might choose to survey executives in organizations who currently or potentially might employ program graduates. These consumers/stakeholders might be asked to assess the qualification and skills of program graduates in their employ. They might also be queried as to new skills or knowledge that the program should provide its graduates. The sample group for curriculum assessment might also include faculty of similar programs in adjacent service areas.

An Alumni Survey

Program graduates could be surveyed as to program quality and relevance to their careers. Questions might include the relevance of the curriculum to their current position and/or its impact on their career advancement. They may also be asked to candidly assess the services provided to them by the program (e.g. advisor access, faculty mentoring, internship placement, instructional quality and so forth).

A Survey of Current Students

Students currently taking classes might be asked to assess a range of factors, not the least of which would be the quality of instruction they receive from the faculty—whether core or adjunct. Students are probably the best source of information regarding advising services, access to their program records, and faculty–student involvement.

Student Focus Groups

Focus groups were made popular by marketing strategists seeking to package products and by political candidates seeking to identify issues that will resonate with voters. Similarly, a well-planned and well-executed student focus group can be an excellent way to get student input on everything from curriculum content, to instructional quality, to student services.

A Faculty Retreat

This is an excellent forum for discussing the data gathered from the various activities noted above. Based on the assessment, the faculty can then develop a mission statement and program goals through an evaluation of program successes and shortcomings, curriculum content, faculty changes, and new or developing needs in the program environment.

Document Preparation and Submission

Preparation for an initial accreditation or reaccreditation of a program is a complex task too large for a single faculty member. Good management of this process in accordance with NASPAA standards requires substantial involvement of the faculty in the accreditation process. Programs must prepare their review documents well in advance of the deadline date in order to have enough time for internal higher-level institutional review. Failure, to submit documents to the accreditation body in a timely fashion can postpone accreditation and require revisiting all of the activities listed above.

The normal NASPAA accreditation cycle is seven years. Clearly, the site-visit team has no interest in reviewing the admission decisions on all students admitted over seven years. The focus is therefore on the year just prior to the visit. A random sample of students admitted during the accrediting year is selected, and the site-visit team is provided access to their individual files. The number of files reviewed is a function of the size of the program. These files are reviewed to determine:

1. The degree to which the program applied its stated admissions requirements.

2. The curriculum presented for graduation by individual students.

3. The timeliness of degree completion.

Where comprehensive exams or thesis/writing projects are required, the review team also may look at content and quality. Assuming the program is able to demonstrate substantial compliance with the various standards it will receive a positive written report from the site-visit team to COPRA, which in turn provides accreditation.

Agency Accreditation

Submitting an agency for accreditation is a much larger undertaking than seeking accreditation for a specific program. This is particularly true if an agency is highly differentiated as to tasks and program responsibilities. Universities, for example, have multiple programs and administrative units that must be reviewed for organization-wide accreditation. Of late, law enforcement associations have adopted accreditation as a way to raise standards generally, but particularly in the agency under review. We use law enforcement to illustrate the agency accreditation process.

In 1979 four professional law enforcement associations cooperated to create the Commission on Accreditation of Law Enforcement Agencies (CALEA).[5] Their aim was to provide a mechanism to upgrade the professionalism of American law enforcement agencies through a rigorous accreditation process. Agencies choosing to seek accreditation, which at present is still voluntary, must commit to several years of serious introspection regarding everything from the agency's purpose, to its organization, to its relationships to external actors. To obtain accreditation, agencies must also undertake systematic program adaptations to correct identified deficiencies. The adaptations may include vigorous training of line personnel and managers and systematic overhauls of the organization's structure.

> CALEA insists that it is: "Seeking to establish the best professional practices; the standards prescribe 'what' agencies should be doing, but not 'how' they should be doing it. That decision is left up to the individual agency and its Chief Executive Officer."[6]

CALEA, like NASPAA, uses a range of standards. Unlike NAASPA, CALEA standards offer a great deal more specificity as to areas covered by the standards. Some of the high points are treated in box 4.1 on the following page.

Personnel processes throughout government agencies are critical, if for no other reason than that operating a merit system of recruitment is a condition of obtaining federal funds.[7] In addition, appropriate structures and processes for protecting employees in the disciplinary process must be maintained. This is especially significant for sworn officers who may have to waive certain legal rights in the internal investigation process. In extreme cases, the information gained in this process could result in criminal prosecution of the officer.

A plethora of other standards deal with such aspects of law enforcement as patrol, criminal investigations, vice drugs and organized crime, juvenile operations, and so forth. This extensive list of standards suggests that when compared to NAASPA, CALEA may have much more defined expectations as to how and what is being done. This may stem in part from the broader mandate of CALEA that deals with law enforcement agencies as a whole rather than addressing idiosyncratic programs within agencies.

Box 4.1   CALEA Standards for Law Enforcement Agencies

Standard 1.0–Law Enforcement Role and Authority

This standard encompasses ethics, legal authority, use of force, and a variety of operating procedures that stem from these categories. Legal authority, for example, includes the authority to carry weapons and the use of force, compliance with constitutional requirements, search and seizure, and so forth. The authority standard addresses relationships to other agencies and has a good deal to do with agency accountability and overhead actors (e.g., city councils or county boards of supervisors). A city charter, for instance, might provide for the police chief to be appointed by the city manager (with the approval of the city council) and serve at the pleasure of the manager. An elected county sheriff, on the other hand, would exercise a great deal more autonomy. In each instance, however, it is the entire agency that is under review. This contrasts dramatically with NASPAA accreditation, whose threshold standard requires that a program be a part of an already accredited university or college.

Standard 11.0–Organization and Administration

Included under this standard are description of organization structure, chain of command (organization chart), and employee accountability and responsibility. The expectation is that the agency will have thought through these elements and provided documentation, including maintenance of accreditation data. CALEA's concern with organizational structure and management recognizes that within the law enforcement community, standards regarding structure, lines of authority and levels of responsibility can vary greatly depending on the history and growth of a particular agency. Not every agency, however, has achieved the highest levels of professional structures and/or managerial policies and procedures. A large urban agency with highly differentiated organization structures (e.g., a patrol division, an investigation division that is further divided between robbery homicide, auto theft, and so forth) would have to meet very different standards than a relatively small agency with a lower level of functional specialization. The CALEA standards and the self-analysis inherent in the accreditation process can prove to be of great assistance in an agency's self-improvement efforts.

Standard 15.0–Planning and Research, Goals and Objectives, and Crime Analysis

The reader will recall that under the NAASPA standards, program goals and priorities must flow from the mission as defined by the individual program. Under CALEA standards, however, a less specific emphasis is placed on mission and goals. CALEA requires documentation of planning activities, an annual update of goals and objectives, and a description of the organization's placement of planning activities. This is not to suggest that CALEA places a low priority on mission; rather, it suggests that a substantial consensus exists regarding mission among law enforcement professionals.

> **Standard 16.0–Allocation and Distribution of Personnel and Personnel Alternatives**
>
> Subcomponents of this standard require the agency to specify the allocation of personnel among various functions and specialized assignments. These include specifying the position management system, workload assessments, and specialized assignments. The standard further specifies that the agency must report on various aspects of the use of reserve officers. The latter includes everything from recruitment and training to performance evaluation and educational requirements.
>
> This personnel standard does not encompass all aspects of the human resources system. Separate standards address classification (standard 21), compensation and benefits (standard 22), collective bargaining (standard 24), grievance procedures (standard 25), and disciplinary procedures (standard 26). Personnel structure, as a standard, has to do with the formal organization for recruitment and training of officers. Some agencies exercise a great deal of autonomy in recruitment and selection, having their own human resource division that develops and administers examinations, training modules, and so forth. Other agencies are dependent on external personnel agencies for these sorts of services.

The operations standard also allows agencies to be in compliance even with considerable variations in the mission. Central to operations is the command structure of the agency. A medium-sized city, for example, might have a patrol division led by a patrol captain with subunits led by lieutenants, one of whom manages a basic patrol and emergency response operation and another who oversees a traffic operation involving motorcycle and radar units. A separate detective division, again led by a captain, could investigate all matters of reported crime (organized crime, drug enforcement, auto theft, and so forth). Larger departments may have subunits specializing in each of the foregoing detective division areas. Very large departments may be organized geographically by precincts, with some investigating functions performed by generalist detectives assigned to the precinct who are supplemented by specialized units (from drug enforcement to gang responses) that operate citywide.

Unlike NASPAA, not every CALEA standard is applicable to every agency. An urban police department, for example, might house its prisoners with the sheriff's department, therefore reducing the applicability of the prisoner standard. A small rural agency might depend on a state criminal division to investigate major crimes, and on a statewide crime lab for investigative results. By the same token, investigation agencies do not engage in traffic patrols or the housing of prisoners.

What accreditation officials look for is a match between the structure and the stated organizational intentions. Furthermore, they look for lines-of-command authority and decision making. The goal is not "one size fits all." Accreditation officials expect professional-quality conduct and training standards, well-developed policy and procedure manuals, and a nexus between what is espoused by the agency and what is observed.

Importance of the Accreditation Process

Accreditation, with its cumbersome self-analyses processes, is an established part of the culture of higher education. NASPAA program accreditation is essential to graduate program credibility. Only programs housed in the most prestigious institutions can ignore the accreditation process with impunity. Programs in relatively unpopulated areas without significant competition for the targeted student population may also ignore accreditation. Law enforcement has come to accreditation relatively recently (in 1979). Agencies that successfully undertake the rigors of the accreditation process find themselves in the rather elite company of the top 20% of law enforcement agencies. Accreditation, however, is by no means required. Law enforcement agencies are created and operate under a variety of state and local policy-making authorities, and therefore it would prove impossible to require accreditation across all jurisdictions.

All accreditation processes share the goal of ensuring program quality. They do so with a common set of procedures:

1. The decision is taken to undergo accreditation.

2. A serious self-examination is performed vis-á-vis the standards of the industries, including systematic documentation of agency efforts at self-review.

3. A preliminary examination is performed by the accrediting agency.

4. A site-visit review is completed by subject-matter experts.

5. Materials are submitted for final accreditation.

A final procedure in this list might include reaccreditation: After a specified length of time (5 to 7 years) the agency repeats the process to determine whether its policies, procedures, organization structure, and so forth are consistent with current standards.

For some (especially those for whom the process is mandated), accreditation can seem like an additional responsibility that diverts agency energy and resources from the "real mission." This cynicism is more evident in the reaccrediting process than in initial application, but nevertheless it tends to undermine the accreditation effort.

For others, accreditation is a serious effort at upgrading the agency, using professional standards as a guidepost. The systematic examination of who we are, what we do, and what we ought to be doing can have positive second-order benefits in the form of building a substantial consensus among agency personnel regarding the mission and their roles in it. The process may also cause personnel to bring the full weight of their collective intelligence to the task of correcting recognized deficits in the agency or program.

Managerial Audits

A decidedly unpleasant examination of organization policies, procedures, and expenditures is characteristic of the managerial audit. While it is possible that the standards of a relevant accrediting organization may be the basis of an audit, it is far more likely that it is generated by critics of an agency's program. The process may involve an external auditor who comes with a set of predetermined methods and questions with the goal of determining if the agency is in fact operating appropriately and efficiently. The auditor surveys managers regarding the mission and goals of their subsystems, how their work is scheduled, how their priorities are determined, and so forth. The auditor may also inquire about expenditure levels and staffing ratios. He or she may follow up surveys by creating focus groups of managers who are asked to identify negative features of the organization. The auditor's report is submitted to the person or persons who retained the auditor's services (e.g., the chief executive, the governing board, and/or the legislature). Unfortunately, the intention of such audits normally is identifying problems, fixing blame, and otherwise satisfying the critics.

Audits that are generated for negative reasons may or may not generate change in an agency. They nearly always have a negative impact on morale, engendering mistrust and mutual animus among actors in the agency as each party seeks to blame the other. However, audits need not be automatically negative. They can form the basis for planned organizational change and quality improvements if program staffs are allowed to participate in the definition of the audit's parameters and in the development of change strategies for which they will be responsible.

Some managerial audits are commissioned by top management or, more often, by funding agencies or legislatures to be sure that an agency is in compliance with its legislative mandate.[8] Very often *compliance audits* focus on purchasing procedures, reimbursement practices, and contracting methods used by the agency. For example, did the agency follow established state bidding regulations? This could include length of time for advertising for contractors, accepting the lowest responsible bid, and treating all bidders equally. Not infrequently, disgruntled losers in the bidding process will complain of nepotism, cronyism that provides the favored bidder inside information not available to their competitors. Were contracts let to the lowest bidders? Are appropriate accounting procedures followed?

Compliance audits frequently are generated by questions regarding management practices in the agency. Even when an agency has met the sorts of compliance criteria listed above, it may not be achieving an appropriate level of service for its clientele or meeting professional standards for service delivery. In such instances, being an accredited agency or program can go a long way towards convincing critics that the agency meets the highest professional standards.

Notes

[1] See Peter H. Rossi, Howard E. Freeman, and Mark W. Lipsey, *Evaluation: A Systematic Approach,* 7th ed. (Thousand Oaks, CA: Sage, 2004).

[2] For an application of the standards notion to education, see The Joint Committee on Standards for Educational Evaluation, with James R. Sanders, *The Program Evaluation Standards: How to Assess Evaluation of Educational Programs*, 2nd ed. (Thousand Oaks, CA: Sage, 1994). Hospitals, mental health facilities, and drug and alcohol facilities must comply with the uniform standards of the Joint Commission on Accreditation of Hospitals (*Accreditation Manual for Hospitals* [Chicago: Joint Commission on Accreditation of Hospitals, 2004]; and *2004–2005 Comprehensive Accreditation Manual for Behavioral Health Care* (CAMBHC) [Chicago: Joint Commission on Accreditation of Health Care, 2004]).

[3] The authors wish to acknowledge the contributions of Peter Vail, L. H. Autrey, and Owen Pollard in the development of this standards framework.

[4] Persons interested an in-depth treatment of all the NASPAA standards are referred to www.NASPAA.com

[5] The associations were the International Association of Chiefs of Police (IACP); the National Organization of Black Law Enforcement Executives (NOBLE); the National Sheriffs' Association (NSA); and the Police Executive Research Forum (PERF). http://calea.org/newweb/AboutUs/Aboutus.htm

[6] This assertion appears on the CALEA home page (http://www.calea.org/content/law-enforcement-program-standards).

[7] For a more detailed discussion of the merit principles, see Ronald D. Sylvia and C. Kenneth Meyer, *Public Personnel Administration*, 2nd ed. (Fort Worth, TX: Harcourt, 2002), pp. 137–46.

[8] For a more complete discussion, see Dwight F. Davis, "Do You Want a Performance Audit or a Program Evaluation?" *Public Administration Review* (January/February, 1990): 35–41.

five

Monitoring and Improving Internal Processes

In chapter 4 we discussed monitoring internal processes to bring them into line with accreditation standards. Frequently, such efforts lead to comprehensive agency introspection to determine the appropriateness of the current mission, to develop a consensus around it, or to improve the efficiency of internal processes. In fact, these sorts of interventions in the organization's processes predate standards-based evaluations. The human relations school of management challenged organizations to upgrade by empowering their employees with meaningful participation in organizational decision making, challenging work assignments, and substantial autonomy.[1] Beginning in the late 1960s the *organization development movement* took human relations management to the next level by devising specific organization interventions.[2] In the 1990s *Total Quality Management* came to the fore.[3] Here the focus was on product/service quality and customer service through employee empowerment. A bemused young Air Force lieutenant decided to ask a major with twenty years of service what it all meant. The major's reply was, "The Air Force wants you to try hard and think about ways of doing your job better."

In this chapter we examine managed change using the example of a children's psychiatric facility to illustrate how an agency can use measurement and analysis to formulate and apply its own quality and performance standards to achieve employee-developed goals.

In our hypothetical children's facility, the staff might undertake a case audit review of the clients who had been served in each of the previous five years as part of its standards-based evaluation. A work group could be formed to examine the case histories of 6% of clients served. The sample could be developed from a list of all clients served. If the agency served 300 clients a year, this would mean an examination of 18 client records for each year. The records could be examined for the appropriateness of diagnoses using the standards of the American Psychiatric Association.[4] The APA maintains a list of generally accepted diagnoses for mental and emotional illness among children. Under each of these diagnoses, typical symptoms are listed. The diagnosis of each of the sample records could be compared to industry standards to determine the appropriateness of the agency's diagnostic and treatment services. The industry in this case consists of children's inpatient psychiatric facilities.

From the analysis the agency might learn, for example, that in the sampled cases, complete or partially inappropriate diagnoses or treatment regimens were applied to 4 clients the first year, 8 clients the second, 2 the third, 5 the fourth year, and 4 in the fifth year. From these data the director might infer that the average error rate was 4.6 or 25.5% of the sample. On the other hand, the director might view the second-year data as potentially aberrant, especially in light of the low figure of 2 errors in the third year. The director might then ask for a more in-depth look at the second year to determine if the bad records showed up by chance or if the unusually high rate of error in the second-year sample (44.4%) truly reflected on the agency's across-the-board performance for that year. Of equal interest is whether the errors noted represent minor failures (e.g., neglecting to note treatment or observations in the chart) versus serious issues such as deviations from prescribed treatment regimens or erroneous diagnoses. The former can be corrected with relatively minor in-house training. The latter should trigger a full-blown program review.

Even without the "aberrant year" the average error in the cases sampled was 3.75 per year for a percentage rate of 21%. Such an error rate would not be acceptable to managers of a mass-production manufacturing process, and the rate should be intolerable to mental health-care professionals, who are directly impacting the lives of their clients. Ill-served clients in a social service agency are impacted as individuals, and the harm can be irreparable. It is also important to note that such a high error rate could endanger the agency's license and the willingness of third-party payers to pay for agency services. Clearly, 21% does not meet the industry standard.

Returning to our historical standards reference point, the director would probably institute measures to correct the problem immediately. He or she might also establish goals and objectives rooted in a historical standard. For instance, the director might set a target of a 3% error rate to be achieved over the next three years. Alternatively, using the history as a base, the director might set a performance standard of 3 percentage points improvement per year over the previous five-year average.

The performance standard is an example of an *engineered standard.* The improvement rate is not specified anywhere in industry guidelines, nor can it be found in federal and state guidelines. Instead, it represents the director's expectations based on his or her professional expertise and experience. If the director wanted to validate the analysis and change expectations, he or she could consult with directors of other like agencies regarding their performance levels and approaches to change. In other words, the engineered standard of the director could be checked against the standards of similar agencies to develop a comparative standard. (To enhance staff acceptance of the changes, and thereby increase the probability of success, the director could engineer the standard in an inclusive manner that maximized participation. Design participation ensures employee buy-in regarding the planned changes. See the section on Solution Development later in the chapter.)

Negative findings of the sampling process reflect badly on an agency's *quality assurance* process, an internal process for checking work on an ongoing basis.[5] Such systems are also a requirement for maintaining agency accreditation. The agency's problems include performance, structural arrangements and processes, and external compliance. It is both unrealistic and insufficient merely to will change in a complex organization. Managers should not expect that staff members will automatically agree with the need for change and be open to management initiatives. Furthermore, a manager can virtually guarantee failure in the change-implementation process by announcing the goals and telling workers that they are responsible for their implementation—in addition to their regular job duties.

Process Intervention/Evaluation

There is only one argument for doing something;
the rest are arguments for doing nothing.[6]

People proposing change will ignore the above tongue-in-cheek aphorism at their peril. Employee resistance to change can be overcome by involving them in the problem-analysis and solution-development stages of the process. Successful implementation of the change can be assured by carefully assigning responsibility for various change components to specific individuals, developing a project calendar with specified dates for achieving change components, and following up the change process with an evaluation.

Process intervention fills a gap left by goal-oriented outcome evaluations. To paraphrase one practicing administrator, we are not interested in whether the impact of X on Y is statistically significant. What we really want to know is, if Y is not happening, what is wrong with X? The level of certainty necessary to animate an administrator is significantly lower than required for publishing academic research. The latter generally requires a confidence interval of 0.5 before accepting that the relationship between variables is reliable. That is, the researchers are 95% certain of the alleged relationship between variables. But it is a poor administrator who would not move to correct a problem that he or she was 75% certain existed. In addition, outcome evaluations reach valid conclusions that are most important to top decision makers rather than line managers faced with correcting program deficiencies. The problem-solving focus distinguishes process interventions from outcome-focused efforts. As we shall see, however, interventions are often based on reports of unacceptable outcome.

Generally, the process intervention model can be described as occurring in four phases, as shown in box 5.1. The first phase, problem identification, is the most crucial element. In this phase the evaluator may use a variety of techniques, ranging from interviews with the agency director and program staff to sophisticated research designs involving survey research and measures of program outputs. The second phase involves developing solutions to the problems identified in the first phase. These solutions may include modest redistributions of resources among organizational units or a complete reordering of agency activities. The third phase involves implementing the solution. In some cases this phase is just a passage of time between the decision to do something differently and the collection of data to determine whether the solution worked. When the solution involves major or even moderate changes, it becomes necessary to devise a change-management structure to ensure that the solutions are not lost in the rush of day-to-day agency activities. The final phase of the process approach involves collecting data to determine whether the solutions were implemented as intended and whether the solutions produced the desired effects.

Box 5.1   The Four Phases of Process Intervention/Evaluation

Phase I: Problem Identification
- The process evaluator meets with program officials and engages in a series of problem identification activities.
- The evaluator presents identified problems to program staff.

Phase II: Solution Development
Program officials and the evaluator select a course of action to resolve agency problems.

Phase III: Implementation
- The solutions are put into operation, with specific individuals taking responsibility for various components of the strategy.
- Management control systems are put in place to see that agreed-upon changes are scheduled and carried out.

Phase IV: Feedback Evaluation
The evaluator and/or program staff engage in systematic assessments of the impacts of the changes on the organization and the program.

Problem Identification

The first task in process intervention is to identify the problem as precisely as possible. In our children's center example, the director asked a work group to sample program records for the last five years to determine compliance with external standards. The agency was found to be out of compliance; however, the equally important question as to *why* should also be asked. Several approaches are appropriate for obtaining an answer to this question, including written or telephone surveys of staff referral sources (e.g., the courts, physicians in private practice, and public clinics) and the parents of current and former clients. The director could assign this task to a specific individual or committee. Alternatively, the agency could retain a process-oriented consultant/evaluator. (For the purpose of discussion, the term *evaluator* will be used to designate the person leading the initiative.) The evaluator could also meet with the staff and parents in informal groups to discuss agency problems and possible solutions. In addition, the evaluator might wish to further analyze the sampled records for problem indicators such as inadequate documentation, incomplete charting, noncompliance with agency quality procedures, and so forth. Each approach has advantages and disadvantages.

Surveys

Formal surveys have several advantages. First, a written survey can ensure input from a representative sampling of the organization's staff and clients. Second, each respondent answers the same query and uses the same construct for formulating his or her response (such as a 1-to-5 scale asking the respondents to agree or disagree with the statement). Third, the data collected from respondents can be applied to a specific problem or problems by carefully constructing the research questionnaire. Unfortunately, one cannot be absolutely certain that the questionnaire addresses the correct problem. This problem can be somewhat alleviated by including a set of open-ended items in which respondents are invited to clarify their responses or raise other issues that concern them.

Drawbacks to the survey approach are that surveys are expensive, time consuming, and require a significant competence in statistical analysis. The decision to undertake a survey research project should therefore depend on the level of information certainty the organization needs and the resources that are available for the project. When possible, the surveyor should avoid canned instruments that contain generic questions directed at predetermined problems that have an overall design intended to apply to all kinds of organizations.[7]

Group Interviews

Group interviews can be carried out inexpensively and within a short time frame. The evaluator in our case would meet with representatives from the various echelons and specialties within the organization, and with parents.[8] Managers and supervisors, for example, may have entirely different perspectives on problems than line staff. Specialists, moreover, may provide useful perspectives on cooperation levels across disciplines about which higher-level managers know nothing. While group meetings are generally economical and effective, consultants must beware of a few common pitfalls.

The Squeaky Wheel Syndrome.   With the group-meeting approach, the evaluator can make qualitative assessments of the nature and intensity of worker sentiments in various sectors of the organization. Unfortunately, the evaluator must take pains to determine the extent to which sentiments expressed by individual participants are representative of the organization as a whole. For example, a group of psychiatric aides might be angry about recent layoffs and are frustrated by their belief that management is attempting to thwart their efforts to unionize. Such an encounter might produce insights regarding the general state of employee morale but offer little regarding diagnoses, treatment, and documentation errors. However, a follow-up discussion with supervisors, either individually or in a group, might reveal that management–worker problems had been ongoing for some time and that employees were angry about management decisions to discipline workers for failing to follow treatment regimes.

Even in the absence of sharp divisions or extreme sentiments, the squeaky wheel phenomenon may occur as a result of a group's tendency to defer to its more vocal members. Unfortunately, these expressions may be an exercise in ego gratification rather than articulations of widespread organization or community sentiment. The skills of the evaluator as a group discussion leader can help control the squeaky wheel syndrome. The ideal group size is between 8 and 10 people. Given a manageable group size, the consultant can guide the discussion, bring the group back to the problem at hand, and generally draw out input from the more reticent members.

The Information Suppression Syndrome.   A situation may arise in which administrative personnel suppress any expression by rank-and-file employees of opinions contrary to their own. In such situations, group meetings may not produce correct information. This process is usually subtle and is characterized by some combination of the items discussed below.

Prior to the evaluator's visit an administrator or division manager may hold a staff meeting and emphasize the importance of presenting a united front and/or not "airing dirty laundry" in public. The administrator might also suggest that the staff confine themselves to responding to the evaluator's questions without volunteering additional information on "extraneous matters." When meeting with the evaluator, the administrator also may engage in a variation on the squeaky wheel syndrome by focusing the discussion on a specific problem and taking issue with anybody who seeks to broaden the scope of the discussion, including the evaluator. Another tactic is to offer "clarifications" on every point made by the staff in order to portray the problem in the most favorable light. After several such clarifications, the evaluator will experience difficulty eliciting staff input.

The best way to control for the information suppression syndrome is to meet separately with staff and with administrative personnel. However, even separate meetings cannot rule out the impact of staff meetings that precede the evaluator's visit. An added benefit of separate meetings is that variations in perspectives are more likely to emerge. In the opposite extreme, an administrator who meets with the evaluator and the staff together may hold back to avoid dominating the discussion. In this case, the evaluator receives only a staff perspective. If the administrator takes an active part in the discussion to offer a broader perspective, the staff might then hold back in the belief that the consultant is seeking only the broad view. Holding separate meetings with administrators and staff can avoid these pitfalls.

Miles' Law.   Recall the quotation from Rufus Miles that was introduced in chapter 2: "Where you stand depends on where you sit."[9] Miles was an official the Bureau of the Budget located in the Executive Office of the President. Miles noted that the very best budget analysts could find the fat in an agency budget, no matter how well hidden. Particularly good analysts were subject to being hired away by the agencies that they monitored—after which these self-same ruthless budget cutters could no longer find any fat in the agency's budgets.

Similarly, bureaucracy is made of interdependent subunit specialties that tend to have a narrow rather than a broad worldview. So in our example, nurses and psych attendants will focus on factors that are very different than those identified by the billing office or the psychiatric social workers. The evaluator should develop queries that are directly related to the subunit specializations. He or she can then build on these insights by asking staff members to speculate on any organizational factors that might contribute to the problems they identify.

Unstructured Input.   A final problem with group interviews is inconsistency of inputs. When these meetings are carried out in an unstructured, open-ended fashion, the members of the organizational community can express whatever concerns them, but these concerns may not be related to the problem at hand. In our example, the evaluator wishes to determine the origins of the problems in diagnoses and treatment. A prudent approach is to maintain a relaxed atmosphere in order to permit all problems to emerge. However, unless the meeting agendas are structured, the discussion may degenerate into a debate over extraneous issues such as salaries and leave policies, inadequate staff appreciation, and so forth. By structuring the discussion, the evaluator can gain specific information regarding staff knowledge of diagnoses and treatment standards; agency policies and procedures for conducting and documenting treatment; and what sorts of quality assurance mechanisms are in place and if, in fact, they are being utilized. Setting aside a portion of the meeting for unstructured input serves the same purpose as the open-ended section of the survey research questionnaire. Both may produce evidence of problems not previously considered by the evaluator or the administrator.

The challenge for the evaluator is to sift through the data and identify patterns and interdependencies in the problems and systems that the staff report. For this reason, that broadly trained evaluators often enlist the help of subject matter experts in interpreting their findings and formulating recommendations. These may be external experts or, more likely, an executive workgroup drawn from the best and brightest in the agency.

Supplemental Procedures

The survey-research and group-interview approaches provide the evaluator with staff perceptions of problems. Because these perceptions frequently do not tell the entire story, however, the consultant may wish to engage in supplemental analysis before submitting recommendations. For example, one might use the **participant-observer approach** to get a first-hand view of the treatment procedures and the division of labor on the wards. In addition, the consultant should always undertake a review of organizational structures and operating procedures to determine whether recent changes could be the cause of the problem at hand. This procedure is called an **interactive managerial audit**. Both these supplemental procedures would enhance the analysis in our example.

The Participant-Observer Approach. This procedure has roots in the research traditions of cultural anthropology,[10] when a participant-observer visits a subject culture and studies how various functions common to all cultures are performed. The methodology has been popular among those who evaluate education programs because it allows the researcher to make qualitative as well as quantitative assessments of program content. The key to the method is to observe subjects as they go about their daily activities while blending in as much as possible so as not to affect the behavior of subjects. For a cultural anthropologist this means living in the village, listening and observing. For education evaluators it can mean sitting in a classroom, attending staff meetings, and taking notes without participating in the discussions or influencing classroom dynamics.

In our children's facility example, the consultant could spend some time in the dormitories, observing the treatment of the children and making note of any activities that are at variance with industry or agency procedures. For example, should a child lose control and become a threat to him- or herself, other patients, or staff, it might be necessary to restrain the child. It might also be necessary to place the child in seclusion. The evaluator would observe whether or not the restraining techniques prescribed in the agency policy manual were being followed. The evaluator could also note whether a child in seclusion was observed on a regular basis and returned to the dormitory as soon as appropriate. The next day, the evaluator could check the record to see if the seclusion incident was properly documented. The consultant also could visit classrooms to get a sense of the agency's educational component. To assess the environment, the consultant might observe the children at play.

An additional benefit of the participant-observer approach is that the staff is more likely to accept the analysis and the consultant's perceptions of identified problems when he or she makes the effort to view the problem from an operational perspective. In the current example, staff interactions with the consultant on the ward should make for greater acceptance of the analysis.

The downside of the participant observer is the danger of "going native." This is a pejorative term used to describe incidences in which the evaluators lose their professional objectivity and become unapologetic supporters of the program. In extreme anthropological examples, the researcher might take a native spouse and take sides in family or group quarrels. Among education evaluators, the danger is that they become such extreme champions of the program that they consciously or unconsciously slant their report data. The importance of maintaining one's professional objectivity and distance cannot be overemphasized.

The Interactive Managerial Audit. This type of managerial audit is distinguished from the method wherein the auditors introduce a prepackaged set of questionnaires aimed at identifying generic problems common to virtually any organization. In the interactive approach, the evaluator links his or her managerial expertise to the program knowledge of the staff and tailors the audit to the specific needs of the agency. To effectively assess organizational structures and operating procedures, an evaluator should be well acquainted with organization theory and the practice of management. In addition, the evaluator should be sensitive to recent changes in program procedures or personnel policies. In our current example, a task force might be formed to further review the sampled records for any patterns of recurring error. Such an analysis might reveal, for example, that the most frequent error in the treatment process was incorrect documentation of the medications given to clients. Such problems can be remedied without reforming all current agency procedures. The pattern could be corrected by in-house training sessions. If, on the other hand, the additional records audit determined a pattern of misdiagnoses and a failure to catch the error in the quality assurance process, the problem is much more severe.

Interactive managerial audits are particularly beneficial to the process evaluator for two reasons. First, they are relatively inexpensive to carry out because they mainly involve discussions between the consultant and administrative personnel, and reviews of operating procedures. Second, and more important, is the fact that analyzing organizational operating procedures is a prerequisite to making implementable recommendations. Suppose, for example, an evaluator learned that written agency policies and procedures were consistent with generally accepted industry standards, but that line staff often seemed to be unaware of the procedures or ignored them in the crush of day-to-day activities. Suppose further that the quality assurance structures and procedures were largely a hollow shell that looked good on paper but were rarely followed. This lack of implementation might be reflected in the minutes of the quality assurance committee. The committee might be meeting only irregularly and spending little time checking case histories for compliance.

Suppose that staff interviews identified morale problems among the staff due to layoffs and that perceived unfair employment practices had led to union-organizing activities by some workers. Even though morale problems do not directly cause quality problems, the development and implementation of any change strategy must involve the employees. Including them enhances the quality of the solutions and leads to good-faith implementation. Ignoring employees or unilaterally imposing solutions may lead to increased distrust, halfhearted implementation efforts, or even outright obstructionism.

Presenting the Findings

Upon completion of the problem identification phase, the task becomes one of presenting the findings to the administrator and senior management. To illustrate this process, we assume that (1) the evaluator employed the group interview approach, the participant-observer method, and an interactive managerial audit; (2) the evaluator concluded that employees lacked knowledge of appropriate procedures; (3) the professional staff was not implementing the quality assurance strategy as prescribed; and (4) educating employees would take months, and seeing the results of the changes might take even longer.

Identifying the problems and having solutions that correctly address them are not enough. The audience (the administrator, the professional and line staff) must be convinced that the analysis is correct. In our case, the administrator recognized that a problem existed and proposed to turn the situation around in three years using engineered standards. The changes, however, will not be self-executing, and having a ready-to-go solution further complicates matters (which would become even more complicated if the changes were announced prior to the arrival of the evaluator). Convincing people that they are being asked to analyze the situation and devise solutions is exceedingly difficult when they believe the administrator has already made a decision.

The evaluator's principal asset in the decision process is the ability to present information in a clear, concise, and nonthreatening manner. In our example, the evaluator might begin by reporting that the follow-up record analysis confirmed the existence of inaccuracies and errors. Next, the evaluator could present the results of the small-group consultations and partic-ipant-observer activities. Finally, the results of the managerial audit—substantial written compliance with standards but lack of implementation and employee knowledge—could be presented.

When presenting a controversial analysis, it is wise to enter the discussions with as much supporting evidence as possible. In the current example, the analysis of written factors is reinforced by the participant-observer findings. Whether an evaluator's expert analysis is accepted depends on how much credibility he or she has with the audience and on the persuasiveness of the presentation. If the administrator remains unconvinced, it might be necessary to undertake the problem identification process again with a new sampling of cases. In the current example, the administrator must be persuaded to engage in team-based solution development and change implementation.

Solution Development

Once the administrator is convinced of the wisdom of a team approach, he or she should announce the formation of a task force that will develop solutions in the short term and oversee implementation of the changes over the long term. Whenever possible, these solutions should be devised in close consultation with the administrator and program personnel.

The goal of the consultative problem-solving model is to generate solutions that are workable, affordable, and acceptable to line personnel. An often unnoticed second-order benefit is staff "buy-in." That is, the staff enthusiastically endorses the proposed changes and actively participates in their implementation. In the children's facility example, there is strong administrative support for instructing workers on correct policies and procedures and for upgrading the implementation of quality control activities. The task force should be representative of the various professional groups in the agency: clinical staff (psychiatrists, psychologists and social workers), nursing staff, and teaching and administrative staff. The task force ideally would convene away from the facility to enhance an objective focus on the problems at hand. The administrator would begin the session with a statement of commitment to the problem-solving process, after which the evaluator would present a findings report.

After the consultant summarized the findings, he or she would ask the group members to share their insights as to the accuracy of the analysis and to suggest other problems that may have been overlooked. Only when the staff is convinced that all relevant problems have been identified should discussion proceed to formulating solutions. At this juncture, the administrator's three-year timetable for correcting the problems should be placed before the group for discussion. Good-faith implementation requires that the staff know when as well as what is to be done. The administrator could direct the task force to generate solutions within the three-year framework, they could ask to generate solutions in a free-for-all discussion and then determine whether three years is an appropriate time frame for change. Assuming the administrator chose the latter option, the task force would next identify changes; set dates certain for their achievement; and assign responsibility for each activity to specific members of the task force and other program staff. If the process energizes the staff, they might well cut the implementation time from three years to fifteen months.

Implementation of Program Adaptations

Managing program adaptations is the single most overlooked phase of the process approach. Whether one is a line manager or a program evaluator, one must recognize that change is frequently resisted and nearly always disruptive. Knowing what the problems are and knowing how one wishes to do things differently are not enough. One also must design a change-management system to minimize the potential for staff resistance and the disruptive effects of the proposed changes on daily operations.

There are two components to a well-run change process: a clear agenda for change and a system for managing its implementation. The adaptations to be carried out in the children's facility have already been described. The focus here is on managing the proposed changes. The essential elements to a successful change-management strategy are the unequivocal support of top management and a clear delineation of responsibility for carrying out the change. The support of top management can be expressed in memos to the staff and orally during task-force deliberations and subsequent staff meetings. The administrator can further show commitment by scheduling a series of meetings in which the responsible staff members are required to report their progress to the administrator.

The success of proposed changes is also affected by the people who carry them out. There are three ways to guarantee failure. The first is to announce the changes along with the expectation that everybody in the organization assume responsibility for carrying them out. The second way to ensure failure is to assign responsibility for the program changes to persons who lack the skills to carry them out. The third way is to assign the responsibility to competent persons with the stipulation that changes are carried out in addition to regular duties. Normally, the most competent organizational members have full desk calendars and program responsibilities that require a full measure of their time. Workloads must therefore be carefully planned and responsibilities shifted to make it possible for the changes to succeed.

The Task-Force Approach

Regardless of the mission of the organization, the change task force should be interdisciplinary and represent the various occupational specialties in the agency. As previously noted, the children's center task force consisted of expert personnel from the fields of education, nursing, and social work, as well as clinical and administrative staff. Task-force leadership should be delegated to the most competent deputy or be assumed personally by the administrator. Task-force membership should also include the evaluator (who also acts as a process consultant), the agency's personnel officer, and the director of employee development. If an agency is too small to have its own employee development specialist, assistance can be sought from the overhead agency or the state department of personnel services. If representatives from either of these agencies are unavailable, an outside training expert could be retained to help plan and facilitate employee training sessions. Finally, the task force should include several paraprofessional employees to ensure everyone's understanding and cooperation.

In addition to assuming overall responsibility for the changes, the task force would act as a sounding board for ideas and as a coordinating body to ensure that various components of the planned changes are carried out on schedule. The task force would also be responsible for preparing the final report to the administrator. In other words, ownership of the change strategy and its implementation should rest squarely on the shoulders of the task-force members.

Work Groups

Actual implementation of the various changes would be carried out by work groups composed of task-force members and other relevant program staff. The appropriate number of work groups varies with the complexity of the change program. In the current example, three work groups could carry out the changes: an employee development work group, a quality assurance work group, and a project coordinating work group. The project coordinating work group would be responsible for coordinating change and evaluating outcomes. Finally, a group could be formed to work with the evaluator to measure the impact of changes.

Employee Development Work Group. This group would be responsible for designing and implementing any necessary training to reeducate program staff on policies and procedures. The work group also would be responsible for carrying out participant-observer visits to the wards and classrooms to determine whether the concepts and procedures being taught in the training group were being correctly applied. Because this group is central to a successful adaptation, the task-force head may wish to chair it personally or at least meet regularly with the group. The other members of the group would include the employee development specialist, two or three nursing supervisors, representatives of clinical staff, and at least two paraprofessionals representing the psychiatric technicians. The evaluator would also work with the group. Membership in the group can be flexible with two exceptions: the training officer, who must be a member of the group to schedule and implement prescribed training; and the evaluator, whose participation is also necessary to ensure that the adaptations undertaken by the group are accounted for in the post-adaptation evaluation design.

The employee development group would begin by prioritizing the problems to be addressed through training. They would then specify actions to correct the problem. Serious deficiencies could also be raised at management meetings, and on-the-job briefing memos could be prepared for delivery at shift changes and in counseling sessions for individual paraprofessionals. For example, correct restraining techniques could be part of in-service training. Documentation of incidents also could be a part of training and could be reinforced at shift changes. The quality assurance group could require supervisors to perform spot checks to assure that staff correctly document their actions.

Quality Assurance Work Group. This group is essential to quality improvement in the short run and to assure continuous improvement over the long term. Agencies in the health-care field are required to operate quality assurance systems as a condition of licensure. In our example, suppose the committee met irregularly, program analysis was sparse, corrective actions were nonexistent, and documentation was poor. The task force might choose to divide the quality assurance work group into two committees: a temporary committee responsible for short-range change and a permanent committee responsible for ongoing oversight. Alternatively, the permanent committee could be responsible for devising and implementing short-range change as well as for preserving ongoing quality. In either case, the consultant/evaluator would work closely with the group as a problem-solving resource and to monitor good-faith compliance. The consultant would also be helpful in identifying indicators to be used in the quality measuring process. The indicators can be process assessments (such as precipitated this change strategy) or outcome indicators suitable for presentation to legislative subcommittees. These indicators can bolster the agency's case with overhead executives responsible for approving program initiatives and allocating limited resources.

The quality assurance committee would begin with the preliminary consultant's report and devise ways to correct procedural deficiencies. This might require in-service training for the professional and paraprofessional staff and systems to monitor corrective action. For the duration of the planned changes, the group would meet weekly to review charts, flag problems, and prescribe changes in procedures. Once an appropriate quality assurance system was in place and the agency was consistently meeting industry standards, the quality work group could shift to biweekly meetings for tracking problems and monthly meetings for analyzing and solving recurring problems or problems requiring interdisciplinary resolution.

Project Coordinating Work Group. This group might include the chairs of each of the other two committees, the consultant/evaluator, the task-force leader, and the various department heads (who must keep abreast of change activities that can affect their operations). Task-force members must bear in mind that the proposed changes are part of an ongoing commitment to program improvement and not an experiment. Thus, the need for the training components, as initially envisioned, may decline rapidly due to heightened awareness and the proactive efforts of line staff. The quality assurance group might find that new problems appear as workers shift their focus to previously identified changes. All too often, analyses are done, training is designed and implemented, and evaluations are undertaken without the benefits of ongoing checks to monitor training quality and appropriateness. Here again, the participant-observer approach may prove useful to the task force. By observing the training in progress and reviewing training materials, participant observers can learn whether the training accomplishes what the task force intended. They can then suggest ways of fine tuning the training to keep it on point with task-force goals. The coordinating group can thus minimize second-order problems. The group would also be responsible for compiling and reporting evaluation data.

The best evaluations are designed in close consultation with program staff. This ensures the accuracy of the design and the usefulness of the data obtained from the evaluation. Even though the evaluator is a participant member of each of the other work groups, staff cannot be sure of the accuracy of the evaluation design without taking an active role in its development.

Regular meetings of the whole task force are necessary to keep the focus on the changes. Regular task-force meetings also serve as a check on the work groups, who may tend to identify their own responsibilities as the principal priority of the task force, if not the agency as a whole. Regular meetings also invigorate task-force members and infuse the agency with a commitment to quality.

Scheduling Tasks and Setting Up a Reporting System

The final detail in the implementation phase of the process model is a schedule for completing the various tasks. The administrator can know whether things are proceeding as planned by scheduling regular progress-report meetings with the project coordinating work group. These meetings would also provide group leaders with access to the administrator, who could then assist in persuading resistant individuals or groups to cooperate with the change program.

The amount of formality needed in the reporting system varies with how complex the proposed changes are and how much personal control the administrator or task-force leader wishes to exercise over the process. In relatively simple change programs (such as the one in our example) the level of control might be limited to a reporting schedule that coincides with the expected completion dates of various components of the plan. For complete change programs, it may be worthwhile to develop a program plan utilizing the techniques of a project calendar as described in chapter 3. In either case, a formal reporting system at the outset gives employees a clear picture of what is expected of them and serves to reinforce managerial commitment to the proposed changes.

A two-part accountability system would suffice for our example. Part 1 is what Richard Beckhard and Ruben Harris termed a **responsibility matrix**.[11] Part 2 is a simple project calendar containing a timetable of project components and due dates for their completion.

The Responsibility Matrix.   Consultants use responsibility matrices to help organizations engaged in change strategies. The matrix is a written record of who is responsible for each planned change (see table 5.1). In our children's center example, the various components of the change strategy are recorded across the top of the matrix; the individuals involved are listed in the left-hand margin. A responsibility matrix uses a four-letter code to delineate responsibilities. The symbol *A* stands for approval/veto authority. An *A* across from an individual's name means that the person must approve of specific activities designed to effect changes. Normally, however, these people accept proposals as written or ask the group to revise proposals in light of issues they had not considered. They should not engage in wholesale redesigns of program changes that are agreed upon by the work groups. Doing so can undermine the entire change effort. Because of the authority an *A* designation represents, it is best to limit its designation to one or at most two members of the organization. Having two people with veto authority over a component of a planned change makes it difficult for those responsible for the project to perform their assigned functions. Additionally, the project manager, who is designated by an *R* (for responsibility) in the matrix, should not have to serve multiple masters.

The project manager (*R*) is assisted by other organization actors, who are designated by an *S* (for support) in the matrix. Those with an *S* designation are also responsible for a project's success, although they usually have other duties that are a greater priority for them. The project manager is responsible for leadership, coordination of work-group activities, and the timely completion of tasks in the group. A project manager may also be assigned to a work group on the basis of expertise rather than rank in the organization, and members of the group may be the project manager's peers or superiors in other organizational matters. Those with the *R* designation must rely on the support of the person with the *A* designation because members of the work group are often drawn from across disciplines. That is, *R*s frequently do not possess organizational authority over those in their groups who have an *S* designation. The person possessing the *A* designation, therefore, must be sufficiently high in the organizational hierarchy to compel cooperation from reluctant members of the work group. Without this type of accountability, persons on project teams can obstruct activities to which they are opposed or allow the press of day-to-day duties to displace the priority that the project should receive.

The final symbol in the matrix is an *I*, for information, which means that persons so designated need to be kept abreast of work group activities. Such information may be merely a matter of organizational courtesy, but it is more likely that persons given the *I* designation need the information to anticipate what impact work group activities will have on their organizational responsibilities. In our children's center example, department heads are ex officio members of the coordinating committee and are given an *I* designation.

The sample matrix in table 5.1 utilizes job titles rather than names of individuals. When creating a matrix for actual organizations, it is best to use the actual names of the participants as well as their titles. To simplify

Table 5.1   A Responsibility Matrix for Changes at the Children's Center

PROJECT COMPONENT

	Training Work Group	Quality Assurance Work Group	Project Coordination Work Group	Evaluation Consultative Work Group
Agency Director	A	A	A & R	A
Director of Nursing	R	I	S	S
Personnel Officer	S		S	
Training Specialist	S	I	S	S
Clinical Professional 1	I	S	I	
Clinical Professional 2	S	R	S	S
Nursing Supervisor 1	S	I	I	
Nursing Supervisor 2	I	S	I	
Nursing Supervisor 3	S	I	I	S
Psych Technician 1	I	S		S
Psych Technician 2	I	S		S
Psych Technician 3	S			
Evaluation Consultant	S	S	S	R

A   Authorization/Veto Authority
I   Information (has no direct responsibility but is kept informed due to the impact of the group on their work)
R   Responsibility (work group leader)
S   Support (active member of the work group)

the illustration, we assumed that there were only four treatment wards in the facility: a male adolescent dorm, a female adolescent dorm, a boys' ward, and a girls' ward. The school facility was deemed to be on site with classrooms that combine several grades. We elected to reserve the approval/veto authority for the agency director. This is possible because of the assumed size of the organization and because the director is presumed to have executive authority over all phases of facility activities. Operationally, the various units are relatively autonomous and the hierarchy is relatively flat. In an organization with a more stratified, stricter hierarchy or a greater diversity of mission, a wider distribution of the approval/veto authority would be necessary.

The Project Calendar.   The second component of the control system is a project calendar that indicates the components of the planned change and the inclusive dates for the various phases of the project. This tool was discussed in depth in chapter 3.

To apply the project calendar to the children's center, let us assume that the task force has allocated fifteen months for completing all phases of the adaptation and for carrying through a follow-up evaluation. Figure 5.1 is a project calendar for changes in our imaginary center.

Across the top of figure 5.1 is the calendar reflecting the planned change in its entirety. The project work groups' calendars and an evaluator's calendar are listed on the left. Each project is tracked by a bar that indicates how the individual project components are progressing. The current date is reflected by the vertical line that runs through the calendar. Each major initiative of the project calendar is outlined below.

The first entry in the calendar is the monthly meeting schedule of the task force here designated as the training work group. This group's progress is tracked in four phases:

- *Phase I:* The group develops a training program targeting the major policy compliance problems and correcting errors in the treatment process.

- *Phase II:* The group conducts training sessions and on-the-job training.

- *Phase III:* The group conducts participant-observer monitoring of training implementation.

- *Phase IV:* The group develops a phase-two training session to deal with second-order problems and emerging problems. The vertical hatch lines in row 28 of the calendar indicate a weekly meeting schedule for this training work group throughout the process.

The schedule of the Quality Assurance Work Group is tracked as follows:

- *Phase IA:* The group conducts an in-depth analysis of patient records for patterns of difficulty.

- *Phase IB:* Simultaneously, the group assesses its record-keeping and program-monitoring procedures.

Figure 5.1   A Project Calendar for the Change Strategy at the Children's Center

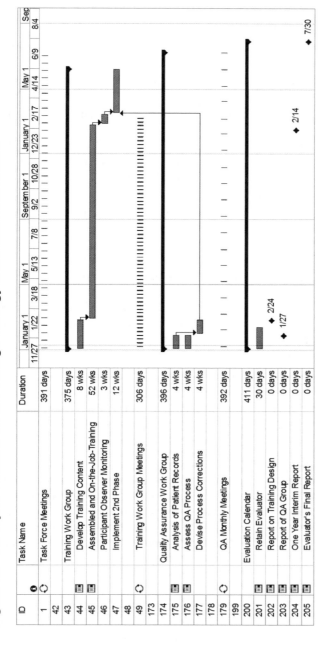

- *Phase II:* The group devises short-term corrections in its own operating procedures to enhance the quality assurance process.

- *Phase III:* The group analyzes patient records for possible progress in correcting identified problems.

- *Phase IV:* The group undertakes a second phase of training to correct problems identified in Phase III.

The short vertical lines in the calendar (line 96) indicate biweekly meetings of this group.

The final element is the evaluation calendar. Because the project involves an action-oriented approach, the activities of the evaluator/consultant are ongoing throughout the project. The three diamonds in this portion of the calendar represent dates on which various reports are due.

- *R1:* The first report due is an evaluation of the training program's design (row 202).

- *R2:* The second report details the findings of the quality assurance activity group and any trends in the patterns of compliance with agency policies (row 203). This report might also contain recommendations based on unanticipated events that arose during the execution of the first phases of the adaptations. The evaluator might also be called on to survey program staff regarding their perceptions of workshop and on-the-job training components and the effects of the training on their job performance.

- *R3:* The evaluator is to provide an interim report after one year (row 204).

- *R4:* The last item on the project calendar is the consultant's final report at the end of the adaptations that includes empirical assessments of all phases of the program (row 205). It reflects a bimonthly meeting of the entire task force.

Keeping on Schedule.   Keeping a project moving is the responsibility of each work-group leader and the task-force director. When slippages in the schedule occur, prompt action is necessary. The administrator must decide whether the slippage is the result of poor cooperation between the work group and its leaders or of unrealistic expectations in the original plan. If the problem is one of cooperation, the responsibility matrix can help direct corrective measures. If the problem is poor planning, schedule revisions are in order.

Managerial aids such as project calendars and responsibility matrices cannot in and of themselves ensure the timely completion of program adaptations, but when combined with a real commitment to change on the part of management and staff, these control aids can be extremely beneficial.

Feedback Evaluation

The final phase of the process approach involves gathering data on the impacts of the change program. The degree of sophistication necessary in this phase varies with the needs and preferences of the consumers, the skills and preferences of the evaluator, and above all, the nature of the changes enacted. In the current case, the evaluator might again engage in participant-observer activities as well as conduct a systematic review of a records sample to determine if the change strategy worked. The evaluation report might prove useful to the director when interacting with the overseeing department and with members of the legislature. If the change strategy worked, the agency should experience increased revenues from third-party payers such as Medicaid and private insurance providers. Such news is always welcome in decision-making circles. Agencies with reputations for positive results find it easier to market their ideas for creative change and to justify budgetary increases.

Summary of Process Evaluation

A four-phase approach to process methodology can be adapted to most organizations. In our hypothetical example of a children's center, we showed how the evaluator must balance the application of empirical data-gathering skills with skills in communication and consensus building, as well as knowledge of organizations and their operation. Flexibility of design is essential for attacking the problems of an agency. A process evaluator might use group interviews, managerial audits, or the participant-observer approach, in addition to survey research and systematic data gathering. Each method has its appropriate applications and limitations—none is universally applicable. The art of evaluation is knowing which methodology is appropriate and applying it accordingly.

When external consultants engage in process evaluation they place themselves at risk because process evaluators are expected to recommend program adaptations as well as point out program malfunctions. Evaluators therefore assume a degree of responsibility for program success as well as for evaluation accuracy. When evaluators share ownership of program adaptations, they are more likely to actively assist in their implementation. Therein lies the principal difference between outcome evaluators and process evaluators. Outcome evaluators emphasize accurately measuring program outputs; process evaluators emphasize problem solving.

Ironically, the education establishment is in the process of shifting to a combination of outcome and process standards for measuring program success. The prerequisites of offering appropriate curriculum content, being appropriately organized, and having the required staffing levels of appropriately credentialed faculty are being supplemented by a demand for outcome assessment. Student learning outcomes are now equally relevant. Thus, in addition to demonstrating that students are taught well, educational institutions must demonstrate that students have learned what was intended. Of course, what is intended will continue to be defined by industry standards.

Notes

[1] Two prominent theorists dominate the field. One is Abraham H. Maslow, author of *Motivation and Personality* (New York: Harper Brothers, 1970) and *Toward a Psychology of Being*, 3rd ed. (New York: Wiley, 2011). The other is Douglas McGregor, author of *The Human Side of Enterprise*, annotated ed. (New York: McGraw-Hill, 2005).

[2] See, for example, Robert R. Blake and Jane S. Mouton, *The Managerial Grid* (Houston, TX: Gulf, 1994); for the latest in its application see Donald L. Anderson, *Organization Development: The Process of Leading Organizational Change* (Thousand Oaks, CA: Sage, 2012).

[3] The father of the movement was W. Edward Deming, *Out of the Crisis* (Cambridge: MIT Press, 1986). See also Dale H. Besterfield et al., *Total Quality Management*, 3rd ed. (Upper Saddle River, NJ: Prentice-Hall, 2002).

[4] See "Complete List of DSMIV Codes" at http://www.psychnet-uk.com/dsm_iv/_misc/complete_tables.htm

[5] See Patrice Spath, *Introduction to Healthcare Quality Management* (Chicago: Health Administration Press, 2009).

[6] F. M. Cornford, *Microcosmographia Academica*: *Being a Guide for the Young Academic Politician* (Cambridge: Bowes and Bowes, 1908), p. 9.

[7] For a more complete discussion, see Floyd J. Fowler, Jr., *Survey Research Methods*, 4th ed. (Thousand Oaks, CA: Sage, 2008).

[8] For an insightful set of readings, see David M. Fetterman, Abraham Wandersman, and Ricardo Millett, *Empowerment Evaluation: Principles in Practice* (New York: Guilford, 2005).

[9] Rufus Miles, "The Origin and Meaning of Miles' Law," *Public Administration Review* (September/October 1978): 399–403.

[10] See David M. Fetterman (ed.), *Ethnography: Step-By-Step (Applied Social Research Methods)*, 3rd ed. (Thousand Oaks, CA: Sage, 2010). See also George W. Stockings, Jr. (ed.), *Observers Observed: Essays on Ethnographic Field Work* (Madison: University of Wisconsin Press, 1984).

[11] Richard J. Beckhard and Ruben T. Harris, *Organizational Transitions: Managing Complex Change*, 2nd ed. (Reading, MA: Addison-Wesley, 1987); see also John O. Kotter and James L. Heskett, *Corporate Culture and Performance* (New York: Free Press, 2011).

part THREE

Measuring Organization Outcomes

The principal focus of most evaluation research is to determine organization outcomes. Originally, legislatures wanted to know what they were getting for their money. They defined programs in terms of their legislative expectations or goals (e.g., eradicate disease, end poverty, make our streets safe, and so forth). They first wanted to know if a program would do what was intended. Second, and of equal importance, was how much money it would cost and whether they wanted to spend that kind of money.

Of course, all disease has not been eradicated, the poor are still with us, and the relative safety of our streets is a matter of considerable debate. Nevertheless, appreciable progress has been made in all these areas. To get program outcomes, evaluators drew upon the techniques of social science research. Chapter 6 details the techniques of carefully defining program goals, and developing appropriate indicators and measures for gauging program progress towards intended outcomes.

Chapter 7 reviews various evaluation designs in terms of their validity, first for measuring what is intended rather than various extraneous factors, and second in terms of the design's validity for meeting the needs of program officials and decision makers. For example, it is possible to construct rigorous program experiments using random assignment of subjects and carefully selected control groups to precisely measure the subject under study. Such rigor is expensive and may be unnecessary and inappropriate for evaluating large-scale ongoing programs.

Chapter 8 presents cost-benefit analysis. Developed by economists, this approach permits decision makers to evaluate program choices using a common unit of analysis: money. Private for-profit enterprises use cost-benefit analysis every day to design programs, secure funding, and manage outcomes. Unfortunately, without a bottom-line profit motive it is more difficult to apply the techniques of cost-benefit analysis, as is often the case in government. Chapter 8 critically evaluates as well as describes this popular tool and its underlying bias towards program options in which the cost is recovered in the shortest length of time. It also lends a considerable advantage to programs with the highest benefit-to-cost ratio.

Finally, we end this section with a ten-point set of tips for evaluators in Chapter 9. These are intended as reference points for the design and conduct of evaluations using process outcome or mixed evaluations. These tips might very well have been presented at the beginning of the book as part of the introduction to the subject. We have chosen to present them last in the belief that the students would better appreciate them after forming a foundation of the theory and practice of evaluation.

six

Conducting an Outcome Evaluation

Some evaluation specialists believe that little can be gained from evaluating programs that are not experiencing problems.[1] The argument is that if everybody concerned with a program (including legislators, program staff, and program clientele) is satisfied, an evaluation is not warranted. The same experts also believe that little can be gained from evaluations of programs that lack clear goals.

Clear goals are absent from many programs because many agencies or subunits of agencies are service operations. These operations may involve services to other agencies or subunits. The missions of service agencies or subunits may vary from day to day, making output measures of goal attainment difficult. This book began with the assumption that most government programs can benefit from an objective assessment of their operations despite the absence of self-evident, quantifiable goals. Moreover, there are instances when evaluations must be conducted regardless of whether the program is controversial or has clearly quantifiable goals. For example, state and local officials who administer federally funded programs may find that evaluations of their programs are a requirement of funding continuation. Moreover, many programs are subject to narrow program guidelines imposed on them by overhead agencies, the federal government, and third-party payers such as insurance companies, making moot the question of whether or not to evaluate outcomes—no evaluation, no money.

We discuss how to conduct an outcome evaluation in two parts. First, we cover the various issues that surround the evaluation process, such as selection of an evaluator, hidden agendas, and negotiation of an appropriate design. Then we provide a model for how to conduct an outcome evaluation and present its applications, using a community health example.

Preplanning the Evaluation

Outcome evaluation strategies are concerned with measuring program outputs. They are sometimes called *summative evaluations*.[2] The other kind of evaluation, known as the process approach, is discussed in chapter 5. *Process* (or *formative*) evaluations focus on how to deliver a program rather than on outputs. The two methods differ in terms of what is observed and how the observations take place. The distinction is more theoretical than practical, because it is often necessary to undertake a mixed evaluation (that uses both techniques) to get a complete perspective on program progress and performance.

Evaluating Start-Up Programs

Program administrators are frequently aware of the need to evaluate at the outset of their programs. This is particularly true when the program is experimental or a demonstration project. In such cases, policy makers want to know whether a new program idea will work before undertaking it on a larger scale. A large police department, for example, might wish to experiment with community-based policing techniques in one or two precincts before going citywide with the application.[3] In recent times, the federal government has allowed individual states to experiment with alternative welfare programs that require such things as work training and job-search skills. These experiments preceded more widespread application. Furthermore, in the mid-1990s Congress passed significant welfare reform legislation that strictly limited time of eligibility, setting time limits on the amount and types of benefits a family could receive. Because the reforms were passed in relatively good economic times, the apparent immediate success of the reforms is worth evaluating in terms of their long-term impacts.[4]

When dealing with experimental programs, retaining the evaluator and negotiating the evaluation design early in the process can benefit both the administrator who wishes to demonstrate program effectiveness and the evaluator who wishes to use the most appropriate measures. Failure to preplan the evaluation constricts the range of available evaluation strategies and the number of available indicators of program success. Carefully designed evaluations of experiments in social policy can serve to iron out the wrinkles in programs before undertaking wider applications. In extreme cases, evaluators may learn that the cost of seemingly good ideas far exceeds their benefits. Persons engaged in evaluation research also frequently possess managerial and programmatic skills. Evaluators with program experience can help the administrator avoid such problems as inefficient organizational structures or inadequately trained staffs.

Impact Analysis

Outcome evaluators also may be asked to conduct an **impact analysis** to determine whether the program is reaching the intended audience. For example, a state legislature might fund a day-care program to assist single parents who receive welfare. The impact analysis might reveal that low-income families were using the program as intended. The analysis might also find that among those taking advantage of the program were low-income persons who were never on welfare. Thus, while the program was a useful public service, it did not achieve the impact intended by the legislature.[5]

Evaluating Ongoing Programs

Outcome evaluations can also be valuable for ongoing programs. In the field of education, for example, how well students perform on standardized reading and math exams (outcome measures) is an excellent indicator of how well a given school is achieving its program goals. Standardized test scores also allow local decision makers to compare student results with those of other schools and with national and state trends. The range of outcome indicators applicable to ongoing programs is more limited than with start-up efforts. Fortunately for evaluators, most programs maintain extensive record-keeping systems that can be used to monitor program progress or to track trends in service levels. Evaluators call these *generic indicators* because they are common to all programs in a given field.

In law enforcement, for example, police departments regularly collect, analyze, and report crime statistics. Often these reports are forwarded to state and federal justice departments for synthesis, which allows decision makers to assess broader trends. By comparing a department's performance to those of like agencies (using generic indicators), local officials can acquire a much better profile of a department's performance than can be gained by limiting the review to local trends. The aggregated data is reported by categories such as violent crimes, burglaries, fraud, and so forth. Utilizing these categories, a given jurisdiction can assess whether or not its trends are consistent with like jurisdictions. (The "how are we doing as compared to what" question).

Another important reason for collecting and synthesizing local data is that it can form the basis for local resource allocations. For example, city X might find that for several years its armed robbery statistics were in decline while crimes of identity theft were increasing. Such a trend would necessitate a reassignment of personnel and would probably also require hiring or training officers with Internet skills. Furthermore, because the problem is so widespread and often national and international, cooperative relationships with adjacent jurisdictions as well as regional and national enforcement agencies may be required. Maximizing the benefits from evaluating ongoing programs may therefore require considerable creativity on the part of the evaluator.

External Factors

Unfortunately, for hard-pressed program administrators struggling to stretch every dollar, new calls for measuring impacts frequently call for new measures. For example, the "no child left behind initiative" that began in 2001 under the G. W. Bush administration significantly added to the cost of program accountability. Under the initiative, to be eligible for federal funds, school districts must demonstrate learning outcomes using standardized tests developed for the purpose. Such initiatives are time consuming and can drain resources from actual education activities; but nevertheless, schools must comply with such legislation in order to meet accountability requirements. The irony is that well-funded school districts that are meeting educational outcomes frequently have outcome measures in place. Poorer school districts that struggle to purchase textbooks and to hire and retain competent teachers have much less divertible resources. In neither scenario does an added layer of accountability enhance educational outcomes.[6]

Most recently, as part of the American Recover and Reinvestment Act, the Obama administration initiated a program of special grants to be awarded to states that created new education initiatives to ensure student success. To compete for grant money, states must first obtain a commitment for 20% of the cost from the private sector. Grant amounts are substantial, and the competition is extreme. The long-term expectation is that these initiatives will serve as demonstration projects of what works, which can then be more broadly adopted.[7]

Choosing between External and Internal Evaluation

The authors do not advocate the exclusive use of external evaluations. To the contrary, both internal and external evaluations can be beneficial, depending on the needs of the agency. Whether to use an internal or external evaluation team, however, is a critical first decision in the evaluation process. As noted in chapter 5, moreover, extensive internal evaluation is a prerequisite for the external review of programs seeking accreditation.

Before the techniques of program evaluation were widely known, choosing an evaluator involved selecting a proposal from among those submitted by various evaluation specialists located outside the agency. More recently, evaluation training has been incorporated into the core curricula of most public administration programs. The age of personal computing, moreover, has given even small agencies the capacity to maintain in-house databases and management information systems. Too, the need for ongoing quality assurance self-assessment has led to a variety of career paths in program monitoring and reporting. The net result is an ever-growing pool of career public servants who can conduct in-house evaluations, so agencies do not necessarily have to contract for evaluation services.

Advantages of External Evaluation

When the audience for the findings is external to the agency an outside evaluation may enhance the credibility of the results. For example, Congress may require evaluation as a condition of program authorization, and state and local authorities may have to provide evaluation information to federal funding agencies as a routine requirement of the accountability system. In such circumstances, an external evaluation can lend an air of objectivity to the findings. The objectivity of outside evaluators is rooted in the fact that they have no vested interest in continuation of the program. External evaluations also may be particularly beneficial when more than one program delivery unit is to be examined. The objectivity of the outside evaluator can allay the fears of bias on the part of competing program units, which might perceive an internal evaluator as a central office assassin bent on making the unit look bad.

External evaluations have the added advantage of bringing fresh perspectives to agency problems that previously may not have been considered. In agencies that do not have regular evaluation units, external consultants may be the most cost-effective way to acquire evaluation expertise, short of hiring new staff or expending resources on training.

Advantages of Internal Evaluation

In-house evaluations may be preferable in agencies that maintain evaluation units or planning units staffed by employees with research skills. The first benefit of an internal evaluation is that the evaluator understands the organization, because the evaluator is privy to past program decisions that are the basis for current operations. Internal evaluators also are aware of the actual program responsibilities of various organization actors, which can save valuable start-up time in getting the evaluation underway.

Internal evaluators' knowledge of the organization may enhance their ability to identify problems and program deficiencies. However, internal evaluators are vulnerable to retaliation from officials who are criticized in the evaluation. Few internal evaluators are brave enough to unequivocally identify managerial error as the cause of program failure. When managerial error or nonperformance is suspected as the cause of program problems, the administrator may wish to retain an outside evaluator.

The Evaluator and Managerial Agendas

Selection of an evaluator is not unilaterally an administrative decision. Evaluators, for their part, must be aware of the motivations behind the commissioning of the evaluation. External evaluators, and to a lesser degree internal evaluators, must resist becoming the pawns of management. In some cases, a number of hidden agendas may underlie the decision to undertake an evaluation.

Evaluations are only as good as the motives of those who commission them. An organization wishing to demonstrate excellence/profitability can sway external evaluators and auditors almost as easily as in-house personnel. The house of cards that was the Enron Corporation hid its financial difficulties from public scrutiny right up to the time of collapse, even though the corporation employed one of the nation's most prestigious accounting firms to audit its record-keeping methods and reported outcomes.[8]

The hidden motive most frequently encountered by evaluators working in the public sector is the program administrator's desire to demonstrate program efficiency and effectiveness regardless of true program performance. In such cases, an administrator might commission an evaluation and demand that the outcome of the evaluation be favorable. Evaluators must then decide whether to sacrifice their professional integrity for an evaluation contract. Program evaluators should also avoid involvement in evaluations that are commissioned for the purpose of injuring one or another program unit. In such cases, administrators are interested only in negative findings and in affixing blame for program failure on one or another predetermined office.

Evaluations may also be prompted by organization critics or dissatisfied workers who take their complaints about the organization to the board. Such complaints result in highly publicized program audits, provoking intra-organizational finger pointing that can be devastating to employee morale and productivity. In the process chapter (chapter 5) we called this "blaming the other victim."

Finally, evaluators should be aware of the proclivity of some officials to seek cover for decisions that they have already made. For example, an evaluation specialist at a midwestern university was contacted by the administrator of a state rehabilitation agency. The administrator expressed a desire for an evaluation of the effectiveness of each of six assessment centers located throughout the state. As she explained, an anticipated fourth year of consecutive budget cuts was making it necessary to close three of the centers, and the administrator wanted some assistance in choosing which to close.

The evaluator indicated that perhaps an impact analysis could be conducted that would determine which centers were most cost effective and which were accessible to the largest number of clients. Based on data as to client location and demand for service, computer runs could be made to identify the most effective way to reallocate resources. The administrator indicated that this was what she had in mind—as long as a particular center remained open in the legislative district served by the chair of the Senate Appropriations Committee. The administrator's agenda was to generate service-based empirical data to support a political decision. The evaluator politely declined to participate.

Hidden agendas can sometimes be uncovered during the pre-evaluation negotiating process, provided the evaluator possesses the requisite interviewing skills. At that point, the external consultant can (1) convince the program manager to abandon the hidden agenda or (2) decline to participate in the evaluation. Internal evaluation staffs are, in all probability, aware of the various agendas that underlie the decision to evaluate. Because internal evaluators generally do not have the luxury of declining participation, they must move cautiously.

The temptation to seek a "whitewash" evaluation of the program may appeal to program managers who maintain internal evaluation units and for whom evaluation is a condition of external funding or accreditation. The tendency in such cases may be to engage in self-evaluation in order to control the findings. Most administrators, however, are honest brokers who are convinced that the program can withstand external scrutiny and that an external evaluation would be more objective. In such cases, the role of the internal evaluation staff is to present the external option to management and then, if necessary, engage in an objective internal evaluation.

When the evaluator suspects that the evaluation is being commissioned to discredit one or another program unit, the external evaluator may decline to participate. As an alternative, the evaluator can take pains to provide objective information on program success and on the performance of various program units. If the unit in question is performing adequately, the evaluation may persuade the administrator not to move against it; if the unit were not performing, an objective evaluation would provide documentation to support administrative actions. Furthermore, as noted in chapter 5, errors can be better corrected with a team-based change strategy aimed at upgrading services rather than by an external audit aimed at affixing guilt.

When an evaluation is commissioned to avoid or postpone needed changes in a program, the best course for the external evaluator is to decline participation. The internal evaluator, on the other hand, should provide as objective an evaluation as possible without compromising his or her professional integrity. If the administrator insists on changes in the evaluation strategy to predetermine the outcomes or demands that evaluation findings be altered after the research is completed, the internal evaluator should consider resigning from the organization. Like their external counterparts, in-house evaluators must adhere to the ethics of their profession.

The decision to commission an evaluation and the selection of an evaluator are pre-evaluation activities. The administrator and the evaluator, moreover, must reach agreement on how the evaluation is to proceed. These negotiations cannot be taken lightly, lest the evaluator become an instrument of management's bad intentions. Assuming that an acceptable understanding is reached, the next step is to design and conduct an objective outcome evaluation.

Defining Program Goals

Program goals operate at two levels. First are the *theoretical goals* of the agency. These are broad statements of legislative or executive intent.

Frequently, theoretical goals are prefaced by the phrase, "it is the intent of the legislature." The theoretical or legislative intents of programs are generally expressed in such terms as improving the quality of life, making the community safer, or improving the environment. Frequently these overarching intentions are reduced to writing in the form of the agency's *mission statement*.

Actual operational definitions of goals are left to career administrators who are commissioned to bring about the conditions desired by the legislature. What the evaluator must focus on, therefore, are *program goals*. These are defined by the program staff to implement the theoretical intent within the limits of available resources.

There is no single perfect evaluation strategy with which to assess all programs. The strategies most frequently treated in the evaluation literature deal with program outcomes. Outcome designs seek to measure the degree of consistency between program intent and program outputs. Ideally, the success of public programs is measured by the degree to which an agency's outputs impact their environment in ways that are consistent with the intent of the legislation that authorized the program. Evaluators frequently find that program officials cannot agree on concrete, measurable definitions of program goals. Translating broad legislative intents into measurable program goals is the difficult first task in the design of an outcome evaluation.

A lack of goal consensus among program officials may be the result of different perspectives on the program. Persons at the top of the hierarchy are interested in broad questions of resource allocation and program impacts. In contrast, line personnel are concerned with the direct impacts of day-to-day activities and may not have given much thought to overall program goals. Because goal consensus is central to the execution of an outcome design, the evaluator must have consensus-building skills. The evaluator can employ a number of goal-defining techniques, discussed below.

The Personal Interview

The most straightforward approach to defining goals is the personal interview. Interviews may be conducted individually or in small groups, depending on the preference of the program administrator and the needs of the evaluator.

The initial contact between an outside evaluator and program staff may be with one or more members of the organization's planning or evaluation staff. Before proceeding with an evaluation, however, the evaluator should meet with the person commissioning the evaluation, usually the program administrator. This meeting should provide the evaluator with clear-cut guidelines as to the type of evaluation the administrator has in mind as well as his or her definition of program goals.

This audience-driven approach recognizes the primacy of customer need over the methodological preferences of the evaluator. The informational needs of program directors are subject to considerable variation. If, for example, the director wants to know the relative levels of service throughout the state, the data-collection protocol and report format would be quite different from the methodologies that are appropriate to testing experimental programs or evaluations that are conducted to comply with a federal reporting mandate.

The evaluator should also meet individually or collectively with the program staff, or jointly with the administrator and the staff. If the evaluator senses that there is a lack of consensus regarding program goals that is not being addressed in the meeting, or that the program staff members are taking the company line and sublimating their own judgments to those of the administrator, follow-up meetings with program staff may be necessary.

Consensus-Building Activities

When a program staff and administrator are unable to agree on the goals of the program, the evaluator must engage in consensus-building activities. Goal consensus can be achieved by means of the group problem-solving techniques popularized by the organization development movement, or by decision methods that do not require assembly by the participants, such as the Delphi Technique.

The Delphi Technique[9]

Mentioned in chapter 2 as an effective forecasting tool, the Delphi technique is also a useful method of achieving goal consensus. Assuming considerable time availability and at least modest resources, the evaluator can conduct a Delphi survey. The process begins by asking each participant to list program goals without consulting the others. The data are returned to the evaluator, who combines the opinions of the participants into a single list of program goals. The list is fed back to the participants, who are then asked to assign a value to the various goals using an interval scale. The scale may be from 1 to 100, using all possible values or only gradations of ten, or the participants may be asked to evaluate the goals using a more simple scale of 1 to 10. The data obtained from this second round are collected and analyzed by the researcher.

Next, each participant receives information regarding the mean value assigned by the group to a particular goal, the range of values assigned to the goal by the group, and the value he or she assigned to the various goals in the previous round. The researcher may want to focus the attention of the participants by substituting the standard deviation of the group for the range of scores (the standard deviation reflects a range within which a substantial majority of the participants fall). Participants then are requested to reassess the weights they assigned in round two on the basis of the group data. If a participant's round-two value for a particular goal was extreme and he or she does not wish to modify previous judgments in light of the group data, that participant is asked to write a justification for the refusal, which is fed to other participants in the next round. The process can be repeated as many times as necessary in order to reach a general consensus on program goals. By the fourth round, however, three to five priority goals usually emerge from the group. The process can be shortened somewhat by asking subjects to both list and assign values to goals in the first round.

The Delphi method may be particularly appropriate when the program staff is widely dispersed, as in the case of a state vocational rehabilitation agency in a midsized state that might have as many as ten regional offices. This approach can bring the collective focus of managers and supervisors to bear on a problem without requiring them to travel to a single location. The Delphi technique may gain in popularity, moreover, given the ease of electronic communications.

Group Problem-Solving Techniques

Time constraints and the preferences of program managers may rule out use of the Delphi approach to consensus building. Instead, the evaluator may wish to employ one of the organization development movement's group problem-solving techniques. Group problem solving is so named because the technique involves bringing the relevant actors together in order to define the goals of the organization in small groups.[10]

The first step is for the evaluator to explain the purpose of the meeting: to develop a set of agreed-on organizational goals for the purposes of program evaluation. The participants are then divided into small groups and asked to generate a list of organizational goals. They are cautioned at the outset that the groups are to discuss various goals until a consensus list is achieved without voting. Voting may be democratic, but it allows group members to decide too quickly based on only limited discussion. The result of voting is usually a majority and a minority; the latter may acquiesce to the group in the goal-negotiating process and later condemn the evaluation findings. The next step is for the groups to report their lists of goals. The evaluator should act as synthesizer of the group outputs. He or she should point out the goals that are consistent among the groups. A surprising level of consensus may emerge even though the small groups act separately. As with the Delphi approach, computer technology can enhance participation among highly dispersed participants. Online chat rooms can facilitate participation but require the evaluator to give up substantial control of the group process.

If substantial consensus is achieved quickly, the evaluator may choose to discontinue the discussions and proceed with the evaluation. If consensus is not reached, the evaluator may ask the participants to form small groups again and rank order the importance of program goals. When substantial goal consensus is not achieved in the first round, the evaluator may regroup the participants so that representative groups with diverse lists may work out their differences. To expedite the discussion, the evaluator may ask participants to discuss only their differences. The process may be repeated as many times as is necessary to achieve a consensus regarding program goals.

Like the Delphi technique, group problem solving can provide a set of consensus goals for an organization. The group approach has the added advantage of allowing the evaluator to establish working relationships with the program staff. By running an effective goal definition meeting, an evaluator can demonstrate professional competence and build a rapport with the staff.

The Importance of Goal Consensus

Although developing a group consensus can be time consuming, the effort is justified if it results in a rigorously defined set of measurable goals. The evaluator should never try to define program goals unilaterally, no matter how well he or she understands the program. Experience has taught evaluation specialists that program officials who cannot or will not reach a consensus regarding the goals of the program are in all likelihood the same persons who will criticize evaluation findings for measuring the wrong thing.

The evaluator's group leadership skills are particularly useful in making certain that the goals defined by the group are those that the agency is presently pursuing. It is virtually impossible to achieve an accurate evaluation if the group defines the goals in terms of what they would like them to be rather than what they are. To conduct an evaluation, one must measure what has been done rather than what *should* be done. If, however, the group feels strongly that the agency should alter its goals to better serve the clientele or carry out the will of the legislature, the goal-setting process should be divided into two phases. In the first phase, the group would identify current goals by analyzing what is being done and why. These current goals can serve as the foundation for the evaluation and provide baseline data for pursuing the goals identified in the second phase, which may be an immediate continuation of the phase-one discussion. Defining first-phase goals and conducting a baseline evaluation before defining what should be done often enhances the planning process.

A Model for Outcome Evaluation

After attaining a consensus on program goals, the evaluator must (1) determine the interrelationship of various program goals with program functions, (2) develop a set of indicators to evaluate the success of the program functions, (3) generate a set of valid measures to make the indicators operational, and (4) design the evaluation so that one can determine what the program outcomes are and whether they have been positive. In the latter case, the evaluator must examine unintended outcomes as well as intended outcomes. A model that illustrates the sequential interrelationships of the steps in the process is presented in figure 6.1. The components of the model are first discussed as generic concepts. They are then presented using a specific application.

Figure 6.1 A Guide to Designing an Outcome Evaluation

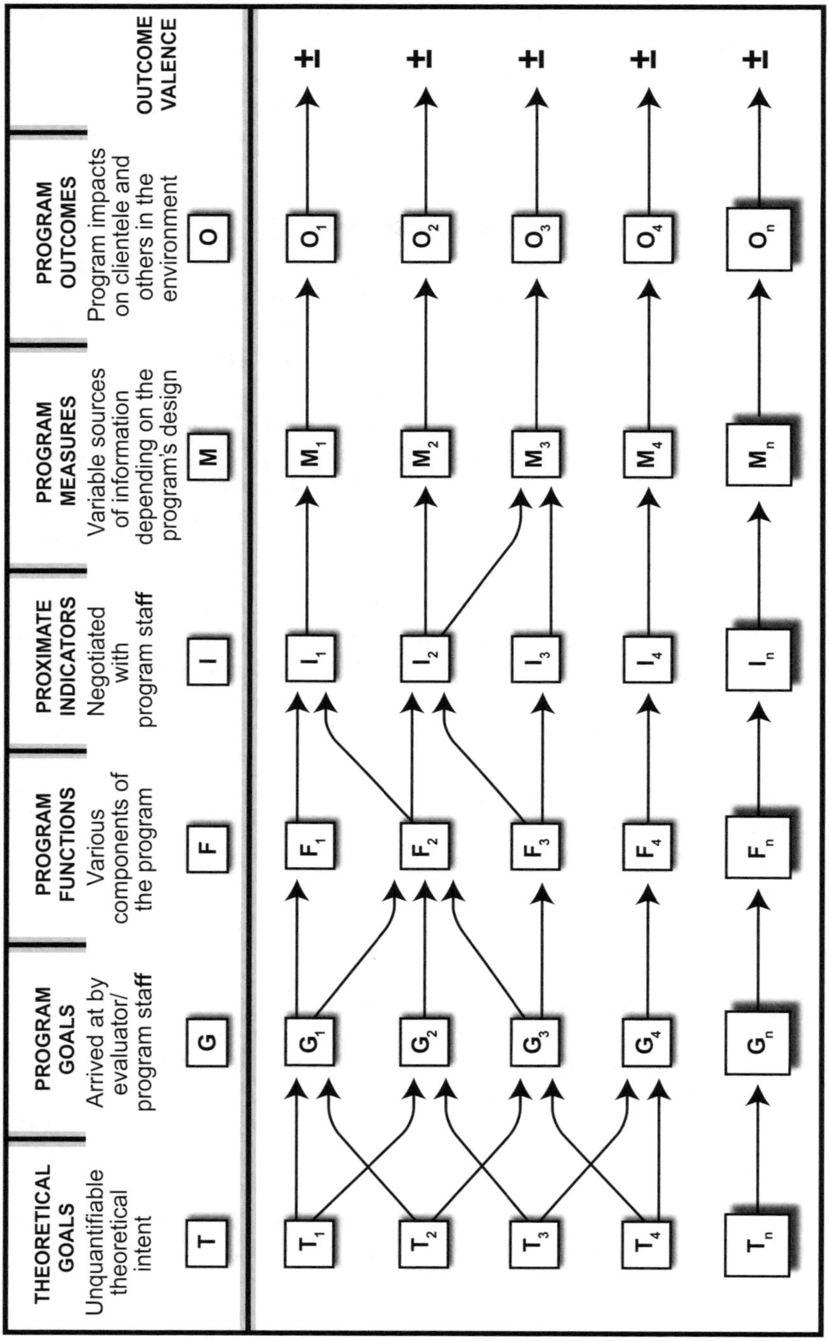

Legislative Intent and Program Goals

As discussed earlier, the legislative intent of the program (which can also be termed the mission statement) is usually stated in broad terms that are not readily quantifiable (column 1 in figure 6.1). Before an outcome evaluation can begin, the evaluator and the program staff must translate theoretical goals into quantifiable program goals (column 2). Defining program goals in close collaboration with program staff can ensure staff cooperation with the evaluation effort and enhance the acceptability of the evaluation finding.

Program Functions

The model may also include a column of program functions or elements (column 3), which are the various components of the program. A university, for example, would have as part of its program components graduate and undergraduate degree programs in various disciplines. Functionally, the components would break down into subcomponents, such as classroom teaching, offering graduate seminars, library and computer services that support student learning, and so forth. When evaluation findings are reported by function, program managers learn which elements of their operation are working and which may need modification. These functional assessments are evaluated in addition to data on how well the program is performing as a whole. Any well-constructed evaluation design can provide legislators and executives with aggregate information that they need to assess the program. Returning to our example of the university, legislators might commission an evaluation to determine the quality of degree programs, numbers served, timeliness of program completion, and whether or not the university maintains a proper balance between its research and teaching functions. By simply identifying an office location, a more program-specific report can be generated for operating managers (but would not necessarily be of interest to the legislature).

Proximate Indicators

Once goals have been defined and functions identified, the evaluator can proceed with developing a set of proximate indicators to assess program performance. Proximate indicators (column 4) are necessary because programs rarely achieve their theoretical goals. For example, the Congress has decided that Acquired Immune Deficiency Syndrome (AIDS) is a major threat to public health. Congress would provide funding to the National Institute of Health (NIH) with the theoretical intent of finding a cure for AIDS. The NIH would fund research projects to identify the genetic properties of the virus and would undertake drug-research studies to develop a cure for the disease and to search for a vaccine to prevent it.[11] As of this writing, there has been no definitive study on the genetic properties of the virus, nor has a drug to cure the disease or a vaccine to prevent it become available. Progress towards the goals, however, has been reported through the use of proximate indicators. Certain combinations of drugs, for example, have significantly increased the life expectancy of those infected. Life expectancy of infected persons is a proximate indicator. Similarly, developing a vaccine that works in laboratory animals is an indicator of progress.

Like goal definition, identification of appropriate indicators is best accomplished in consultation with program staff. The range of available indicators is governed by the purpose and timing of the evaluation, the resources available for evaluation, and the preferences of the evaluator and the program staff. If, for example, the program is experimental, the evaluator can arrange with the staff to gather data throughout the course of the experiment that will be used in the evaluation. When evaluating ongoing programs, generic indicators are often the only practical approach.

Generic Indicators

A generic indicator is a type of data that is routinely gathered by the program. Police departments routinely record the number of arrests they make by type of crime. Health agencies record instances of public health diseases. Emergency rooms track the types of services they provide as well as patterns and trends in the data. Schools routinely test children for progress in reading and math, and they use national testing instruments that allow comparisons to other districts and programs. While generic indicators may not be as tightly tied to goals of the evaluation as the evaluator would prefer, they often provide excellent data for assessing program outcomes without the expense of setting up experiments or demonstration projects.

Attitudinal Indicators

Other popular indicators are client satisfaction and staff perceptions of program operations and success. These indicators can be valuable for assessing both start-up and ongoing programs. Surveys of the target groups render assessments from those closest to the program and those most affected by it. For example, a community policing program intended to get officers out of their patrol cars and into the neighborhood might have the goal of improving police/community relations. A citizen survey of the target community would be a good gauge of program effectiveness. The survey might also indicate whether the program was being implemented properly, by including items on the frequency and types of police contacts experienced by the respondents. A survey of the officers involved would indicate their perceptions of the program and whether they believe it to be worthwhile. They also might be asked to assess the commitment of fellow officers and supervisors toward the program.

Attitudinal indicators should not completely replace other indicators. Nevertheless, when evaluation results reveal that the program is not achieving its desired ends or is doing so at a less-than-optimal level, attitudinal indicators can point to why this is so and may suggest corrective actions. Furthermore, accrediting agencies often specify that programs must demonstrate customer satisfaction as a mandatory program outcome. Finally, customer satisfaction is a highly valid indicator when customer service is built into a program's mission statement and operating principles.

Program Measures

Program measures (column 5 in figure 6.1) reflect the operations that the evaluator will undertake to convert proximate indicators to formal measures of program performance. This may involve the construction of experimental and control groups within the clientele served by the agency (addressed in chapter 7). Alternatively, measuring agency performance may involve simple comparisons of organization performance before and after program implementation. Measures may also be after-only measures of ongoing programs. Data gathered on the program may be analyzed singly or in comparison with data from programs of similar organizations, or with data from program subunits that are not engaged in the program or have implemented the program intent differently. Finally, measures may be based on existing organization records or on records of external accounting agencies, or they may be specifically tailored for the program. A variety of evaluation designs are possible and are limited mainly by how much program administrators are willing to spend and how much information is needed.

One of the most consistent errors committed by students addressing the case studies in this book is the tendency to overevaluate. It is theoretically possible to spend more money measuring a program than the cost of its actual operation. Returning to our example of community attitudes about the police, a realistic cost per survey is forty dollars. This covers the cost of survey design, conducting the actual interview, and coding and analyzing the data. Therefore, it would be highly impractical to survey every resident served by a precinct or even every person requesting police services in a given year. This is why evaluators use sampling methods.[12]

Program Outcomes

The purpose of the entire evaluation strategy is to correctly identify and assess program outcomes. Outcomes can be categorized as primary and secondary. Primary outcomes are direct program impacts; secondary outcomes are spillover effects that a program may have on clientele, other groups, or organizations. Program administrators are sometimes able to anticipate secondary outcomes. Whether or not secondary outcomes are anticipated, the evaluator must be aware of their potential and allow for them in the evaluation strategy. For example, the societal goal of providing health-care benefits to the poor through the Medicaid program has the secondary impact of providing a disincentive for welfare recipients to seek low-paying jobs that do not provide medical benefits. How to adjust the system in light of this unforeseen negative occasioned much legislative debate. The universal health-care coverage that will come in to full effect in 2014 should ultimately remove this secondary disincentive to work.[13] Sometimes program administrators will strive for a primary outcome to achieve a secondary one. In World War II, United States supplies of gasoline were plentiful to address the needs of the war effort. The Japanese invasion of Southeast Asia, however, had severely limited the nation's supply of rubber. Thus, by rationing gasoline, war planners achieved the secondary outcome of reducing demand for tires.[14]

Outcome Valence

The final component of the model, outcome valence (column 7 in figure 6.1), may be positive or negative. A positive valence indicates that program efforts have achieved progress toward accomplishing program goals. The valence is negative when progress toward stated goals is achieved but agency clients or others are suffering negatively from the program in ways that were not anticipated by officials or by the evaluator. Programs that have no apparent impact can also be seen as producing a negative valence insofar as they are not performing. Returning to our World War II rationing example, a positive valence was the development of synthetic tires. A negative valence outcome was a black market in tires.

Audience Considerations

Arriving at outcomes and assessing their valences is the purpose of evaluation. They come into the equation only after the evaluation is designed and carried out and the data is analyzed. How the data is assembled and disseminated is a function of the *audience* of the evaluation. An evaluator working for the state legislature may be called upon to develop a comprehensive report for analysis by legislative staff members or provide an executive summary for legislators. The evaluator may be asked to testify in a legislative hearing. The focuses of such reports are normally program outcomes and impacts. When the audience for the report is primarily program officials, the report should include specific recommendations for change as well as impact analysis. Evaluations generated for program accreditation or federal accountability purposes should be formatted to meet the requirements specified by the mandating agency.

Applying the Model to a Community Health Program

The preceding discussion of goal definition was, of necessity, generic. Here we use a hypothetical community health program to illustrate more concretely the steps in an outcome evaluation. A community health program might have as its *theoretical goals* the upgrading and improving of community health and the quality of life. General health and the quality of life are difficult to quantify without translating theoretical intent into *program goals*. Therefore, the community health program might be divided into three program goals: locating and suppressing health hazards, providing diagnostic and treatment services to the community, and immunizing citizens against communicable diseases. The interrelationship between theoretical and program goals is illustrated in figure 6.2,[15] through scientific notations (T_1 and G_1).

Such notation is preferable to the arrows shown in figure 6.1 when the relationships in an evaluation design are complex and overlapping. A theoretical goal may be related to more than one program goal, which could complicate the designation of interrelationships. The T_2 designation next to G_3, for example, indicates that this goal is how the agency operationalizes the second theoretical goal, but it is unrelated to the first. A theoretical goal that is linked to more than one program goal indicates that the former must be translated into more than one program goal.

Program functions are organizational activities to carry out one or more program goals. In the present example, the program functions include air- and water-quality assessment and activities intended to prevent and suppress environmental health threats to the community (F_1 and F_2 in figure 6.3). Functions involve the location and suppression of health hazards, such as pest infestations (F_3), and providing direct diagnostic and treatment services to the community (F_4), like prenatal services (F_5) and routine immunizations (F_6). In addition, special immunization projects (F_7) might be assessed separately from routine immunization services.

The inclusion of program functions is not essential to the conduct of an outcome evaluation. A community health agency's overall effectiveness could be evaluated by developing an indicator for each goal *without* tying

---

Figure 6.2   The Relationship between Theoretical and Program Goals

THEORETICAL GOALS	PROGRAM GOALS	RELATIONSHIP OF PROGRAM GOALS TO THEORETICAL GOALS
T_1 Upgrading quality of life	G_1 Locating and suppressing health hazards	T_1 T_2
	G_2 Providing diagnostic medical services	T_1 T_2
T_2 Improving community health	G_3 Immunizing citizens	T_2

it to a specific program function. However, including functions allows program managers to readily apply evaluation results through program adaptations. Inclusion of functions in this discussion is an expression of the predilection of the authors of this text for design strategies targeted at managers. That is, managers would be provided with decision-oriented evaluation information that could be used to design program adaptations.

In our health-care example, the prevention and suppression unit might be staffed with medical and environmental specialists who are responsible for finding and suppressing health hazards in the community. Such hazards might range from poor air and water quality to rats in concentrations that present a health problem. The diagnostic unit might be staffed with persons responsible for conducting health clinics where citizens could obtain medical advice and preliminary treatment for a range of health problems, from communicable diseases to prenatal care for expectant mothers. The diagnostic units might simultaneously provide immunization services for a variety of diseases. Special immunization projects could operate on an ad hoc basis when outbreaks of specific diseases occur, or at the start of the school year when large concentrations of children become available for treatment.

Because health-care operations are complex and interrelated, the range of activities discussed above only scratches the surface of health-care services. There are enough, however, to demonstrate the relationship between program goals and program functions (see figure 6.3).

In addition to temporary or experimental efforts, government programs are established to provide continuing services. Most programs achieve only partial success in alleviating their targeted problems. In the community health example, eradication of a disease through immunization of the public would indicate program success, but if the program reduced the rate of the disease by only 80%, one could not realistically label the program a failure.

The evaluation specialist has a number of indicators available for measuring program progress short of complete success. In our community health example, the proximate indicators of water- and air-quality unit success might be the incidents of water and air pollution that the unit identified during a specified period. Indicators of hazard prevention might include the instances of pest infestation reported by the hazard-prevention unit and the volume of reported diseases attributable to pest infestation. The success of the diagnostic unit might be measured using the indicators of the amount of prenatal service provided and the amount of communicable disease diagnosis in which the organization engaged. The indicators of immunization services success might be the instances of communicable diseases in the community over time and the type or quality of immunization services delivered.

Secondary services to the public could also be a valid indicator of program success. For example, the evaluation might disclose that the prenatal

Figure 6.3   The Relationship between Program Goals and Program Functions

PROGRAM GOALS	PROGRAM FUNCTIONS	RELATIONSHIP OF FUNCTIONS TO GOALS
G_1 Location and suppression of health hazards	F_1 Water-quality monitoring	G_1
	F_2 Air-quality monitoring	G_1
	F_3 Pest-infestation investigation and suppression	G_1
G_2 Providing diagnostic medical services	F_4 Diagnostic and treatment services	G_2
	F_5 Prenatal services	G_3
G_3 Immunizing citizens	F_6 Immunization services	G_3
	F_7 Special immunization services	G_3

clinics spent considerable time counseling expectant mothers with regard to available welfare and birth-control services.

Figure 6.4 on the following page indicates linkages between program functions and proximate indicators. In reality the relationships are rarely so simple, because program units engage in mutually supportive services. For example, the investigation unit might be responsible for locating persons who had come in contact with clinic patients treated for communicable diseases. Examples of these diseases are infectious hepatitis and the various forms of venereal disease. Indicator 9 (communicable disease rate in the community) would therefore be an indicator of the success of the investigation unit as well as of the diagnostic clinics and immunization projects. An excellent example of program interdependence and mutual support is the response of local, state, federal, and international health organizations in their efforts to contain the spread of Severe Acute Respiratory Syndrome (SARS). Suspected victims had to be isolated and treated and their movements tracked to identify the origin of the disease and other potential victims.[16]

Disease rates and rates of compliance with federal and state air- and water-quality standards are examples of generic indicators for which the

Figure 6.4   The Relationship between Program Functions and Proximate Indicators

PROGRAM FUNCTIONS	PROXIMATE INDICATORS	RELATIONSHIP OF INDICATORS TO FUNCTIONS
F_1 Water-quality monitoring	I_1 Incidence of water pollution	F_1
F_2 Air-quality monitoring	I_2 Incidence of air pollution	F_2
F_3 Pest-infestation investigation and suppression	I_3 Incidence of pest infestation	F_3
	I_4 Incidence of pest-related diseases	F_3 F_4
F_4 Diagnostic and treatment services	I_5 Quality of health-diagnostic and treatment services	F_4
F_5 Prenatal services	I_6 Quality of prenatal care	F_5
F_6 Immunization services	I_7 Incidence and quality of client counseling	F_4 F_5
F_7 Special immunization services	I_8 Communicable disease diagnoses	F_3 F_4
	I_9 Communicable disease rate in the community	F_3 F_4 F_6 F_7
	I_{10} Type and quality of immunization services	F_6 F_7
	I_{11} Client satisfaction	F_3 F_6
	I_{12} Staff perceptions	F_1 F_7

agency routinely collects data. Also note the inclusion of the attitudinal indicators of client satisfaction and staff perceptions. The latter may serve the purpose of needs analysis as well as that of program measurement. The staff might report, for example, that they believe the agency must begin offering evening services. They might also note that the clinic should undertake special services to new target populations, such as treatment and referral services to persons infected with HIV or nutrition counseling and referrals to poor persons—especially new immigrants with poor English skills.

Once the proximate indicators have been selected, the next step is to devise a set of *measures* to put them into operation. However, the measure selection process may result in a rethinking of the indicators because data are not available.

The design employed and the timing of the evaluation governs selection of an appropriate set of measures to put the indicators into operation. When the program under investigation is temporary or experimental, the evaluator can gather baseline data before the program is initiated. The measure of program success would be the changes resulting from the program as measured by a comparison of data gathered at the end of the program with the baseline data. Statistics on disease rates in the community gathered before and after implementation of an immunization program would be an example of this type of measure.

When evaluating an ongoing program, one may wish to utilize a combination of measures that are gathered from program-record and ad hoc measures that are created solely for evaluation purposes. The latter frequently involves surveys of program clients and staff. Such surveys are popular because they are convenient and because a number of indicators can be put into operation in a single survey. Both records and survey measures can be illustrated using the community health example.

Air- and water-quality enforcement programs could be measured by collecting samples of air and water in various parts of the jurisdiction over time. When combined with a geographical analysis of enforcement activities, the air- and water-quality data would constitute a measure of how effectively enforcement activities were distributed in the district. The effectiveness of the agency over time could be determined by comparing results to federal and state water- and air-quality standards.

The effectiveness of the investigation unit in locating and eradicating pest infestations could be accomplished by a review of program records and health-care statistics. The agency's own records could provide information on the number of pest infestations investigated by the unit, the measures that were taken to eradicate the pests, and the frequency of reported infestations over time. Most states require that health-care providers, such as doctors and hospitals, maintain copious records on certain diseases and that this information be reported to local public health officials. These records could be reviewed over time to determine whether there had been a change in the incidents of diseases related to pest infestation.

The numbers of prenatal service clients, communicable disease diagnoses, and clients counseled could be measured by a review of clinic records and surveys of program personnel and clientele. Clinic records would reveal what types of services were rendered and whether expectant mothers were utilizing the health clinics in lieu of retaining private physicians. Clinic records might also indicate whether persons seeking treatment for communicable diseases came on their own initiative, on the advice of another, or because the investigative team located them and asked them to seek help at the clinic.

Members of the clinic staff could be surveyed to determine how they allocate their time, their perceptions of the quality of services rendered by the clinic, and what suggestions they have for upgrading services. Clients could be surveyed as to the quality of treatment they received, how they were treated by program staff, and any referrals they received from the staff.

Measuring the success of the immunization programs might involve a review of records for the jurisdiction and available state and national data. The evaluator might review the records for several years prior to and after the introduction of various immunization programs as well as data on state and national disease trends. Such a time-series analysis would indicate whether changes in local disease patterns could be attributed to immunization programs or to a general change in the occurrence of a disease.

Finally, quality-based indicators can be analyzed using the compliance standards of health-care accrediting agencies. This could be done by the program staff or by a group of external peer reviewers brought in for the evaluation. Most evaluation generalists, however, lack the in-depth knowledge necessary to conduct such reviews unilaterally.

The relationships between indicators and the various measures (see figure 6.5) can be straightforward, one-to-one relationships, but sometimes they involve complex relationships, as when the success of clinical services is assessed by three separate indicators that are put into operation by four measures. The measures, in turn, may serve multiple purposes. Measure 9 (the staff survey) would measure the quality of prenatal care, the incidents of communicable-disease diagnosis, and the amount of counseling service provided to clients. The survey would also gather staff perceptions regarding changes necessary in clinical services.

The next step in the evaluation strategy is to consider the interrelationships between measures and program outcomes. Because program outcomes can be either positive or negative, the evaluation should provide for either outcome valence. When the data sources are such things as health statistics, either valence may appear in the analysis. When employing survey questionnaires, the evaluator must construct the instrument so that it probes for negative as well as positive program results.

A program produces a positive valence when satisfactory progress toward a stated goal is accomplished. Negative valence occurs when the program produces results that are in the direction opposite from that

Figure 6.5   The Relationship between Proximate Indicators and Program Measures

PROGRAM FUNCTIONS	PROXIMATE INDICATORS	RELATIONSHIP OF INDICATORS TO FUNCTIONS
I_1 Incidence of water pollution	M_1 Water and air sampling studies	I_1 I_2
I_2 Incidence of air pollution	M_2 Record analysis of enforcement patterns	I_1 I_3
I_3 Incidence of pest infestation	M_3 Time-series review of program records on infestations	I_3
I_4 Incidence of pest-related diseases I_5 Quality of health-diagnostic and treatment services	M_4 Time-series review of records on pest-related diseases	I_4 I_5
I_6 Quality of prenatal care	M_5 Time-series review of clinical records	I_5 I_8
I_7 Incidence and quality of client counseling	M_6 Multiple time-series review of local, state, and national records	I_9
I_8 Communicable-disease diagnoses	M_7 Review of program records	I_9
I_9 Communicable disease rate in the community	M_8 Client survey	I_5 I_6 I_{10} I_{11}
I_{10} Type and quality of immunization services I_{11} Client satisfaction I_{12} Staff perceptions	M_9 Staff survey	I_6 I_8 I_{10} I_{12}

intended. Programs that produce no apparent change can also be thought of as negative.

Most direct outcomes can be inferred from the goal-definition phase of the strategy, but not all outcomes can be anticipated. Programs may also produce secondary outcomes that can be either positive or negative. In our community health-care example, a positive secondary outcome would be the counseling of expectant mothers with regard to the availability of social services. Secondary outcomes may be new problems that stem from a successful program. Such unanticipated problems often involve other programs or other units of government. For example, federal highway programs enabled persons employed in the central city to live in single-family suburban dwellings and commute to work. The negative impact of the program was the loss of the middle-class taxpayer to the central city. In our health-care example, the unit involved in investigating pest infestations might identify areas of the city where whole blocks were unfit for human habitation. Condemnation of these buildings could produce the secondary outcomes of a shortage of low-cost housing for the poor or the disruption of an ethnic community.

All programs have the potential for producing secondary outcomes. Some of these can be accounted for in the design strategy. For example, during consultations over program goals and indicators, the evaluator can interview program officials regarding their knowledge of secondary outcomes. Secondary outcomes can also emerge as a result of open-ended items in surveys of program staffs and clients. However, program resources and the desires of program administrators limit the extent to which an evaluator may assess spillover effects of a program. Correctly identifying outcomes and their valences is the final step in an evaluation strategy.

Notes

[1] Chief among the proponents of this position is Carol H. Weiss in her classic text, *Evaluation Research: Methods of Assessing Program Effectiveness*, 2nd ed. (Englewood Cliffs, NJ: Prentice-Hall, 1997).

[2] Peter H. Rossi, Mark W. Lipsey, and Howard E. Freeman adhere to this distinction in their classic, *Evaluation: A Systematic Approach*, 7th ed. (Thousand Oaks, CA: Sage, 2004), especially chapter 5.

[3] Michael Palmiotto, *Community Policing: A Police Community Partnership* (New York: Routledge, 2011).

[4] For a complete discussion see WELPAN, "Welfare Reform, How Will We Know if It Works?" at http://www.ssc.wisc.edu/irp/welpan/welpan.htm

[5] For a more complete discussion of impact analysis, see John G. Grumm and Stephen L. Wasby (eds.), *The Analysis of Policy Impact* (Lexington, MA: Lexington Books, 1981); Patricia Spakes, *Family Policy and Family Impact Analysis* (Cambridge, MA: Schenkman, 1983). See also Lawrence B. Mohr, *Impact Analysis for Program Evaluation* (Thousand Oaks, CA: Sage, 1995). For a health-care example see Martin H. Birley, *Health Impact Assessment Principles and Practice* (London: EarthScan, 2011). For impact analysis in public administration, see W. Johnson, *Public Administration: Partnerships in Public Service,* 4th ed. (Long Grove, IL: Waveland Press, 2009), pp. 132–317.

[6] President George W. Bush signed "No Child Left Behind" into law on January 8, 2002. For a linked discussion of the pros and cons see US Department of Education, "No Child Left Behind," at http://www.ed.gov/nclb/landing/jhtml?src=pb

[7] To learn more about the act see "Nation's Boldest Education Reform Plans to Receive Federal Innovation Grants Once Private Match Is Secured," www.ed.gov/news/press-releases/nations-boldest-education-reform-plans-receive-federal-innovation-grants-once-pr

[8] For a fuller discussion of the Enron matter see *Financial Times*, "Enron: The Collapse" at http://specials.ft.com/enron/

[9] For a health-care application see Sinead Keeney, Hugh McKenna, and Felicity Hasson, *The Delphi Technique in Nursing and Health Research* (Somerset, NJ: Wiley-Blackwell, 2011).

[10] Scott A. Myers and Carolyn M. Anderson, *The Fundamentals of Small Group Communication* (Thousand Oaks, CA: Sage, 2008).

[11] The fight against the disease has grown so much in importance that it has a specialized journal, *AIDS Research and Human Retroviruses*.

[12] See Louis A. Rea and Richard A. Parker, *Designing and Conducting Survey Research,* 3rd ed. (San Francisco: Jossey-Bass, 2005).

[13] For a more complete discussion, see *Medicaid Reform: A Twentieth Century Fund Guide to the Issues* (http://epn.org/tcf/). For a discussion of the 2010 health-care reforms, see *The Affordable Care Act 2010: Public Law 11-252 of the 111th Congress* (US Government Printing Office), www.gpo.gov/fdsys/pkg/PLAW-111pub/152/

[14] See Doris Kearns Goodwin, *No Ordinary Time: Franklin and Eleanor Roosevelt: The Home Front in World War II* (New York: Simon and Schuster, 1994).

[15] For a more specialized perspective see Willemijn Schefer, "Priorities for Health Services Research in Primary Care," *Quality in Primary Care*, 9(2) (2011): 77–83; Christina Bielaska-Duvemay, "Vermont's Blueprint for Home Community Health Teams," *Health Affairs*, 30(3) (2011): 383–86.

[16] For a compete discussion see *Science Magazine*, "Science Magazine: Special Online Edition: The SARS Epidemic," http://www.sciencemag.org/features/data/SARS/

seven

Research Validity and Evaluation Designs

This chapter amplifies the discussion of measurement begun in chapter 6. As evaluators seek to apply their indicators in the form of quantifiable measures, they must consider various validity and audience issues. Of critical importance is making sure to measure the actual impacts of the program rather than some extraneous factor. Evaluators are also concerned with who will read the evaluation report and to what end. A great deal of measurement precision is necessary before recommending to Congress that an experimental welfare program be mandated nationwide. Somewhat less precision is necessary to assure program administrators that the initiatives they have undertaken have achieved the desired end.

We begin by discussing *design validity* as it relates to the needs of the evaluator, program staff, and external consumers. We then turn to the various threats to achieving a valid design. Next, various designs are presented, beginning with experimental designs and followed by nonexperimental approaches such as time-series, nonequivalent control-group, and matched-pair designs. The chapter concludes with the participant-observer approach and designs that mix outcome and process measures. Evaluators should view their design options as a tool kit. There is no one design that is best under every circumstance.

Validity

Design validity can be divided into three broad categories: internal, external, and programmatic validity. Internal validity asks whether the evaluation measures what is intended. External validity asks whether the findings can be generalized—that is, whether other researchers can replicate the methodology and rely on the findings. A second external concern is whether other program administrators can extrapolate the conclusions of the evaluation to their own programs. Finally and perhaps most important is programmatic validity that asks whether the evaluation generates relevant information that is useful to program officials as they seek to make prudent decisions about their programs.

Internal Validity

Internal validity is the principal concern of all researchers. Social scientists generally seek to ensure that their research designs actually measure what is intended; moreover, they want to employ the most powerful measure available to ensure the quality of their findings. In evaluation research, however, **internal validity** involves the additional concerns of correctly identifying and measuring program goals.

Correct identification of program goals can best be accomplished in consultation with program staff. Because program goals are often vague, missing, or contradictory, failure to engage in goal consultation may produce a methodologically valid research design that measures phenomena peripheral to the program. For example, an assessment of a training program that taught unemployed persons the techniques of job hunting, résumé writing, and interviewing should incorporate a control mechanism for changes in the general economy as well. Suppose that participants in the program were very successful at obtaining employment during a time of economic growth. Officials and evaluators could not be sure that they were measuring the impacts of only the training program. By comparing the success of participants to job seekers who did not receive the training (by use of a control group) the effects of the economy can be ruled out.

External Validity

External validity involves the interdependent concerns of replication and inference. *Replication* is of particular concern to research purists because the implicit audience for the findings is their research peers, who may wish to replicate the research. This is especially true in the scientific community where medical protocols and treatment regimes for various diseases may lead to medical breakthroughs, government patents, and highly profitable proprietary drug formulations. But before a drug or procedure can gain approval by the Food and Drug Administration, others must be able to replicate the methodology and verify the outcome. To assure replication of the methodology and findings, the design and conduct of the research must be documented systematically. In the social sciences, design precision makes it possible to have repeated replications that may result in a body of data sufficient to build a theory regarding the phenomenon in question. Studies are replicated to ensure that the findings are not unique to a particular time or place.

Another concern of external validity is *inference*, or whether the findings of the evaluation can be generalized to all similar programs. Inferential or theoretical knowledge is the goal of research in both the physical sciences and the social sciences. Investigators therefore seek to discover relationships among elements in the phenomenon under investigation. For example, if multiple replications of research findings demonstrate a consistent relationship between Element *A* and Element *B* (for example, poverty and malnutrition), researchers will infer that, other things being equal, when *A* is present *B* will occur.

Evaluation researchers often do not share the scientist's concerns about replication and inference. If they did, identical research designs would be used when several evaluation teams examined separate delivery units of the same program (e.g., housing subsidies across jurisdictions). Such replication would make a meaningful assessment of program success possible. Replication is particularly valuable when dealing with experimental programs. For example, various states experimented with work requirements for welfare recipients. The use of common evaluation designs would facilitate after-the-fact comparisons between programs. Without consistent evaluation strategies, decision makers cannot be sure that program officials are pursuing identical or even similar program goals or that there is any commonality among program structures. The use of accepted and replicable evaluation designs would be very useful to evaluation consumers as well as to evaluation professionals.

Program Validity

Evaluation specialists must also answer the research questions in a form that is understandable and acceptable to the audience for the evaluation. The audience may include political executives and legislators as well as program staff. Because these consumers of the evaluation are not evaluation experts, findings must be clearly expressed. In addition, external consumers may have program expectations that are different from the goals of program administrators. Designing an evaluation that is acceptable to all audiences should, therefore, be of critical concern to the evaluation specialist. Failure to take into account the interests of all concerned may doom an evaluation to controversy or, worse, to being ignored from the outset.

This book emphasizes the importance of tailoring evaluations to the needs of program administrators and their staff because they care the most about program results. On the other hand, legislatures and oversight agencies have been guilty of requiring elaborate program reports that go unread. Those who implement programs are more interested in knowing what can be done more efficiently than they are in precision of measurement. They are more likely to cooperate with an evaluation that they understand and helped design than one imposed upon them without consultation. They are also likely to prefer evaluation reports that contain concrete recommendations for change over evaluations that use sophisticated statistical techniques without providing recommendations. It would not be unreasonable for an evaluator commissioned by the state legislature to look only at outcomes to provide a separate set of recommendations to the program administrators as a matter of professional courtesy.

Expectations may also change after the evaluation is complete and the report filed. A nongovernmental community-outreach charity operated a program designed to empower immigrants from an Asian culture in raising their children in the context of American culture and institutions. The program dealt with accessing health-care services, interfacing with schools, and information sessions on American norms regarding school attendance, nutrition, discipline and so forth. An evaluation was commissioned to determine if in fact the training and public service announcements impacted the target community. A bilingual outside evaluator conducted a survey of clientele to measure their knowledge of what was expected of them in American culture. It also tested whether training participants retained and utilized the information contained in the training seminars. The results of the study were positive in virtually every aspect of the program. The director of the agency thanked the evaluator, then promptly requested an additional report with all of the statistical data removed so that findings could be used for fund-raising. So, the evaluation measured what was intended and agreed upon in advance, utilizing measures directly applicable to program decision making. Unfortunately, the program director redefined the evaluation audience and report format after the fact. In the spirit of public service, the evaluator drafted an executive summary without requiring a second contract.

Threats to Validity

There are a number of specific threats to internal and external validity that researchers seek to avoid. Certain factors in the formulation and conduct of an evaluation can serve to invalidate the findings. These factors may be elements in the environment over which the researcher has no control, but threats to validity are more likely to stem from the methodologies employed by the researcher.[1]

History

The term **history** describes problems that result when the program's environment changes after the program is introduced. When external changes occur simultaneously with the implementation of the program, the impact of the program cannot be separated from the environmental factors. These factors may distort the apparent impact of the program and lead the researcher to believe that the program is a success or failure when the researcher is actually measuring two different phenomena. For example, law enforcement officials in a local jurisdiction might note an upswing in violent crime statistics among adolescents. This could be due to social decay in the city and an increase in gang activity. Part of the increase, however, might stem from an increase in number of adolescent males in living in the community. The data could be enhanced by controlling for the percentage of adolescents in the population as well as the numbers of crimes the group commits. These data could then be compared to findings from jurisdictions with similar population demographics.

The best way to rule out history and several other validity threats is to compare results of program participants to a **control group** *of like persons who did not take part in the program.* Returning to our job search training example, the control groups could be created in the form of an experiment by randomly assigning persons registering for work to the training group and a control group. A less cumbersome methodology might involve comparing training participants to everybody else receiving unemployment benefits in the county. In other words, if everyone registering for work were required to participate in the work readiness program, comparisons could be made to unemployment recipients in an adjacent county or to statewide aggregate data. In this example, the history factor that the evaluators would wish to control for is economic upturns or downturns.

Fortunately for evaluators, many ongoing programs routinely collect data on program outcomes. Police departments routinely collect and report crime data to state and federal officials. Health officials collect data on communicable diseases, and so forth. Thus, an experimental patrol program could be compared to programs in cities of similar size throughout the state and nation to see if variations were due to the program or to general trends. Similarly, an increase of childhood diseases for a local public health district could be compared to like districts. If an increase was noted, the agency could seek to learn why: Was the upswing due to poor performance in local immunization programs, or had a historical factor such as an influx of immigrants from third-world countries caused the change? In either case, immediate program adaptations would be appropriate.

Maturation

Another potential threat to validity, **maturation**, reflects the passage of time and the accompanying changes in the subjects under study. Controlling for maturation is particularly important in research projects involving children because children grow stronger, taller, and more capable of reasoning and learning with the passage of time. For example, children's vocabularies and cognitive development are affected by age. Simple before-and-after tests of subjects in experimental reading programs, therefore, would be impacted by the effects of maturation. Children participating in the program should therefore be compared to their age cohorts who do not participate. Merely gathering before-and-after data on the experimental children's group will not yield valid results. Control groups are the best way to rule out the effects of maturation.

Maturation also can affect adult subjects insofar as it refers to development over time. Workers who participate in program planning decisions and develop strategies for improving operations frequently gain a sense of empowerment that carries over into their daily work routines, resulting in increased productivity. So were the improvements in productivity and morale due to the operational changes or the inclusion of the rank and file in formulating the changes? Realistically, most executives are preoccupied with improving productivity regardless of the source of the improvement, unless the operational changes were to be duplicated in another division without consultation. In the latter case a control group would be greatly beneficial.

Maturation, however, is not always positive. Maturation could reflect negative changes, as when an adult becomes hungrier or grows more cynical over time. The long-term unemployed frequently become discouraged and give up searching for work, regardless of the training that they received.

Testing

Pretesting subjects can affect their performances on subsequent tests. **Testing effects** are particularly important in testing children, because the pretest may be a learning experience for them. A math skills test, for example, allows children to practice their math and possibly improve their performance on the posttest as a function of the pretest learning experience. Among adult subjects, testing may alert them to the fact that something is going to change. Subjects become sensitized to the variables being studied. This phenomenon, sometimes known as the *Hawthorne effect*, is likely to occur in testing experimental management or personnel programs.[2] The act of testing may lead to a change in the climate of the workplace, which in turn may alter work outcomes. For example, workers generally accept their supervisor's managerial styles and idiosyncrasies as long as the manager's behavior is not viewed as unreasonable by workers. That is, managers who are too demanding can expect resistance. Likewise, managers who are lax in their expectations may find that *laissez-faire* management results in no productivity whatsoever.[3] But when workers are asked to assess their supervisors regarding leadership, approachability, and overall effectiveness, workers may begin to scrutinize managerial behavior in light of the test. If supervisors were subsequently sent to a training program aimed at improving their leadership and their subordinates were again surveyed, the results might be skewed due to the earlier measurement. That is, worker expectations could be expected to increase merely by the fact that they have been asked their opinion.

Before-and-after testing on the subjects can have an impact independent of the effects of the experiment. A carefully constructed design can control for the impact that testing can have on the experiment (see the discussion of experimental designs later in this chapter). In the management training example an evaluator might wish to use a control group and/or an after-only survey to control for the impacts of the test.

Testing is most important when the evaluator wishes to know the impact of a particular intervention (such as a reading program or managerial training). Line managers might also give a pre- and posttest to determine the level of employee knowledge of a subject critical to the organization before and after training them. If the goal is employee knowledge, it matters little whether they gained the knowledge from the pretest or the training; in either event the agency has achieved its goal. A good example of this positive impact of training is the "rules of the road" tests that drivers must pass to obtain a license. If the test allows a maximum of six wrong answers, those who do not meet the standard can either study the driving manual or go over their exams to learn the rules before being retested. Similarly, an Air Force officer once confided to the authors that before his subordinates were allowed to operate information-gathering satellites, they must pass a knowledge test. Those who fail the test must complete a training regime and then be tested again. The officer asserted that he cared little whether a satisfactory performance on the second test was a function of the training or of having taken the first test. All the Air Force cared about was that the knowledge was instilled.

Instrumentation

The **instrumentation** threat occurs when the measuring instrument is altered. For example, a police force altered the statistical reports on residential burglaries by deleting garage break-ins from the data reported as household break-ins. In the next year's report residential break-ins would be down, even though there was no actual crime reduction. An instrumentation change may be mandated by a change in public policy, as when the Clinton administration began to incorporate financial and other services into US trade statistics that previously counted only manufactured goods and commodity sales. The new numbers better reflect the current state of trade. They also alter the apparent deficits and advantages with various trading partners.[4]

The most recent controversy surrounding instrumentation arose from the No Child Left Behind program begun under President George W. Bush in 2001. The law called for measuring the competence levels of children at various grades. The goal was to achieve 100% competence in every state by 2014. States, however, were permitted to develop their own performance standards provided that they met the federal requirement by 2014. In August of 2011, President Obama suspended this expectation to avoid defunding states making satisfactory progress that would still be unable to meet the ultimate goal of the program. The controversy surrounds whether or not the president has the authority to change a standard defined in law.[5] Programs must be absolutely transparent when making such changes and when reporting their findings in order to prevent consumers from having an unrealistic impression of program performance. This can be done by footnote or by generating data, beginning with the new criteria, that is reported separately from previous years.

Variations in findings may also result from turnovers in the research staff or even changes resulting from different people performing the evaluation, as when the experiment involves the observation and scoring of participants' performance. In such cases the principal evaluator should be sure that all observers apply the rating scale uniformly (*interrater reliability*). For example, the senior author once conducted interviews with children who were told stories involving moral dilemmas. The interviews were recorded, then scored after the fact by pairs of evaluators who applied a scale linked to Jean Piaget's developmental paradigm.[6] When the raters did not agree, A third evaluator listened to the recording separately. If the third person did not agree with one or the other or believed that the child's response was too ambiguous to scale, the child's responses were deleted from the findings of the research.[7]

Turnover in evaluation staff is another type of instrumentation change that can be addressed by carefully orienting incoming staff regarding goals of the research and the rationale for the measuring instruments used. New staff must also be apprised of the proper methods for applying the research instruments. Prolonged contact with the program and its staff may cause changes within an observer over time.[8] An objective evaluator may become a program advocate. This problem is particularly acute when the evaluator's personal assessment of subject performance is the measure of program success. Such problems can be corrected through careful training and reliability checks on the raters.

Statistical Regression

When extreme performers are the experimental subjects, **statistical regression** may threaten validity. This is because on any given test, individual performances will vary as a matter of luck. On a good day a superior student will guess correctly on the answers he or she does not know, and on a bad day the opposite will occur. The same is true at the other end of the continuum: Those scoring the lowest on the exam will do so partly as a result of inability and partly as a result of bad luck. Thus, results on the after-experiment test may vary simply because right and wrong guesses tend to even out over time. Extreme cases therefore can be expected to regress towards the mean on the second test. Using *outliers* (extreme performers) in an experimental program can bias the findings. Suppose that a researcher selected the poorest performers on a reading examination for inclusion in a special tutorial program. Because random changes would cause some of the students to improve their performances on the second test, regardless of the merits of the program, a before-and-after test of the poorest performers would not show which students' performances could be attributed to some other cause and which were a result of program participation.

Consultations with program staff can help avoid the problems of statistical regression. Program staff may believe that the targets of the tutorial program should be the neediest. The evaluators must therefore explain the importance of data reliability. The best way to ensure the validity of the test is to select students of varying abilities on a random basis for inclusion in the experimental and control groups.

Selection Bias

Making comparisons between groups that are erroneously believed to be equivalent is called **selection bias**. Suppose, for example, that the police department in City A instituted a new crime detection training program. One year later the arrest and conviction rates of the officers working for City A were compared with those of City B. This after-only design could not guarantee that the differences in performance were a function of the training program. Officers in City A may have been better at crime detection *before* the training program was instituted.

Selection bias is a possible problem whenever participants in an experimental program are volunteers. For example, drug addicts who volunteer for an experimental behavior modification program to reduce drug dependency cannot be compared with another randomly selected group of addicts. The volunteers are more motivated to do something about their addiction, which distinguishes them from other addicts. A more appropriate experiment would be to assign volunteers randomly to the experimental program and to a placebo control group. Of course, such a study could only be generalized to persons wishing to end their drug dependency because unmotivated addicts would resist participation.[9]

Selection bias may also impact the inferences made from evaluation data. Elite educational institutions obtain their ranking, in part, based on their selectivity. An institution whose students are recruited from the upper 3% of the S.A.T. test takers are thought to have high standards and, ergo, quality programs. They also receive high ratings for their graduation rates and the success of their alumni. Both of these outcomes are impacted by the front-end selection bias—that is, they only accept outliers from the high-performance end of the spectrum.

Experimental Mortality

One of the most vexing problems for evaluation researchers engaged in comparisons of pilot programs is **experimental mortality**. "Mortality" in this case refers to subjects dropping out of a program. Subjects with low-level motivation might drop out of our experimental job training program at higher rates than persons in ongoing programs simply because the pilot program requires an extra effort from them. The threat to validity is that subjects who remain in the pilot program are more motivated than subjects in the comparison group. The probability that this group will find jobs at a higher rate is therefore increased as a result of the elimination of the unmotivated rather than as an effect of the program.

An additional problem can result from the good intentions of program staff who may add subjects to the experimental group to replace the drop-outs after the experiment is underway. The additions would not receive the same length and type of training and might therefore lower the performance level of the experimental group. The staff might also add subjects out of a desire to extend program benefits to the largest possible group. The humanistic impulses of the staff might also incline them to extend program benefits to their most needy clients, which would add the problem of selection bias to that of mortality. Whatever the motivation, the principal effect of subject additions or substitutions is contamination of the research findings. Staff must be aware of the need for preserving the purity of experimental conditions. Close cooperation between program and evaluation staffs throughout each phase of the experiment can help avoid such problems. After the experiment runs its course the staff can extend the program to all clients, but substitutions before that time will never permit the manager to conclude that the program had the desired effect.

Interaction of Selection with Other Variables

If selection is based on factors other than random assignment, it can interact with other variables to compound the problems of validity. For example, a test to determine the impact of a teaching method on college sophomores, juniors, and seniors suffers from several potential **interaction effects**. The most obvious is the maturation variable. Juniors and seniors are not equivalent to each other, or to sophomores. Each successive year in school increases the probability that a student will develop quality study habits. The ranks of the lower classes, moreover, are populated by a greater number of persons who refuse to take school seriously and who will eventually drop out. The way to rule this out is to compare seniors to seniors, juniors to juniors, and so forth. The program evaluator should examine any nonrandom selection process and ask if selection interacts with mortality, regression, instrumentation, testing, maturation, or history. If so, the study must be redesigned or the conclusions qualified.

Selection bias can frustrate evaluators of ongoing programs simply because the subjects have already experienced the condition one wishes to measure. For example, a study wishing to know how well a ten-year-old prison education program had achieved its goals of preparing prisoners for productive lives and reducing recidivism must work backwards. Prison officials would be unlikely to authorize an experimental program for additional years so that the researchers could randomly select prisoners and assign them to the education program and control groups. Officials would much prefer a review of current records.

Selection bias could be problematic in this instance for several reasons. First, participation in the education program would probably have been conditioned on good behavior. This problem is called *creaming* because only the best behaved are eligible. Second, all participants are self-selected because they all actively sought participation. Findings would have to be reported with the caveat that those undergoing the education program were not equivalent to the larger prison population. Furthermore, an after-the-fact evaluation might not yield good data on recidivism due to selection bias. Very often, model prisoners are serving life sentences for murder. Lifers most probably would also have seniority for program participation as well. Thus, the number of prisoners who completed the education program and then reentered society might be quite small. Officials and evaluators might therefore wish to examine the records of participants with those of others serving life sentences, checking for differences in behavior, and survey the two groups regarding their quality of life in prison. Many prison systems begin by putting violent offenders in highly regimented, secure facilities that are expensive to operate. Prisoners are then transferred to less secure, more comfortable prisons based on their conduct. Thus, officials might compare progress within the system as a benefit in addition to recidivism reduction.

Four Threats to External Validity

External concerns are important when the research findings are to go beyond the specific setting of the program. Successful pilot programs result in large expenditures for wider applications. A false positive evaluation of a program could result in millions of wasted dollars. For this reason alone, the researcher must provide for as much external validity as possible.

Interactive Effects of Selection Bias and the Experimental Variable

A major threat to external validity is the interactive effects of the experimental variable and selection bias. To make sure that such effects do not occur, one may use a selection process based on random assignment to the experimental conditions from a population sufficiently large to assure representativeness. For example, testing the benefits of a particular type of weight-training equipment for football players using only the University of Notre Dame football team as the experimental group would jeopardize the generalizability of the results. Members of the team are exceptionally dedicated athletes attending college on scholarships. A sizable portion of them also aspire to careers as professional athletes. The subjects are probably more motivated to train than would be the case with college teams generally. Even if the Notre Dame team were divided into an experimental and a control group, one would still be comparing outliers to outliers.

The interactive effects of the experimental variable and selection bias can also be illustrated by the aforementioned job-training program. Suppose that the research team sought to control as many conditions as possible to isolate the effects of the program and therefore the evaluation team requested volunteers from existing programs. Suppose that the evaluation team then divided the volunteers into an experimental group and a control group, the experimental group receiving the special training and the control group continuing as they were. Selection bias has occurred because both the experimental group and the control group are volunteers. Both were selected from among persons sufficiently motivated to participate in existing jobs programs and to volunteer to be part of the experimental program. The study is apt to show that the experimental program produced results not much greater than those of current programs. While the experimental group was receiving job-readiness training, the equally motivated control subjects would be looking for work. Again, creaming has occurred, comparing outliers to outliers.

Program officials, however, are much more interested in whether the job readiness training is likely to work than they are with whether their data can be relied upon to a statistical certitude. Thus, they might go ahead with the experiment with the caveat that the findings should be extrapolated with caution to the greater welfare community. If the researchers are only interested in assessing the impacts of the job readiness training on the ability to find work, they might choose the less expensive option of comparing the training participants to the aggregate success rate of persons registering for work who did not receive the training. Comparisons could then be made using the proximate indicators of speed in finding work, ability to retain a job, and the starting salary of the participants compared to the average starting salary. The measures would not be precise, but they might well be sufficient for measuring the impact of the program and whether it was worth continuing.

Reactive or Interactive Effects of Pretesting

Pretesting subjects may make them more or less susceptible to the effects of the experimental condition. For example, cholesterol testing of persons on an experimental drug would be required throughout the experiment to monitor the impacts of the drug. Knowing that they would be tested on a daily or weekly basis might cause participants to more closely regulate their diets and cut down on the intake of foods high in cholesterol. The US military counts on the interactive effect of testing to reduce the use of drugs by active-duty personnel. Troops are less likely to use drugs recreationally if they never know when they will be randomly selected for a drug test.

Reactive Effects of the Experimental Environment

Reactive effects of the experimental environment that cannot be duplicated in the nonexperimental condition can also invalidate research findings. For example, the presence of the evaluation team may cause the subjects to deviate from normal behavior, and subjects who know that they will be posttested may put forth extra effort. Such a situation can be problematic for managers of large programs seeking to set realistic performance standards. This can best be achieved by observing workers performing the task. However, if they are aware of the observation they may alter their regular work patterns in order to look good to the observer, or they might slow down if they know a standard is to be set—for example, workers who must record the time when a piece of work arrives and leaves their desks.

The US Postal Service utilizes time and motion studies to determine the appropriate number of addresses to assign a given postal route. This is accomplished by having an evaluator accompany the carrier and take note of how long it takes to service a route, given the volume of mail being carried. One need only compare the hour at which their personal mail is delivered on days when the carrier is being observed to the normal delivery time to witness the reactive effect. Workers who complete their routes quickly can expect to have them increased.

The experimental environment also may be so controlled that it does not reflect circumstances in the real world. For example, much of our knowledge about human performance and psychological motivation has been gained in laboratories, using homogeneous subjects. Persons seeking to apply this knowledge of human performance to real-world groups are frequently frustrated because tasks, reward systems, and accountability operate differently under experimental and real-world conditions. Experimental groups composed of student volunteers from the same age cohort may be more cooperative or be willing to take greater risks than groups composed of supervisors, subordinates, and peers. Real-world group decisions are influenced by relationships among group members that existed before they began the current task. Moreover, much deference is given to the views of supervisors of real-world work groups even when they do not produce the best ideas in the group. Risk taking and the degree of cooperation, moreover, may have been defined and limited by the organization. Given these factors, program innovations that prove promising under experimental conditions should be pilot tested under operational conditions before being broadly applied.

Multiple-Treatment Interference

Another threat to external validity is **multiple-treatment interference**. Because the application of consecutive treatments is cumulative in the subjects, the researcher frequently has difficulty isolating the effects of subsequent treatments from those of earlier applications. Suppose that a manager wished to study employees' productivity under different reward systems. Is maximum productivity achieved when they are compensated on an hourly basis as individuals, when they are compensated on a piecework rate, or when they are compensated as a unit on the basis of group productivity? The manager might experiment by paying workers by the hour for one week, individually by the piece for one week, and then as a group for one week. At the end of each week both productivity and job satisfaction would be measured. The data on employee productivity and satisfaction when paid by the piece as individuals would be tainted by the employees' prior experience of being paid by the hour as individuals. Similarly, employee productivity and attitudes toward compensation by the piece as a group would be colored by the previous two experiments. The most that could be learned from the experiment is how groups react when subjected to the three treatments in the same order. The pitfalls of multiple-treatment interference can be avoided by conducting three simultaneous, separate studies of workers who were randomly assigned to each of the three conditions.

Design Selection

Evaluators must generate evaluation strategies that rule out as many validity pitfalls as possible while producing data that are both understandable and useful to the program staff. Evaluation costs and evaluation timeliness also impact the choice of designs. Evaluations commissioned to facilitate decision making normally do not enjoy the luxury of long-term study. Decision makers are more interested in identifying and solving problems than in design purity. Selecting a cost-effective design that is rigorous enough to avoid validity threats is a prime concern of evaluation specialists as social scientific researchers. Effectively balancing design rigor against program needs is an art form.

The evaluation designs presented in this section are not classified according to rigor. We do not attempt to judge their relative merits. The yardstick by which evaluation designs should be measured is how applicable they are to the needs of the program, not their methodological sophistication.

Experimental Designs

Experimental design is the evaluation method that most closely approximates the rigorous standards for research found in the physical sciences. Experimental designs feature **random selection** of subjects from the population under study. Random selection is necessary to rule out such validity threats as volunteerism, creaming, and so forth. Random selection also enhances an evaluation's external validity because results can be extrapolated to the population from which subjects were drawn. Suppose a drug company wanted to test a new birth control drug for its efficacy in preventing pregnancy and document any side effects the drug might cause. The experiment might begin by asking for female volunteers who wished to become pregnant. The volunteers would first undergo physical exams to determine if in fact they are capable of becoming pregnant. They could then be divided into experimental and control groups. The first group would receive the experimental drug. A second group would receive a placebo. Neither group would know whether they were actually receiving the experimental contraceptive. A one-year comparison between these groups would reveal the effectiveness of the drug at preventing pregnancy. Members of the two groups could also undergo periodic physicals during the experiment to identify negative side effects. Of course, one clinical trial would not satisfy the Food and Drug Administration. Before the drug could be marketed, the experiment would have to be repeated several times, holding conditions constant.

In the field of education, the results of an experimental reading program on randomly selected elementary school children could be generalized to similar children who did not participate. Because the children were selected randomly, the impact of the experiment would be measured on children with various levels of initial ability, much like those that exist among school-age children generally. Evaluators could therefore state with relative confidence that a statewide adoption of the program would yield similar results. Of course other factors such as class size, teacher training, and school and home environments would be expected to cause variations in results. Nevertheless, the variations would not be attributed to the quality of the program.

Random selection is important whenever generalizability is a concern. In point of fact, a great deal of social science research does not engage in experimentation. Survey researchers often are interested in what the public thinks about a particular product, service, political issue, or candidate for office at a particular point in time. They must be concerned with random selection of those they interview, even though no experiment is involved,[10] for the simple fact that they wish to ensure that their findings reflect those of the population from which the sample was drawn. Findings can then be compared to parallel surveys to improve confidence in the findings. Furthermore, by asking the same sorts of questions year after year, trends in attitudes can be assessed over time.

Random assignment ensures that history, maturation, selection biases, and the like do not threaten the validity of the data. In addition, the experimental strategy carefully controls the exposure of subjects to the experimental condition. Of course medical experiments, like birth control methods, need not concern themselves with volunteerism or creaming. Participants would of necessity all be volunteers consisting of women of childbearing age with no objection to becoming pregnant.

The Classic Experiment

The classic pretest-posttest experimental design can be illustrated as follows:

$$R \quad O \quad X \quad O \quad \text{(experimental group)}$$
$$R \quad O \quad \quad \quad O \quad \text{(control group)}$$

The two *R*s represent two groups of subjects who have been randomly assigned to the experimental and control-group conditions. A pretest is administered to both groups before the experimental condition is introduced. The *O*s in the second column represents the pretest observation of both the experimental and control groups (e.g., a baseline reading test). Only the upper row contains an X, which represents the experimental condition and thus indicates the experimental group. The absence of an X in the second row identifies it as the control group. Both the upper and lower rows contain an O in the last column, indicating the posttest measurement. In our birth control example, the volunteers would undergo a pretest consisting of a medical exam to determine if in fact they were able to conceive a child. After the pretest, they would be randomly assigned to either the experimental or the control group. The subjects would then undergo the experimental condition. The last step is a post-experiment posttest to measure the changes in the subjects that can be attributed to the experimental condition. The process is visually illustrated in figure 7.1.

To further illustrate the experimental method, suppose that one wished to learn the impact of jogging on pigs that have high-cholesterol diets. The researcher might randomly assign pigs of comparable age, weight, and sex to the experimental and control conditions. In this case, X would represent jogging. All pigs would have complete physical exams at the outset, which would constitute the cholesterol pretest that is designated with an O. Pigs with other abnormalities would be screened from the test.

The next step is conducting the experiment, which requires that both the experimental group and the control group be fed diets high in cholesterol. The groups would be housed separately to ensure the purity of the experimental conditions. (It would not do to have a control subject undergo the rigors of jogging.) The experimental pigs would be taken out jogging each day for increasing distances until the test conditions of jogging fitness were reached. The control group would not jog. (Presumably some of the pigs might play golf, tennis, or some other sport.)

The final test would be to give the experimental and control groups complete physical examinations again to determine the level of cholesterol in the bloodstream and the overall cardiovascular condition of the subjects. The before-and-after condition can be represented as follows:

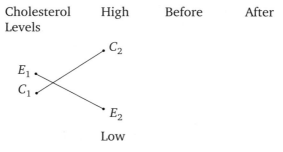

The dots at E_1 and C_1 respectively represent the cholesterol levels in the experimental and control subjects before introduction of the experimental variable of a high-cholesterol diet. E_2 and C_2 represent the posttest cholesterol levels in the two groups. The researcher would measure the

Figure 7.1 A Diagram of the Experimental Research Process

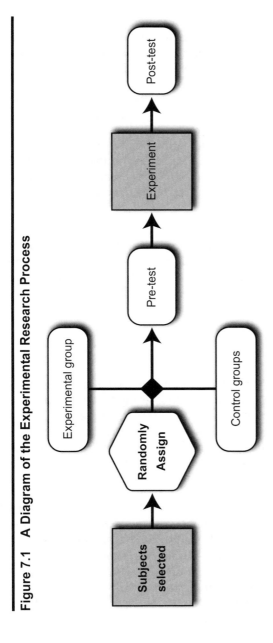

relative changes in cholesterol level between the two groups to determine the effects of jogging on subjects on high-cholesterol diets. The plot indicated above shows that jogging resulted in reduced cholesterol levels despite the increase of cholesterol in the diet. The control group, which did not jog, experienced increased cholesterol levels.

The test could be enhanced by introducing additional experimental and control conditions. For example, the researcher might also want to compare the above results with pigs that were fed regular diets but did not jog, pigs that received a normal diet and did jog, and a group that received a low-cholesterol diet but did not jog. The number of variations on the design would be limited primarily by the number of questions the researchers wished to investigate and the number of pigs the research budget could afford.

The Solomon Four-Group Design

With human subjects, the impact of testing becomes an important consideration, especially when the experiment calls for the measurement of learning. To absolutely ensure against the interactive effects of testing, one might use the Solomon four-group design. This design uses two experimental and two control groups that can be represented as follows:

$$
\begin{array}{ccccc}
R & O & X & O \\
R & O & & O \\
R & & X & O \\
R & & & O \\
\end{array}
$$

Assignment to the various conditions is done on a random basis and is indicated by the Rs in the first column. The first group receives a pretest, undergoes the experimental condition, and then receives a posttest. Group Two receives only the pretest and the posttest and acts as a control on Group One. Group Three undergoes the experimental condition but receives only a posttest. Group Four receives only the posttest.

The methodology is cumbersome, but it does rule out the interaction effect of testing and X (the experimental condition). Differences can be measured between Group Three, which received only the experiment and the posttest, and Group One to determine if X interacted with testing. Group Four provides information on comparable subjects who have undergone the same maturation and historical conditions without the experimental or testing impacts. Comparing Group Two and Group Four would provide a pure measure of the impact of simple testing on posttest performance without the impact of X. In addition to being cumbersome, the costs associated with the Solomon four-group design are substantial only for a marginal increase in validity over what can be obtained by the much simpler posttest-only design.

The Posttest-Only Design

A simpler method for ruling out the effects of testing on X is the *posttest-only* approach, which involves random assignment to two groups, the administration of the experimental condition to one group, and the administration of a posttest to both the experimental group and the control group. The posttest-only design is diagrammed as follows:

$$R \quad X \quad O$$
$$R \qquad\quad O$$

The Mutual-Control Design

A researcher may design two discrete experiments so that the experimental group in one condition acts as the control group for the other experiment, and vice versa. The mutual-control design has been used with success in educational situations. The design can be achieved by randomly assigning students to two groups, A and B. For example, Group A undergoes mathematics training but is not given a pretest. Group B undergoes reading training but does not take a reading pretest. At the end of the first training cycle, Group A is tested for mathematics gain and Group B is tested for reading gain. Each group then becomes the control group for the other by using a pretest-posttest approach in the second round of training. In the second round, Group B begins math training but, unlike members of Group A in the first round, takes a pretest. Group A begins its reading training and takes a pretest. The pretest scores from the second phase become the control-group scores for the first round. The design can be represented as follows:

| Math | R_A | X | O | | Math | R_B | O | X | O |
| Reading | R_B | X | O | | Reading | R_A | O | X | O |

These education evaluators would have to be sure that not too much time elapsed between the first and second rounds of the experiment to limit the impacts of maturation. Presumably, the experiments could be run in consecutive semesters if time was not an obstacle.

Advantages and Disadvantages of Experimental Designs

The benefits of experimental designs are the confidence one gains in the internal validity of the findings and the range of variables that can be tested using additional experimental conditions and control groups. Moreover, rigorously designing, implementing, and documenting the experiments enhances external validity. Other researchers can duplicate the research conditions and test the findings. Others can also weigh the relative values of experimental approaches to a problem. In our birth-control example, the scientific community could assess the relative effectiveness of several birth-control drug experiments conducted on different groups at different times. This is possible only when they are confident in the experimental rigor of the processes. The high cost of drug development is offset by the profits they normally gain from having exclusive rights to produce and market the formulation.

Evaluators of social programs must weigh the cost and difficulty of sustaining the experiment against the relative importance of the knowledge to be gained from the experiment. Sustaining experimental conditions over a period of time is the principal difficulty in applying these designs in evaluation research, especially when the subjects are free to come and go or drop out of the experiment. On the other hand, experimental designs can be especially useful when subjects are not mobile, as is the case when subjects are long-term patients in mental institutions or convalescent hospitals or when the subjects are prisoners. In such cases, however, generalizations can only be made to these particular populations.

While random selection may not always be possible, it is well worthwhile to utilize a control group whenever possible. Control groups—even nonrandom control groups—are valuable when there is a high possibility of contamination from the threats caused by history and/or maturation. As noted in the previous chapter, many agencies are required to collect and maintain data on a variety of generic indicators. Establishing control groups that rule out history, therefore, may merely mean including report data on similar organizations in the evaluation. Maturation can be dealt with similarly. For example, a program of counseling fifteen- to eighteen-year-old gang members might report spectacular success rates if the only measure was continued gang membership after counseling. A control-group design might indicate that as adolescents mature they tend to discontinue gang membership without counseling. What was attributed to program success was actually the result of maturation.[11]

Staff concerns for program delivery can also pose a threat to sustaining the experimental condition for the duration of the evaluation. Suppose that an experimental drug-treatment program was the subject of study. Outpatients at the drug-treatment center would be assigned to either the treatment group or the control group on a random basis. Suppose further that the period of experimentation was to be two years. If the program seemed to be a success on the basis of an interim report, the staff might press for immediate delivery of the benefits to all patients in the center, including the control group. If program administrators yielded to staff pressure, the evaluator would have no alternative but to terminate the experimental conditions. This problem can be avoided by laying out the need for preserving the experiment at the outset of the design phase and by eliciting a staff commitment not to press for early termination of the experiment.

An Example of Experimental Design

Despite the possible problems with experimental designs, there are circumstances in which one or more pilot programs can be worth conducting by using the experimental method or a close approximation of it. The drug rehabilitation program is an example of such a program. Suppose that one wished to determine whether a halfway house for drug users is more beneficial than outpatient centers, where treatment and counseling normally take place. The first step would be to identify the variables that might affect program outcomes. Researchers might consider whether the halfway house is to use heroin substitutes, whether to utilize social workers or persons in recovery as counselors, and whether the halfway house will conduct in-house job training or operate a job placement service.

The next step would be random assignment of subjects to the experimental and control conditions. One could generate a list of potential participants from the existing centers, contact the persons in question, and invite them to participate in the program. Persons who agreed would be assigned to either the experimental or the control conditions. Control subjects would continue as they had been at the regular treatment center. Experimental subjects would participate in the halfway-house experience.

Two potential dangers to the success and validity of the study have already appeared. First, it is unlikely that persons who are assigned to the control condition will agree to increased scrutiny (for example, psychological tests) when they see no apparent benefit. An alternative would be to select a random sample of participants from among those agreeing to participate in the study. Clients in the regular treatment program could be used as a control group. This, however, would limit the range of measures that one can use because there is no direct access to the control group.

The second threat to the validity of the outcome is that the volunteers who enter the halfway house must be selected from among those agreeing to participate. They therefore are not equivalent to volunteers for medical experiments, where the mental attitude and emotional stability of the volunteers have no effect on their physiological reactions to treatment. On the other hand, volunteers selected from among heroin users may have the motivation to terminate their drug dependency. It is also possible that the same persons would have achieved a high success rate at the drug treatment center if they had not participated in the experimental program.

The research, therefore, is not purely experimental, even though the conditions are more controlled than in some of the nonexperimental designs treated later in this chapter. Given these limitations on experimental purity, it would be best to run several tests of the program simultaneously. If a heroin substitute is to be used in conjunction with the halfway house, a separate group could be given the heroin substitute but receive counseling at the regular treatment center. Similarly, halfway houses without the substitute could also be run and the use of professional counselors in recovery could be varied. Increasing the variation in conditions would strengthen the findings.

Once the experimental conditions have been designed, the next step is to identify proximate indicators of program success. The number of cases in which the subjects experience complete freedom from drug addiction, if taken alone, would be a stringent test of program success. Other goals of the program could be making addicts productive citizens, reducing crime, and minimizing the return to complete addiction. Additional proximate indicators of program success might include the ability of a subject to hold a job and the number of arrests of control- and experimental-group members. A final indicator might be the rates with which subjects abandon various forms of treatment to resume the life of complete dependency on heroin.

The findings of the above design would provide decision makers with information about the efficacy of expensive labor-intensive programs before large expenditures of public funds were poured into wider applications of the program. Unfortunately, funding limitations do not always permit experiments that are rigorous enough to isolate all the potential impacts individually. Public officials must therefore be convinced that rigorous experimentation is a necessary decision-aiding tool in the process of forming policy.

Nonexperimental Designs

The systematic data-gathering techniques and rigorous measures found in experimental design are also incorporated into nonexperimental designs. They are not, however, constrained by the requirements of random assignment and maintenance of experimental conditions. **Nonexperimental designs** are particularly attractive to program evaluation specialists because evaluators are frequently required to begin their research after a program has been in operation for a number of years, which makes experimentation impossible. Even some pilot programs are so broad-based in scope (e.g., city or statewide) that random assignment is impossible. Fortunately, time-series designs and other nonequivalent control-group designs, matched-pair designs, and the like (discussed later in this section) can provide officials with information about the success of the program without the complications and cost of experimentation. Nonexperimental designs have the added advantage of applicability after the fact.

Time-Series Designs

This type of design enjoys widespread popularity with evaluation specialists.[12] First, time-series designs are easily applied. Second, a variety of data exists for some programs. As we noted earlier, health care, law enforcement, and social programs as well as schools routinely gather information using generic indicators. Perhaps the greatest reason behind this design's popularity is that it may be applied after a program has begun. The design can be illustrated as follows:

$$O \quad O \quad O \quad X \quad O \quad O \quad O \quad O$$

The Os indicate that data on the program were collected on a number of occasions before the change was instituted. In reality, the preprogram observations are gathered retrospectively, utilizing program records and other available statistics. The Os (points of data collection or data points) are normally done at systematic intervals of time such as weeks, months, quarters, or years. These intervals are constrained by when generic data are collected. Agencies that collect and store data on a monthly basis can be retrospectively examined by month, quarter, or year. Weeks would not be possible. The frequency of data-point inclusion also depends on the speed with which the program changes are expected to come into effect.

The reason for several observations before and after the introduction of X is to rule out episodic, random, up-and-down swings in data. If the researcher is confident about the stability of the indicators or when only the immediate impact of X is to be measured, the evaluator may wish to conduct a simple before-and-after test, which is illustrated as follows:

$$O \quad X \quad O$$

However, the researcher can have much more confidence in the data by taking the additional measurements. A midwestern state passed a law allowing the highway patrol to confiscate the driver's licenses of suspected drunk drivers, thus suspending their driving privileges pending a court appearance where a judge would determine whether to return the license or to impose a more lengthy forfeiture. Data on confiscations and alcohol-related traffic accidents in the months immediately following the implementation indicated a significant drop in both. Longer-term impact, however, showed a leveling off, then a decline in confiscation and an increase in accidents. Initially the officers enthusiastically embraced the new tool, but their interest subsequently waned.[13] Time-series analysis added more realistic impact information.

Application of time-series methodology can be further illustrated using the example of an innovative patrol program in a hypothetical police department. The evaluator could obtain data on various measures for several years or months before and after introduction of the new system. Time-series measurement of crime rates, citizen complaints, speed of response to emergency calls, and conviction rates due to citizen cooperation could be gathered. (The latter three measures would be subject to the existence of record-keeping systems for such data.)

A key problem lies in interpretation of the data and knowing when to declare the program a success, a failure, or merely a good intention. Suppose that the evaluator gathered data for the six months preceding and following the introduction of the new patrol program. A plot of the data might resemble the following:

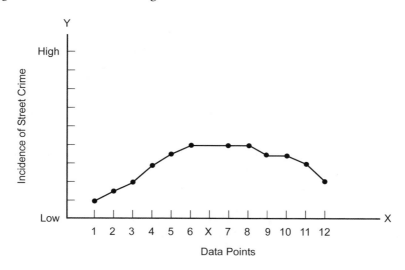

The incidence of street crime are represented on the Y (vertical) axis of the above illustration. The X (horizontal) axis represents the various observations (data points) over the twelve months. An X between the sixth and seventh data points on the X-axis represents the introduction of the experimental program.

The illustration shows that after an initial period of leveling off, street crime in the district dropped. The researcher cannot be sure, however, if the drop is a result of the program or of history. History can be controlled by the introduction of additional time-series data from other precincts, a neighboring city, or cities of comparable size and demographics, or by comparing the pilot precinct with national statistics. The researcher's best bet is to gather data on other precincts or to compare the findings with statewide or national statistics. Other cities of comparable size, for example, may not be keeping monthly records or may have introduced programs that could have an impact on the findings.

The multiple time-series design can be illustrated as follows:

O   O   O   X   O   O   O
O   O   O   O   O   O

Assuming that the researcher decides to compare the experimental precincts with national figures, the plot might resemble the following:

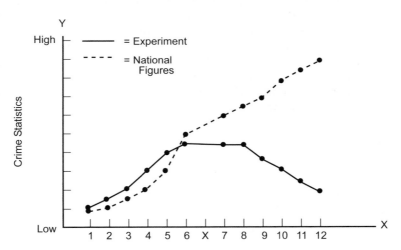

The multiple time-series findings indicate that the street crime rate in the experimental district changed from being slightly higher than the national average for this category of crime to slightly below the precinct's own preprogram average. The drop in relation to the national figures indicates considerable change, because the slight decline in the local rate occurred during a period of increase in national crime figures.

Once the evaluation is complete, it must be determined whether the program was successful. This is done by the manager, who assesses the indicators (such as crime statistics, citizen complaints, and so on) in the aggregate. Unfortunately, citizen complaints, emergency response rates, and the rates of street crimes cannot be forced into a one-dimensional measure of the program. The problem of interpretation might be further compounded if some indicators showed no change or if the program had an effect that was the opposite of what was anticipated. For example, the evaluator might learn that the program reduced the rates of such street crimes as muggings, assaults, and purse snatchings. Other crimes such as the number of family disputes, burglaries, and homicides might not have been affected. The evaluator might also learn that the program had cut the response time in emergencies but that the overall conviction rate went down.

The results obtained from this hypothetical evaluation are mixed. Maintaining evaluator neutrality is particularly important in such cases. In some cities, good police work is defined as short emergency response time. In others, reduction in street crime is a goal. The function of the evaluator is to present the data in a straightforward, understandable format. Decisions regarding program continuation, expansion, or cancellation are the province of management. Cities that want to impact domestic violence, for example, may wish to train officers in the latest techniques of crisis intervention and the referral of victims to counseling and other assistance agencies. Increasing conviction rates may have more to do with follow-up investigations by detectives than with the response of street patrol officers. Evaluators may rest assured that advocates and opponents of various program alternatives will attempt to enlist the support of the evaluator.

Nonequivalent Control-Group Designs

This type of design is another variation of non-experimental evaluation strategies. (Strictly speaking, multiple time-series analysis is also a nonequivalent control-group approach.) All nonequivalent evaluations compare the results of the program to those of similar organizations, groups, and the like. No attempt is made to randomly assign subjects to the experimental and control-group conditions. Nonequivalent designs can be diagrammed as follows:

$$O \quad X \quad O \qquad\qquad X \quad O$$
$$\text{or}$$
$$O \qquad\quad O \qquad\qquad\qquad O$$

The diagram represents the pretest/posttest and posttest-only designs. Conspicuously missing from the diagram are *R*s, which would signify random assignments to the conditions.

The use of nonequivalent control-group strategies can be illustrated with the example of the alternative patrol pattern. Suppose that the police chief wished to know the impact of the alternative patrol pattern on citizens' perceptions of the police and officers' perceptions of citizen cooperation. In this case, the posttest-only design would be preferable to the pretest/posttest design for three reasons. First, the additional data gained from the pretest might be only marginally beneficial when the additional costs are considered. Second, the pretest step would necessitate ruling out the impact of testing on the subjects. Finally, a pretest-posttest design would require that the evaluators posttest the same subjects who were surveyed in the pretest. Many of them may have moved in the interim.

Carrying out the posttest-only design would involve construction of two survey questionnaires to measure citizen and police perceptions. The citizen questionnaire would survey a randomly selected sample of citizens living in the experimental precincts. The evaluator might also wish to gather a separate subsample of merchants in the experimental area. Merchants are disproportionately the victims of certain categories of crime and consequently experience a disproportionate amount of contact with the police.

The nonequivalent control group for the survey might be a random sampling of citizens living or operating businesses in a roughly equivalent precinct, or the evaluators could sample attitudes in the city generally. Police perceptions could be measured by sampling officers in the experimental precinct and a control precinct or by surveying all the officers in the experimental and control precincts. Sampling is only beneficial when dealing with large populations where surveying everyone is prohibitively expensive.

Analyzing the data would involve comparing the mean responses of the respondents living in the experimental precinct with those of the control group. Similar comparisons would be made between officers in the experimental precinct and their control group. The evaluators would interpret substantially better attitudes among the experimental officers and public samples as a positive indicator of program success. Conversely, better attitudes among one or both control groups would reflect negatively on the program.

There are instances when even roughly equivalent control groups do not exist. In chapter 2 we offered the example of an NGO dedicated to anti-sex-trafficking activities in Vietnam. A major component of the NGO's efforts is a scholarship program to keep high-risk girls in school by paying their school expenses (fees, uniforms, and books). The program also offers tutoring to help them academically. Finding an equivalent control for a backwater program in a developing country is impossible. While there are at-risk girls throughout the country, they are not identified as such by school officials. The evaluator therefore chose three control groups: dropout rates in the general student population of Vietnam; participant performance compared to that of their age cohorts in the participating schools; and dropout rates in the United States. To measure the efficacy of the tutoring program the evaluation surveyed the tutoring staff, which was made up of public school teachers working after school. Student academic and discipline performance year after year were used as indicators for the efficacy of the tutoring program. That is, did students as individuals improve their grades in light of two hours a day of extra study? Their discipline records also were tracked year after year, and they were aggregately compared to the general student population.

Matched-Pair Designs

This type of design falls into the category of nonexperimental designs because it does not rule out the effects of sampling, history, and maturity to the degree that experimental designs using random assignments do. The matched-pair approach assigns subjects to various experimental and control conditions on the basis of some common characteristic that the evaluator wishes to measure. In education evaluations, the characteristic frequently is the grade in school and/or the performance of the subjects on an indicator such as reading or math ability. In adult organizations, one might use pay grade in order to get a vertical snapshot of the program's impacts on various echelons of the organization.

For example, suppose that the experiment called for testing a new reading program. The researcher might proceed by assigning the children to the experimental and control groups on the basis of year in school and reading level. Thus, the reading scores of students would be used to gain test and control groups that reflect the spectrum of reading abilities. Two children from the top percentile might be assigned to test and control conditions. Then two children from the next percentile could be assigned. Ideally, the researchers would select the sample to reflect the distribution of reading abilities in the district—that is, the bulk of the students would be drawn from the average reading-ability range. By so doing, the additional factor of regression would be controlled. Thus, three factors that could influence the findings are controlled. Other factors, however, could affect the outcome, such as home environment, classroom atmosphere, individual intelligence, and learning disabilities. Matched pairs may be preferable to other nonequivalent control groups, such as the teacher to whom the student is assigned or the school attended. Complete random assignment, however, is the only way to assure maximum internal validity.

In some circumstances the matched-pair design is applicable to noneducational programs. Suppose one wished to assess the efficacy of a supervisory training program. Suppose further that the goals of the program were to improve organizational efficiency and employee morale through improvement of supervisory skills and leadership. The evaluator might choose employee attitudes toward their supervisors as the primary measure of morale. The managers of the participants could also be asked to rate the leadership/supervisory skills of the participants vis-à-vis their nonparticipating peers. The units of work produced per unit of cost might be the measure of productivity.

The first step would be to select from among program participants and their peers a sample that was stratified according to position in the hierarchy. For example, if the training program were in a federal agency, the Government Service rating of the participants would be a rough indicator of their level of responsibility. Thus, if the sample of program participants contained two managers at the rank of G.S. 11, the researchers would then select two G.S. 11s who had not undergone the training for inclusion in the control group. The process would be repeated for each G.S. level until matched pairs of managers from each level of the hierarchy had been achieved.

The next steps would be administration of the employee morale questionnaire and assessment of unit productivity in relation to costs. The data would allow comparisons between program participants and their peers in the organization. The design would also allow measuring the impacts of the training between various levels of the organization.

The above findings might be questioned, especially if program participants were far superior to the control group. Critics might question whether the researchers ruled out the possibility of creaming in the initial selection process. Creaming in this case would mean that participants had been selected on the basis of previous superior performance. If creaming had occurred, the evaluation could not determine if the superior performance was attributable to the training program or to the native abilities of the participants.

Creaming is a threat to the validity of the training program and therefore also a threat to the validity of the evaluation, regardless of the design strategy employed. It could be ruled out merely by interviewing the training staff and upper-level managers before the evaluation began to ascertain the selection criteria used in the training program.

Matched-pair designs frequently involve the examination of employee files. Thus, employee retention and promotion rates might be an added indicator of the benefits of the program. Matched-pairs is a comparatively low-cost option when the goal is to assess the value of the program to the agency and there is no intention to extrapolate the findings to other organizations.[14]

The Participant-Observer Approach

Examples of the participant-observer research design in process evaluation are presented in chapter 4. The discussion here is confined to the method and its internal and external validity.

The participant-observer method is used to assess process. A change in process, however, may be the central goal of the program. For example, an education program might be established to provide training on the latest teaching techniques with the expectations that it would improve classroom teaching methods and, implicitly, better student performance. Before student performance can be improved, however, the methods taught in the training program must be implemented in the classroom. The only way to assess the application of the methods is to go to the classroom and observe. Similarly, suppose that a police department trained its officers to engage residents more closely by getting out of the cars. Observing officers in their day-to-day routines is the only way to know if the officers are making a good-faith effort to apply the techniques that they learned.

The measurement instruments of participant-observer evaluations are the professional insights of the observer. The observer might also have a set of objective criteria on which the subjects are to be rated. The observer would visit the classrooms of teachers who had undergone training and assess them on the basis of the objective criteria. Additional reliability could be gained by having two or more observers rate each teacher independently using common criteria. These independent observations could then be combined into a single assessment of the teacher's overall performance. Officer application of the community engagement program may be assessed by simply having the evaluator do ride-alongs with patrol officers.

The validity of the findings of participant-observer methodology cannot withstand rigorous questioning regarding instrumentation or the biases of the raters. Nevertheless, cultural anthropologists have used the approach to enrich our understanding of the day-to-day dynamics of cultures that are different from our own. There is simply no way to measure, with questionnaires and experimentation, who communicates with whom regarding social or economic problems confronting a group. Similarly, participant-observation can enrich an evaluator's understanding of organization dynamics that might otherwise be overlooked. The contact gained through the methodology, moreover, may enhance the evaluator's credibility with program staff, which could increase their acceptance of the findings. Ironically, this latter strength of the methodology is also its greatest weakness in the eyes of critics who fear that over-involvement with program staff can cause the evaluator to consciously or unconsciously slant the report. Furthermore, observations midway in a program allow for corrections if the program is not being operated as envisioned in the design. Of course, program corrections midway would completely invalidate the data of a program employing strict experimentation.

Whether the findings can be generalized beyond the organization studied is also questionable in a statistical sense. The strength of this methodology lays in its validity for addressing problems that program managers want solved. Acceptance of the findings from participant-observer methodology rests in part on how the program staff perceives the evaluator's expertise. For example, if a nationally known educator attests that in his or her professional judgment an education program is an unquestionable success, the program staff is very likely to accept the judgment. More important, such expert testimony before school boards or legislators would probably carry the same weight as empirically gathered data. An expert assessment of program failure would also carry a great deal of weight. Generally, however, if the expert is retained by the agency he or she will advise as well as judge. The program staff can thus make adjustments based on the expert's advice in order to bring program procedures into line with program goals.

Mixed Designs

Programs are rarely so one-dimensional that they warrant a single research methodology. Nothing, moreover, precludes combining outcome and process methodologies to advise program staffs as well as measure program success. Evaluations that mix their designs provide more comprehensive understanding of how programs operate and what they achieve.

The basic patrol program is an example of how the two methodologies can be combined to good use. In conjunction with the program staff, the evaluators could define the goals of the program in a way that provides for a rigorous outcome evaluation. The evaluators could also provide feedback on an ongoing basis by accompanying program participants on routine patrol and by advising program officials on whether the officers were implementing the program as written. Program officials could then adapt supervisory procedures to ensure compliance, revise the program plan, or reconsider the entire program concept.

These midstream adjustments could be taken into account in the time-series design by extending the number of measurements after the introduction of X. In the case of the pretest-posttest design, interim data could be gathered. The methodology is not pure, but if the program is a success, the adaptations are justified. Such adaptations would not be permissible in one of the experimental designs, regardless of whether the program was functioning as expected.

Evaluating other aspects of the program might involve surveys of staff and clients to operationalize the indicator (staff perceptions). Sampling of individual case records for content and standards compliance might also enhance the nexus between program content and outcomes.

The range of available evaluation designs extends from experimental designs to the participant-observer approach. Combining methodologies, moreover, generally adds to the program relevance of the design. The order in which the various designs were presented here was in no way intended as a judgment of their relative worth. Experimentation was presented first because the design discussion followed the section on evaluation validity and because experimentation is the design least sensitive to the problems of internal validity. As we have demonstrated, experimentation is not always possible or desirable—especially when the evaluation is undertaken after the program has been in operation for some time or when the evaluation is commissioned to assess a specific program adaptation.

The variety of program evaluation strategies available and the complexity of programs now requiring evaluation make it mandatory for the evaluator to acquire a full range of evaluation skills. The evaluator who insists on using a specific design to the exclusion of all others is like the repair person who specializes in work on a particular brand of washing machine—he or she runs the risk of being very lonely.

Notes

[1] The discussion of threats to validity relies heavily on the taxonomy of threats developed by Donald T. Campbell and Julian C. Stanley in *Experimental and Quasi-Experimental Designs for Research* (Chicago: Rand McNally, 1963).

[2] The Hawthorne effect is so named as a result of studies conducted on workers at the Hawthorne Works of Western Electric Company during the 1920s and 1930s. The Hawthorne research team concluded that some of the work-related behavior of the subjects was a result of their knowing they were being treated differently than normal. The findings of the Hawthorne experiments were reported by F. J. Roethlisberger and W. J. Dickson in *Management and the Worker* (Cambridge, MA: Harvard University Press, 1939).

[3] See Chester Barnard, *The Functions of the Executive*, 30th Anniversary ed. (Cambridge, MA: Harvard University Press, 1968), Introduction by Kenneth R. Andrews.

[4] For a full discussion, see Executive Office of the President, Council of Economic Advisors, *Economic Report to the President*, 50th ed. (Washington, DC: US Government Printing Office, 1996), especially chapter 8.

[5] See Sam Dillon, "Overriding a Key Education Law," *New York Times*, August 8, 2011.

[6] For a discussion of the theory see *Piaget's Theory of Cognitive and Affective Development: Foundations of Constructivism*, 5th ed. (Independence, KY: Wadsworth, 2003).

[7] Ronald D. Sylvia, Howard Hamilton, and Husain Mustafa, "Political Moral Judgments of Children," *Polity* (Spring, 1981): 384–409.

[8] This phenomenon, also known as "going native," is precisely why some researchers argue that outcome evaluations which use objective measures are the most valid approach to evaluation. In addition, virtually every evaluation text argues for the importance of maintaining the evaluator's detachment and professional objectivity.

[9] For a discussion on the variations in methadone treatment, see Jan Gryczynski, "Dropout from Interim Methadone and Subsequent Comprehensive Methadone Maintenance," *American Journal of Drug and Alcohol Abuse*, 5(6) (2009): 394–98.

[10] See Sharon L. Lohr, *Sampling: Design and Analysis* (Florence, KY: Duxbury Press, 2009); see also Floyd J. Fowler, Jr., *Survey Research Methods*, 4th ed. (Thousand Oaks, CA: Sage, 2008).

[11] See Walter B. Miller, "The Impact of a Total Community Delinquency Control Project," *Social Problems*, 10 (1962): 168–91; and Edwin Powers and Helen Witner, *An Experiment in the Prevention of Delinquency: The Cambridge-Sommerville Youth Study* (New York: Columbia University Press, 1951).

[12] See Paul S. P. Cowperwait and Andrew V. Metcalfe, *Introductory Time Series* (New York: Springer, 2009); see also Helmut Lutkepohl, *New Introduction to Multiple Time Series Analysis* (New York: Springer, 2010).

[13] For an example of this type of study using time-series analysis see Steven H. Feimer, *Administrative Per Se: Public Policy Impact Evaluation Using Interrupted Time-Series* (Unpublished Doctoral Dissertation, 1987, AAT8721965).

[14] Helen Weems and Ronald Sylvia, "A Quasi-Experimental Evaluation of Tuition Reimbursement in Municipal Government," *Review of Public Personnel Administration* (Spring 1981): 13–23.

chapter eight

Cost-Benefit Analysis

Cost-benefit analysis uses monetary cost and benefits to plan programs, evaluate their outcomes, and assess the effectiveness of organization processes. The general approach is to identify and quantify both the negative impacts (the costs) and the positive impacts (the benefits) of a proposed project and then to subtract costs from the benefits to determine the net benefit—thus the name **cost-benefit analysis.** To put the procedure in context, the monetary return on investment becomes the principle standard against which proposals are judged. The standard has two built-in biases. First, the method prefers programs with the shortest time to recover the investment cost and begin showing a return (profit). So, a government utility located near a mountain pass with a lot of wind might choose wind power over a solar power project based on construction costs. Windmills require the purchase of less land and can be constructed relatively quickly, thus shortening the amount of time necessary to begin generating power. Conversely, a utility located near a desert might choose solar because space would be less of a problem and the number of days of sunshine per year would boost profitability. Either option would have lower startup costs than an offshore facility to generate electricity utilizing ocean currents. Unfortunately, when short-term benefit-cost ratios are the driving criterion, none of the three can compete with power-generating facilities that burn fossil fuels.

Second, the standard is most applicable to programs in which benefits and costs can be weighed in the same unit of measure: money. Thus, the costs of routing an urban freeway through a poor neighborhood are much lower than one that passes through an affluent area simply because of the lower price associated with buying property along the route in the poor neighborhood. However, choosing routes based solely on the basis of construction costs does not take into consideration the displacement of low-income homeowners. The government would, of course, pay fair market value for the acquired properties, thus providing the displaced with just compensation for the greater public good. An unanticipated second-order impact, however, is that the displaced homeowners cannot find comparably priced houses in other neighborhoods. It is also unlikely that their incomes, despite the equity that they get from their former homes, will be sufficient to qualify them for loans on more expensive properties. They thus join the ranks of renters, producing another second-order impact of driving up the cost of rental property for all renters. The foregoing is to say nothing of the issue of equity raised by the initial decision to displace the poor over the affluent (i.e., the lower values of their property do not change the fact that people with lower incomes value their homes as much as the wealthy value theirs).

When used appropriately, however, cost-benefit analysis can be a valuable decision making tool. The method is most appropriate for evaluating alternatives towards a previously agreed-upon end. Suppose, for example, that a city council found itself with a considerable amount of cash from a redevelopment district[1] and decided to build a sports facility to raise the city's profile, create jobs, and renew a blighted area downtown. Analysts could then weigh the costs and benefits of several options. Alternative A might be a multi-purpose indoor facility that could be used for basketball, hockey, and also as a concert venue. Alternative B could be an outdoor sports facility to be used exclusively for one sport, such as football or baseball. Alternative C might be a dual-sport outdoor facility for both baseball and football. The actual construction costs of each could be readily calculated.

These types of decisions are complicated by the fact that locating or relocating professional sports franchises are highly dependent on decisions by other bodies that do not have a tangible interest in the city. The number of teams in the various sports and where they are to be located is decided by the owners' associations and the various sports leagues. The odds are especially long against the success of either of the dual-purpose alternatives. The indoor facility would probably not be able, in the near term, to attract a National Hockey League (NHL) team and a National Basketball Association (NBA) franchise. Similarly, while alternative C, a dual-purpose outdoor facility, could accommodate larger crowds and raise the city profile with two national audiences, it is highly unlikely that the city could attract both a Major League Baseball (MLB) and a National Football League (NFL) football team. Even the single team option is complicated by the same decision bodies. Suppose, for example, that the City of San Jose wanted to attract either an MLB or NFL team. Assuming that either league was contemplating an expansion, the selection of San Jose as a location would be opposed by the nearby owners of the San Francisco Giants and Oakland Athletics baseball teams. Also, a new football franchise would be opposed by the San Francisco 49ers and the Oakland Raiders NFL franchises. Those owners would no doubt recognize the potential competition for their fan bases as well as added competition for television revenues.

Consideration of their constituent financial interest would also occupy the minds of council members. Land owners and real estate developers would have concerns regarding facility location. Environmental groups would weigh in on the issue of air quality impacts and increased traffic congestion on game days. Traffic would also be a concern for commuters not attending the game. The constituencies of various council members are another factor influencing the decision, as is the sports preferences of local citizens. In the end, San Jose finally settled on an indoor facility because the NHL was expanding and permitted the creation of the San Jose Sharks franchise.[2] When the Sharks are not playing, the facility is leased for musical concerts, circuses, and so forth.

The reader should bear in mind that cost-benefit analysis is value neutral and therefore no better or worse than the analyst conducting the study. It can be a valuable tool when used as one among several decision criteria. Businesses use it every day to decide whether to expand or contract, or whether to build a new facility locally or in another state or country. Business executive are cautious in its use because they are called to account for the economic impacts of their decisions by boards of directors, shareholders, and the marketplace. Unfortunately, elected public officials are held to much less rigorous accounting for their actions; if congressional reelection statistics are any indicator, members are reelected at a rate over 80%.[3]

Our discussion begins by describing cost-benefit analysis in the context of the rational comprehensive planning process, followed by a step-by-step explanation of how to conduct such an analysis. The discussion then turns to the controversy surrounding its application. We conclude with a set of tips for evaluators and consumers of cost-benefit data.[4]

Cost-Benefit Analysis and Rational Planning

Cost-benefit analysis is used routinely by government and business executives to plan resource allocations. It can be used to choose between program options or for deciding whether a project is a worth undertaking. It is less appropriate when used to justify a program or project about which there is no general agreement. It is completely inappropriate when used to decide between programs with different goals (e.g., whether to build a missile defense system, a highway, or to fund a hot lunch program in schools).

In the planning process decision makers specify organization goals over the short and long run, or they define a problem to be solved. These decision makers then assess various alternatives for achieving the goals or solving the problems. Alternatives are considered in terms of their primary and secondary outcomes, and all costs are considered. Cost-benefit analysis is thus a powerful tool for choosing between alternatives. All else being equal, decision makers may choose the alternative that costs the least. Unfortunately, in government all else is rarely equal, so decision makers must closely scrutinize the assumptions that underlie policy recommendations.

Furthermore, prospective users should be aware of four general assumptions that underlie the application of cost-benefit analysis.

1. All major program impacts can and will be identified. Suppose that a city set as a goal the beautification of its public parks and other grounds. The alternatives to be considered might be whether to assign the beautification activities to in-house personnel or to contract with private companies to provide the service. The current trend in rethinking government spending might require government agencies to bid against private providers to determine the most economical approach.[5] A bid-submission approach might determine that the private contractor could landscape and maintain the grounds at a lower rate than could the city department. Before jumping on the privatization bandwagon, however, decision makers should closely examine the factors underlying the bids.

Does the private company provide its employees with health-care benefits? If not, the city may be engaging in *cost shifting*. Both government and private-sector employees need medical services. In the case of the government, city employees are compensated for these costs (usually through an insurance plan). Private gardening contractors, however, normally pay their workers on the lower end of the wage scale and do not provide them with a health-care plan. It is unrealistic to believe that such workers will obtain their own private-sector health-care insurance. Thus, in all likelihood, they will seek services at city-subsidized health-care facilities. In the case of serious illness they may be unable to pay for the services they need. By letting the contract to the private employer, therefore, the city has shifted its health-care cost for the affected workers from its insurance pool to its public hospitals. In other words, it may appear that the cost of using a private contractor is less, when in effect it is the same or possibly even more. The most responsible approach in such cases is to require all bids to factor in health-care costs for workers.[6]

Cost shifting also can be a serious problem in large government agencies where division goals and department mandates may conflict with one another. For example, the manager of the education support division of the US Department of Defense takes bids for an overseas educational program. University A proposes sending its own degreed and highly-qualified faculty to the various off-site locations for short-duration courses; University B proposes staffing sites on a more permanent basis with short-term, part-time, often less qualified faculty. The manager believes that University A's plan is the best way to guarantee quality control—that is, to ensure quality education for off-site military personnel. Because travel costs are included in the bid, University A's proposal initially appears to be the more expensive plan, since it would involve frequent travel by university teaching staff to and from the off-site locations. However, while University B's travel costs are lower, its off-site faculty (and perhaps, in some cases, their spouses and children) would require housing as well as access to commissaries, medical treatment, and other services associated with semi-permanent "base residency"—all of which in the long run make University B's plan the more expensive of the two plans. The manager knows that these other costs are not part of the education support division's budget, although the overall Defense Department budget will eventually pay for them. Because the Department of Defense has issued a mandate that cost containment should be of paramount concern, our manager may choose Plan B because the costs associated with the semi-permanent staffing plan will be *shifted* to the budgets of other divisions in the Defense Department. Although the choice of Plan B will actually be more costly to the Defense Department, the manager appears to have met the Defense Department's cost-containment mandate when the lower bid is submitted. The shifted costs are, in this manager's mind, somebody else's worry.

Overhead costs are another problem for governments using progressive accounting and budget procedures that seek to assign costs for legal services, operations and facilities (buildings, equipment, and utilities), and administrative support services to line departments. Continuing the beautification project example, if the Parks Department were forced to add its portion of the city's overhead cost to its bid, it could never compete with a private contractor who does not have (or need) the range of services that a large city has. In addition, private contractors are able to fine-tune their bids by absorbing such additional costs into existing operations. Thus it is important to determine whether the Parks Department's bid contains unrealistic overhead costs that do not apply to the private contractor and to limit city overhead costs to the actual incremental increase that such a project would add to the budget. Cities sometimes address this issue by selecting the lowest "responsible proposal" rather than picking the lowest bidder per se.

2. Impacts can be measured using a common unit of analysis. Cost-benefit analysis is rooted in economic theory, so the common unit of analysis therefore is normally money. Costs and benefits are measured in dollars. However, some things have social benefits that are difficult to quantify in dollars, even though their costs can be readily enumerated. A school district, for example, may choose to reduce the ratio of students to teachers in grades one through six. The decision would be put before the school board on the grounds that lower student/faculty ratios would increase the individual attention each student receives and improve students' learning capacity (which would be reflected in improved scores on achievement tests).

The costs are easy to calculate in terms of additional faculty to be hired and facilities to be renovated to accommodate the new classes. It is virtually impossible, however, to calculate the value of increased attention or the net benefit of a two-point average performance improvement on standardized tests. Such measures, however, may be ends in themselves appropriate for measurement in a not-for-profit organization.

The difficulty lies in determining the incremental dollar value of a unit of quality improvement in government generally, and particularly in educational and social programs. The quality improvement movement currently in vogue argues that obsession with cost containment can sacrifice overall product and service quality. These, in turn, lead to loss of customers, overall market share, and long-term profitability.[7] Some quality-oriented organizations measure their success by using the indicators of reduction in customer complaints, increases in on-time deliveries, and improvements in market share as well as profits. Realistically, market share is not transferable to a government context because its services are financed through taxation and are available to all eligible persons.

3. People know what they value now and will value in the future. When faced with economic choices, most individuals can use their own values to assess alternatives. Managers, especially in the public sector, make economic choices based on the missions of their organizations. Police departments, for example, will allocate funds with direct law-enforcement activities as a priority; streets departments will set their resurfacing priorities based on need and traffic volume. Public organizations, moreover, are not permitted to unilaterally alter their organizational direction, since their missions reflect the priorities of elected officials. Police officials, for example, are not at liberty to bid on security contracts to local businesses in order to improve the department's cash flow.

The conflict over values inherent in cost-benefit analysis occurs when it is applied to macro-level problems about which no substantial consensus exists. What society values now and what it will value in the future is presumed to be an aggregate of the values of individual societal members. The cost-benefits of allowing old-growth logging in national forests, for example, presume to reflect how much average citizens value forest preservation compared to the creation of local jobs, enhancing the treasury through collecting logging fees, and lowering the cost of lumber. There is no accurate way to determine precisely the amount of environmental degradation the public will accept to achieve economic ends. It is even less reasonable to presume that the public has thought about the long-term consequences of harvesting old-growth forests. Using cost-benefit analysis for such decisions is simply inappropriate.

The 2011 controversy between the Obama administration and conservative members of congress is a prime example of the dilemma of selecting between short- and long-range societal benefits. On one side are the Keynesians,[8] who argue that in times of economic downturn it is important for the government to incur debt in order to provide stimulus through tax cuts, the bailout of troubled industries, and so forth. On the other side are those who see increasing long-term debt obligations to be so great a threat that no short-term stimulus is acceptable.[9]

4. Generally speaking, people want to maximize cost-benefit ratios. All else being equal, people will act in an economically rational fashion. However, as previously mentioned, all else is rarely equal. Individuals frequently will not contact multiple lenders to determine the lowest credit interest rates before applying for a car loan. Still fewer will greatly consider resale value when purchasing an automobile. Similarly, city council members who perceive a public fear of crime may vote to hire additional police officers rather than to replace aging fire equipment, despite the fact that local crime is declining.

The pitfalls of cost-benefit analysis notwithstanding, it can be a valuable tool for program assessment. It is most valuable when it is limited to assessing economic factors in the decision process (i.e., providing decision makers with program cost estimates among options for delivering a service that decision makers have chosen to provide). When cost and benefits are used to decide whether to provide the service, analysts may be more prone to manipulate the numbers to support their preferred option. The costs and benefits, along with political and social considerations, can then be placed before those who must make informed decisions regarding the public purse.

The Techniques of Cost-Benefit Analysis

Utilizing the planning process discussed in chapter 2, the following step-by-step techniques apply to cost-benefit analysis: (1) The problem to be solved or the goal to be achieved is defined as precisely as possible; (2) all alternatives are assessed in terms of their primary and secondary impacts on the target audience of the program and on society in general; (3) an alternative is chosen and implemented; and (4) the success of the program is evaluated.

Identifying the Project

Cost-benefit studies must carefully define the project. For example, a study of "all the welfare programs provided by a state" to measure their benefits and costs is so vague that it is meaningless. Does such an analysis include only traditional welfare programs, or does it include related programs such as vocational rehabilitation and veterans' preferences? Do programs that are not normally considered as welfare but contribute to maintaining the well-being of temporarily disadvantaged citizens (e.g., unemployment) fall under this definition? Definitions that are too narrow should also be avoided.

Identifying a project precisely cannot be done by formula. Project identification requires attention to legislative intent, administrative regulations, and agency implementation procedures. Perhaps the most effective method of identifying a program for cost-benefit analysis is a consensus-building group process involving program managers to identify the crucial aspects of the program. No matter how the identification is done, every cost-benefit analysis (and every program evaluation) should contain, at the beginning of the report, a description of the crucial elements of the program.

One planning caveat to remember is that cost-benefit analysis is not appropriate until decision makers have defined the goals of a program or specified a problem to be solved. When applied in the first phase of the project, the values of the planners can bias the numbers. Returning to our sports facility example, city officials might inappropriately utilize cost-benefit analysis to determine whether to build the facility. While analysts can carefully estimate the construction costs of the facility, they could determine the cost that the city will incur when borrowing the money. They also could precisely define the impact on the city's credit rating, and so forth. Opponents of the project, however, may object out of an unwillingness to commit city resources to a particular program due to lost *opportunity costs*. That is, once the city's future revenues are committed to a particular project through the issuance of bonds, the money is no longer available for other projects and programs.

In our sports facility example the facility was to be paid for by tax revenues from the Redevelopment District. If, however, a city chose to curtail its redevelopment-funded building programs, the tax revenues from the district would be available in part to fund education programs and government in general. The opportunity cost is compensated somewhat by the use of a discount rate (see below) that is factored into the decision. Nevertheless, discount rates account only for the funds dedicated to the project. They do not make value assessments on whether the program should be undertaken in the first place. The sports advocates may seek to justify their policy preferences by projecting an early cost recovery through ticket sales, sales tax enhancement, the creation of new jobs, and the attraction of suburban dwellers to the city for sporting events. This, arguably, would increase restaurants' business and the opportunity for increased retail sales in the city center. Both presumably would create more jobs and increase sales tax revenues. Project supporters tend to overestimate such benefits, and they may use optimistic cost estimates. Opponents will engage in the opposite tactic. Both uses of cost-benefit analysis are inappropriate for the expenditure of public funds. The problem stems from a propensity to estimate costs and benefits in a manner that supports the estimator's position.

Negative government experiences proceed from the fact that the estimators are not usually held responsible if their cost-benefit estimates are overly optimistic or pessimistic. Simply put, it is not their money. This is not the case with private companies, who use cost-benefits every day to make policy choices with their own or their stockholders' resources. By definition, private organizations are driven by missions that implicitly seek maximization of cost-benefit ratios. Furthermore, the careers of executives ride on how well their planning assumptions predict outcome. At least that was the conventional wisdom. Unfortunately, recent history has been full of examples of creative accounting and erroneous assumptions designed to deceive investors and enhance the value of publicly traded stocks, real estate investments, and their derivatives.[10]

In the public sector, cost-benefit analysis always has the potential for manipulation by policy advocates. Once the decision to act is taken, officials can make good use of cost-benefit numbers. Nevertheless, even when projects are narrowly drawn, decision makers must check the figures closely for the biases of advocates in the assumptions underlying the figures.

Listing the Impacts

Cost-benefit analysis can be particularly useful in the second step of the planning process. The analysts list all projected impacts of the project, both positive and negative. They then develop monetary estimates of the impacts. Net benefits are determined by subtracting the cost of the negative impacts from the benefits of positive impacts. The process is straightforward, but it too is based on assumptions. First is the assumption that all impacts can be evaluated monetarily. More difficult is the accurate projection of future costs in multiyear projects. During the late 1970s, for example, government programs that included weapons systems, dam projects, and highway construction were approved using estimates that underestimated the inflation rate and the governments cost of borrowing money. Programs quickly ran out of funds and had to be put on hold until supplemental appropriations could be secured. Such problems can be avoided or lessened through careful analysis.

Two major problems face the analyst. The first is where to find the information: What sources and methods can help anticipate and forecast impacts? The second is how to classify the impacts: What schemes will help the analyst avoid "double counting" impacts while providing a way to separate the impacts into meaningful categories?

Collecting Data

Collecting data on potential impacts is difficult and time consuming. The type of data gathered depends to some extent on the levels of expertise of program staff and the amount of money and time available for the study. Wherever possible, impacts should be identified both by experts and by interested parties, whether citizens or special-interest groups. Methods for collecting data include using program staff or contracting with outside experts, conducting literature searches and surveys, consulting citizen advisory committees, and brainstorming with colleagues or decision makers.

Data sources that provide clues for potential impacts and trend information needed for forecasting include statistical reports prepared by various levels of government, census materials, and reports on similar projects.

An expensive way to obtain information on possible impacts is to conduct a pilot study. Currently, experiments are underway to allow students in underperforming schools to enroll in neighboring districts or in private academies using vouchers that guarantee a certain level of funding from monies earmarked for the troubled district.[11] This sort of preliminary examination is well worth the expense before billions of dollars are expended. However, funding and time for this type of preliminary effort are rarely available. Smaller undertakings usually lack the resources to extensively pilot test programs. Fortunately, their potential negative impacts are also limited.

Classifying Data

The analyst should set up a systematic approach for classifying each identified impact. Pre-established categories can be confusing because some impacts are not amenable to ready categorization. A well-thought-out classification system can prevent "double counting." For example, if a new shopping center in a section of the city results in increased property values for houses in that area, the analyst should not count the increase as a benefit. The increase really represents the additional convenience and opportunities for jobs, entertainment, and shopping that are important to consumers. These are the benefits that should be incorporated into the analysis. Property values and enhanced opportunities cannot *both* be included in the analysis because they represent a stream of effects rather than two separate benefits.

Cost and benefits can be classified as internal or external effects. This classification is sometimes refined as to whether their impact is primary or secondary. *Internal effects* are those that are specifically linked with the goals and objectives of the project. *External effects* are those that fall outside the definition of the project and are usually not given a monetary value in the analysis. The decline in the violent crime rate as the result of a successful drug-abuse treatment program is one example of an external effect.

Often called *second-order consequences*, external effects are excluded from many analyses because they have no monetary impact on the project being analyzed. Analysts could specify program benefits and costs ad infinitum, but at some point they must assume that all other benefits and costs are trivial or cancel each other out. However, certain external effects (particularly second-order benefits or costs) should *not* be excluded if they impact the project financially.

Identification of internal and external effects (costs and benefits) should follow certain steps. First, all internal costs, such as operating costs and fixed overhead expenditures, should be estimated. Second, such external costs as regulation compliance must be identified. Third, direct benefits intended by the agency are specified. Fourth, external benefits (e.g., positive second-order consequences) should be outlined. Fifth, each of the benefits and costs must be examined to determine whether it is a real effect or a pecuniary effect. **Pecuniary benefits and costs** change the financial outcomes or effects for the public or society without specifically affecting individuals and should be deleted from the analysis. (For example, the tax revenues and jobs created by a new suburban mall should be included; the reduced cost of commuting for shoppers is a pecuniary externality and should be eliminated.) Sixth, the manager must determine whether the benefits and costs are tangible or intangible effects. These terms are frequently used by groups that disagree with the values placed on impacts in a cost-benefit analysis.

Impacts are also examined as to whether they are tangible or intangible. **Tangible effects** can be easily assigned a monetary value based on market information. **Intangible effects** are effects for which the market does not supply good information. Some analysts break this down further, using the term **incommensurables** to describe effects that, while difficult to quantify and measure, can be valued in at least a relative measure. The analysts then reserve the term *intangible effects* for impacts that are not economic in nature, such as saving a human life or preserving democratic processes. Some contend that there are no intangible effects—that using one technique or another can treat all effects as tangible. Some analysts omit either intangible impacts or minor impacts, or both. Whenever impacts are excluded from the analysis, the report should specify them and the reason for their exclusion.

Making Monetary Estimates

After all data have been collected and classified, the analyst must next assign monetary values to program impacts. Cost-benefit analysis, especially the process of making monetary estimates, is derived from a branch of economics called **welfare economics**.[12] Welfare economics assumes that the welfare of a society depends on the well-being of the individuals in that society and nothing more. When considering policy choices the analyst must be concerned with the value that individuals place on the consequences or impacts of a policy. The "social welfare" can then be determined by adding up, or summing, all the individual statements of value. This is a sound idea if one can accept the assumption that individuals can accurately place values on program effects. It would also help if there were a mechanism for inquiring what all members think rather than creating a best-guess estimate. Although this assumption fits well with democratic principles, recent threats to the environment and to personal safety indicate that individuals can be misled by lack of good information regarding policy consequences. Moreover, the values some individuals place on program effects can be unduly influenced by such problems as deviance or envy, which cause them to choose options that may be personally harmful or detrimental to the general well-being of society. Examples of this type of deviant counterdecision are failure to use seat belts, continuing to smoke cigarettes in spite of known health hazards, building homes in known floodplains, and buying expensive items to "keep up with the Joneses."

Pricing Techniques

Although welfare economists have never successfully measured the benefits an individual receives from a project, they have generally agreed on a substitute—voluntary transactions. If Citizen A voluntarily buys Product X from Citizen C for five dollars, it is obvious that Citizen A believes that Product X is worth at least five dollars. Willingness to pay therefore becomes the general criterion for establishing value. This assumes that rational individuals seek more rather than less of a desired product and seek less rather than more of an undesired product.

Market Prices

The first technique used for estimating value is **market pricing**. By using market prices to measure individuals' values—and thus social values—economists assume that the market is a perfect reflection of supply and demand. Cost-benefit analysts make the case that some segments of the market are near ideal and that often there is no other information available. Critics are reluctant to accept this necessary assumption. Just such a controversy could arise in determining the cost savings of investing in an alternative energy source. Would it be accurate to calculate the savings based on the average cost of petroleum products using a world market number, or should the figures be adjusted downward to reflect the portion of the cost savings derived from lower-cost domestic fuels from old fields?

The analyst measures social value by using market information on the price and quantity of a good or service to put together the familiar demand curve (see figure 8.1). The logic underlying demand curves is that rational people seek to maximize their personal wellbeing. In a perfect marketplace, the price that the *rational* person would be willing to pay for a product would be exactly equal to its price. This price would be at point *B* on the demand curve line in figure 8.1.

If a project produces an increase or decrease in the availability of a good or service, the change can be valued as equal to the quantity of change multiplied by the market price. The social value of a project, then, is simply the sum of these changes multiplied by the price. Since a market demand curve represents the total of all individual demand curves, it tells the analyst how much of a product would be desired at a certain price by the public in general.

For example, the National Transportation Safety Board requires that all automobile bumpers be able to withstand a five-mile-an-hour collision with no resulting damage to the vehicle. One benefit of this regulation is

Figure 8.1   A Typical Price-Quality-Demand Curve

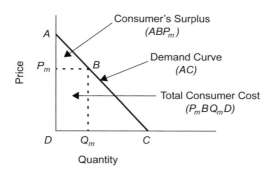

that fewer vehicles are damaged in low-speed accidents. The market-price value of such an accident being avoided is the cost of repairing the vehicle. The total of this benefit is therefore the product of the number of accidents without damage and the cost of repairs had the accidents occurred.

Shadow Prices

When market prices exist but seem inappropriate or are clearly biased, as in monopolies, shadow pricing is a valuable technique. For example, in 1974 the US Justice Department filed an antitrust suit against AT&T (*US v. AT&T*, 1974), alleging that it was essentially a monopoly. This led to the "Bell System Divestiture," a breakup of AT&T into seven regional holding companies. There was no way to factually assess the potential social value of breaking up the phone company before the fact. Market data did not exist on how much consumers were willing to pay for local or long-distance services, nor could cost savings accurately be determined. Analysts use approximate valuations of true values for goods and services when there is no market for the good or service. **Shadow pricing** is accomplished by substituting the value of a similar good for the actual good being considered.

Analysts also use shadow pricing to determine social values in matters involving human safety. There are, for example, no accurate market figures on the value of a human life. Shadow pricing based on lifetime earnings, social contributions, and so forth might be devised by an analyst to calculate the social value of human lives saved by wearing seat belts (see the discussion of incommensurables later in this chapter). The rationale for computing shadow prices is that, in situations where market prices are not available or are inappropriate, the analyst must substitute a value (shadow price) that he or she believes should explicitly evaluate the benefits and costs in question. The manager must realize that shadow prices can cause controversy because they reflect the subjective judgment of the analyst. The analyst's report should explicitly identify the assumptions underlying the shadow price and the procedures used in the calculations.

Biased Market Prices

Market prices accurately reflect social value and people's willingness to pay when the market exhibits purely competitive characteristics. In a purely competitive market there are so many buyers and sellers that no single person can affect the market price, all goods are equally substitutable, consumers have perfect information, and producers have freedom of entry and exit. Whenever the market deviates from perfect competition (which is always), market prices deviate from social value.

In monopoly situations, for example, one seller determines the market price of a good. In this case the seller can and understandably will restrict production and charge prices greater than the "normal" market price. The more people desire the product and are unwilling to do without it, the higher the price the monopolist can charge. In an oligopoly situation, the results are similar but not as extreme. While all economists agree that monopoly and oligopoly prices are too high, they do not agree on how to adjust the prices to reflect social value. There are, however, ways to approximate market prices.

Determining the social value is of critical importance when the price of the goods in question changes dramatically without a corresponding change in the quantity available. Instead of using the quantity-to-price ratio to determine the net benefit produced by such a change, the analyst should use the change in the consumers' surplus to determine the net benefit to the consumer. The *consumers' surplus* is the excess amount of utility that individuals obtain because they do not have to pay as much as they would be willing to pay to buy the quantity desired. For example, if completing a project will decrease the price of water to consumers (from P_1 to P_2), consumers will get a surplus or extra benefit represented by the shaded area in figure 8.2.

Market prices can also be too low, for example, when government subsidizes the price of a good. Gasoline prices in the 1960s were subsidized, and today grain prices and food prices in many countries are subsidized. The cost-benefit analysis must adjust the value of these goods upward.

Other market conditions that can cause deviations from normal price/quantity ratios are government actions in the form of taxation, regulation, and price controls. These generally can be incorporated into the market price analysis by making explicit the extent of the price differential but using the market price nonetheless. Government price controls bias the market by setting artificial floors or ceilings on goods, thus creating a gap between the market price and the social value of such goods. The actual effects of these government actions usually depend on the supply conditions; such action does not always create a discrepancy between market prices and social values. When, for example, the federal government

Figure 8.2   The Relationship of the Consumer Surplus to Normal/Price/Quantity Ratios

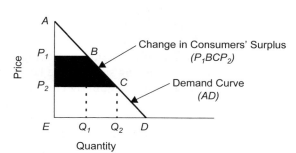

engages farm price supports (sets a minimum price to producers) the end result may be excess capacity without a drop in price. In the case of dairy price supports, for example, the price of milk to consumers did not change even when dairy herds and milk production outstripped demand.

The problems associated with the subjective nature of shadow prices raise the question of whether the analyst should even try to correct for biased market information. Although the unnecessary use of shadow prices should be avoided, the analyst must, nonetheless, be alert to markets that are clearly biased. In such cases, the analyst must supply information on deviations from social value. Other factors in the evaluation may also be undervalued or overvalued if they are rated at their actual market prices. For example, inputs to production, such as labor costs, are often biased in project evaluation estimates. If a project creates jobs, these new jobs are benefits only if the jobholders would otherwise be unemployed. Even if the people who were hired for these jobs were previously unemployed, thus creating a benefit, they would not have been likely to remain unemployed over the whole period of the project (unemployment seems to be cyclical), so labor costs must reflect job-market conditions during the project. In a similar manner, capital and land that otherwise would not be used during the life of the project should be valued at zero social cost when included in a project evaluation. Each instance of shadow pricing must be documented and fully justified by the analyst. Then the policy makers must decide whether the shadow prices are consistent with their own view of the program and its environment.

Absence of Market Prices

In some situations market prices, even biased ones, simply do not exist. Shadow prices are frequently used in two situations lacking market prices—externalities and public goods.

Externalities are effects that involuntarily accrue to outsiders. Air pollution is a classic example of an externality, because we cannot determine the market value of an incremental increase in air quality. Analysts must decide which external effects are to be included in the calculations. Only real changes in production or consumption opportunities should be included. In all cases, there is no compensation for costs borne by outsiders, and there are no fees collected for benefits enjoyed by outsiders. The Los Angeles commuter, for example, gets no economic credit for being able to see the San Gabriel Mountains as a result of scrubbers having been installed on industrial smokestacks, thereby reducing smog in the Los Angeles basin.

Putting a price on noise is the most frequently cited example of how difficult it is to create market prices for external effects. While analysts can measure the *amount* of noise or level of noise with relative ease, they have enormous difficulty putting a *price* on each unit (decibel) of noise. Conducting a survey would be one solution, although the reliability of individuals' statements about their willingness to pay for quiet is likely to be low. In fact, the issue is really one of compensation rather than willingness to pay. That is, if "peace and quiet" is a right under government protection, the proper concern for the analyst is how much money a citizen would accept to waive the right to peace and quiet, or how much money would compensate for the loss of peace and quiet.

The absence of noise is an issue that falls under the realm of *public goods*. The issue of public goods creates additional problems in the pricing of externalities. Public goods are goods provided or protected by the government and consumed by many people at the same time—for example, clean air, mosquito control, national defense, wilderness areas, and highways. These types of goods and services can be characterized in three ways:

1. The use of a public good by one or more individuals does not affect its availability to others.

2. Public goods are in theory nonexclusive in that, once the public good is provided, citizens are not selectively excluded.

3. Public goods will not be provided by individuals if it is left strictly up to them, even though such goods provide a net benefit to society as a whole.

Try as they might, economists have been unable as yet to develop a model that can be applied to valuing public goods. The reason for this is the individual's alleged rational behavior. Theoretically, citizens use a gaming approach when asked how much they are willing to pay for a good. By undervaluing their interest in a public good, individuals hope to be able to take advantage of the good without having to take any responsibility for providing it. Thus, individuals act as "free riders" by consistently underestimating their willingness to pay for public goods.

Faced with this problem, analysts have several less-than-ideal choices. They can take a survey, knowing that the information obtained will be biased. They can substitute the market price of a similar private good (e.g., using the price of books to determine value of library circulation), but this substitution would have to be well documented through analogous reasoning. Using the *initiative* or *referendum* processes in which people vote to tax themselves to provide a benefit is an alternative that has received increasing support from citizens.

The feasibility of initiatives for project evaluation depends on the political unit, citizen interest, and so forth. Initiatives, moreover, are ballot propositions written by advocates of a specific policy. For instance, California voters endorsed the public good of guaranteeing that the proportion of the state budget allocated to fund public elementary and secondary schools and community colleges could not be below the current percentage. However, they were not asked to indicate levels of service cuts in road construction, higher education, and prison construction that they were willing to accept as a result of the allocation. By contrast, in the referenda process policy makers formulate a policy, then send it to the voters for ratification. Under a California law (created by an initiative) proposed new taxes must pass by a two-thirds majority.[13] These "supermajorities" are difficult to obtain; nevertheless, their passage represents a substantial consensus.

In summary, shadow pricing is a technique for uncovering deviations from market prices that are important enough to be presented to the decision maker. It should be used with caution. Shadow pricing is not appropriate for use on externalities and public goods. All shadow pricing should be well-documented, both to justify the decisions made by the analyst and to inform the manager of the extent and direction of the biases in market prices.

Shadow pricing is controversial because no analyst is value neutral. An analyst who believes a market price is biased has an obligation to document the bias and adjust the social values accordingly. Critics also point out that elected leaders are not apt to read the fine print and tend to rely too heavily on the numbers provided in the final tally, overlooking the assumptions made and the cautionary statements offered.

Incommensurables

An even more controversial area for cost-benefit analysis is the quantification of **incommensurables**. These are effects for which no market exists, such as human life, health, clean air, and recreational opportunities. In new areas of social regulation, such as worker health and safety, environmental protection, and consumer protection, the major benefits are incommensurables. As a result, cost-benefit analysis must face the problems involved in valuing incommensurables if it is to play a role in these growing areas of government action.

The best example of problems in valuing incommensurables (somewhat similar to the problems in pricing externalities) is in the area of human life. Government policies that save lives (traffic safety, worker safety, and the like) do provide some benefits. Analysts who accept the principle of willingness to pay might "logically" attempt to determine how much compensation a person would want before that person would give up his or her life! Of course, willingness to pay would not yield an appropriate monetary value for a human life, because most people are unwilling to accept any amount of monetary compensation in exchange for their lives.

Often, *willingness-to-pay measures* are constructed by reversing the estimation process. Rather than asking individuals how much compensation they require, an analyst asks how much an individual would be willing to pay to avoid a cost or to attain a benefit. For example, an analyst might ask residents how much they would be willing to pay in taxes to eliminate noise from a nearby airport. While this approach works for some effects, it has serious problems when applied to valuing lives or injuries. Each individual's willingness to pay is limited by that person's income, thus giving greater weight to the preferences of wealthy citizens than to those of the poor. This violates both the norms of democracy and the principles of welfare economics.

Another approach used to estimate the value of a life is the *proportionate risk approach*. Individuals are asked how much compensation they would accept to be subjected to a 1% greater risk of death on the job. In industrial safety, for example, a person might be told that Job A pays $10 per hour and Job B has a 1% greater risk of on-the-job death. This individual would then be asked how much the wages should be for Job B. Let us assume that his or her answer is $1 more per hour, or $2,080 per year. The analyst then assumes that if 100 workers are exposed to this greater risk, one will die during the year. The required compensation for one life, therefore, is $2,080 × 100 = $208,000. The manager should be aware that the proportionate risk approach has a few problems. Getting survey responses from workers on questions of this nature is extremely difficult. In addition, translating the proportionate risk to an individual into an actual number of deaths may well change the workers' calculus. Very often analysts guesstimate this cost as they make decisions about levels of liability insurance to purchase.

Another method often used to place a value on an individual's life is the *consumption method*. By assuming that an individual's contribution to society can be measured by what the individual produces, the cost-benefit analyst then estimates the value of an individual's life as the amount of money that individual would earn for the rest of his or her life (no consensus exists; however, economists currently place the value between $3 and $7 million). Under this approach human beings are treated exactly like government programs and valued according to the future income/benefits they produce. The consumption approach to valuing human lives creates the greatest ethical problems for decision makers because it places a higher value on men than on women, on whites than on blacks, on professional workers than on blue-collar workers, and on the able-bodied than on the disabled. The criticisms of this approach are extremely difficult to counter.

An example of the problem is the government difficulties in arriving at a fair level of compensation for the victims of the September 11, 2001, attacks on the World Trade Center. To experience this dilemma firsthand, ask yourself how to factor in the potential lifetime earning of a twenty-five year old stockbroker versus the future earnings of a forty-five year old secretary. Should the families of police and firefighter rescue workers who were killed while trying to save others be compensated more because of the rescue workers' bravery in entering the damaged towers after the attack? Finally, how should the future earnings of an unemployed student visiting her mother on the day of the attack be calculated?

Compensation to the families of victims of the 9/11 attacks was partially calculated as the consumption approach, in which the family of a thirty-five-year-old stockbroker was compensated at a much higher rate than that of a thirty-five-year-old janitor. This caused considerable criticism based on the "a life is a life" argument. As a result, downward adjustments were made for persons with considerable assets, triggering protests of unfairness based on why survivors of victim A (who saved) should be paid less than those of victim B (who did not). The arguments might have been more extreme if the minimum compensation levels not been so high with an average award of approximately $1.8 million.[14]

The above-mentioned methods are only a few of the ways that can be used to value human life. Mark Thompson discusses twelve different approaches, each based on different assumptions.[15] An easy, noncontroversial way of valuing human life is not likely to be found soon.

Even though valuing loss of life or injury is an enormous problem in cost-benefit analysis, such values are critical in producing studies that evaluate the impacts of the expanding technological sector of our society. Conditions of risk and uncertainty dominate such evaluations and create dilemmas both for the experts trying to assess the impacts and for the decision makers trying to use such assessments. The issues that have to do with valuing such impacts are so deeply embedded in philosophical and/or religious traditions that the credibility and legitimacy of such estimates will continue to be debated.

Discounting the Values

Estimating the values of effects does not stop when current values are determined by market pricing, shadow pricing, or some other technique. Few projects result in costs and benefits that occur immediately after implementation. Most projects have impacts occurring over a period of years following implementation. Cost-benefit analysis uses discounting to incorporate the effect of time on both the costs and the benefits.

Discounting is based on the theory that people will not pay as much for something that will not be available until a future date. In other words, people prefer to sacrifice a benefit in the future in order to have a benefit in the present. Decision makers must also factor in the impacts of expending limited resources on a particular project because, once committed, the funds are no longer available for other uses. For example, a city calculates that over the next ten years it can afford to accumulate no more than an additional $25 million in debt. (These calculations would be based on current commitments, the interest rate that it will have to pay to borrow the funds, and projected tax revenues.) Suppose the council was debating whether to build a new municipal golf course at a cost of $5 million. In addition to construction costs and recreational benefits to citizens who golf, the city must factor in the impacts of the $5 million commitment. After all, once the money is expended it is no longer available for other worthwhile purposes. Discounting accomplishes this end using the concept of *present value*. The discount rate has an enormous impact on the net present value. The formula for calculating present value is

$$PV = \frac{FV}{(1+d)^t}$$

where PV is the present value of the future benefit, FV is the stated value of the future benefit, d is the discount rate, and t is the number of years. If the discount rate is set at 5%, a person who has been promised a benefit of $100 from a project next year can calculate that the $100 in today's value is worth only $95.24. In the case of the person who was offered $100 next year, the present value would be determined as follows:

$$PV = \frac{100}{(1+.05)^1} = \$95.24$$

The discount rate is helpful because it reduces items that cannot be compared—costs and benefits occurring in different years over a time period—into a common monetary unit. This unit is the present value of the costs and benefits regardless of when they are predicted to occur. Discount rates look and function like interest rates.

In for-profit enterprises, the discount rate is readily derived from the cost of borrowing money for capital projects. Managers know how much a new facility costs to build and operate. Their cost-benefit projections regarding increased market-share profitability will be guided by their willingness to take risk. The problem is more difficult in the public sector because variations in the discount rate (*rate sensitivity*) may determine project viability and because cost-benefit analysts must also determine something called the *social discount rate*.

Rate sensitivity does not quarrel with the use of discount rates so much as it simply points to the extreme sensitivity of final benefits and/or costs to the discount rate chosen. Even a variation of 1–2% in the discount rate can make the difference between one project and another. This coincides with a second problem: The appropriate rate to use is the one that produces the actual present *social* values for the project.

The social discount rate should be an accurate measure of the rate at which society will trade present costs and benefits for future costs and benefits. Finding this rate and getting agreement on it is difficult. A number of sources exist for choosing the rate, and no one rate seems to have proven itself as *the* social discount rate.

Sources of Discount Rates

Examples of the rates that have been proposed for use as the social discount rate are market interest rates usually associated with government bonds, banks, or savings and loan associations; marginal productivity of investment; corporate discount rates; the government borrowing rate; personal discount rates; and personal preferences for social discount rates. Each of these examples has further nuances—for example, there are usually several different market interest rates available, depending on the amount of risk to the lender. Economists and policy analysts have their favorite social discount rates, the justification for which is usually based on a belief in either high or low discount rates.

Low or High Rates

Low discount rates favor projects whose benefits occur in the more distant future. On the basis of work by economist A. C. Pigou, proponents of a low discount rate argue that because individuals selfishly weigh their own interests too heavily compared with those of future generations, the government must intervene to correct their shortsightedness by acting as a trustee on behalf of future generations through the use of lower discount rates that make long-term projects more feasible. Those arguing for a high discount rate state that to get a meaningful analysis, the true opportunity costs of a project must be considered. They point out that the higher rate will knock out many long-term, capital-intensive projects, freeing money for private business forays into the economy and for more short-term public projects.

Problems with Discounting

The most basic question is whether discounting makes any sense in evaluating public projects. Particularly in safety and environmental issues, such as nuclear power development or wilderness preservation, critics have made a strong case for the folly of discounting or weighing the future less heavily than the present. Besides, they point out, the low discount rates used cannot handle benefits and costs for periods exceeding approximately 50 years. Such lengthy time frames become unrealistic because society cannot comprehend the value of such distant benefits. For example, if governments do not move to reduce mercury content in the world's oceans, the long-term impact on certain fish species could be catastrophic. Although people can relate to this danger emotionally, calculating the loss of swordfish in year X in terms of current dollars becomes an exercise in futility.[16]

The impact of any given program does not remain constant year over year, especially with multi-year projects. They must also allow for the interest that the money spent on the project might generate if the project did not exist. Analysts use the device known as the discount rate to make this adjustment. Analysts are really on the spot here. Economists have not been able to agree on the social discount rate but the federal government does so. Currently, the discount rates for government programs are tied to the Treasury Department's long-term borrowing rate, which fluctuates, making the discount rates better reflections of the true cost of investments in public projects. As of February 18, 2009, rates were set for 2011. The current official discount rates for federal project planners are as follows:

Table 8.1   Nominal Interest Rates on Treasury Notes and Bonds[17] of Specified Maturities (in percentages)

3-Year	5-Year	7-Year	10-Year	20-Year	30-Year
1.4	1.9	2.4	3.0	3.9	4.2

This solves the problem for the analyst, but not necessarily for the manager.

Comparing the Costs and Benefits

Once important program effects have been given a monetary value and discounted, the next step is to compare them. **Net present value** (*NPV*) is the method of comparison most often used to evaluate the alternatives. It combines a number of factors that influence the real monetary value of a project. By discounting any costs and benefits that will occur in the future, *NPV* considers the problem of time in evaluating the current value of the project to society. The formula for calculating the *NPV* would be

$$\frac{B_t - C_t}{(1+d)^t} \ldots + \frac{B - C_n}{(1+d)^n}$$

where B_t is the monetary value of benefits at time t, C_t is the monetary value of costs at time t, d is the discount rate, and n is the number of years of the project's life. This means, for example, that the *NPV* of a two-year project that yields a net benefit of $100 the first year and a net benefit of $50 the second year would not be evaluated as worth $150. Using the appropriate discount rate (5% for example), the *NPV* of such a project would be $140.35:

$$NPV = \frac{100}{(1+.05)^1} + \frac{50}{(1+.05)^2}$$
$$= 95 + 45.35$$
$$= 140.35$$

If the analyst has already discounted each of the individual effects, the *NPV* formula simply translates into total discounted benefits minus total discounted costs. If the *NPV* is positive, a project is said to return benefits. When comparing two project options, decision makers normally will choose the option with the most benefits over its costs.

Net present value is not the only bottom-line figure that the manager can see in a cost-benefit analysis. Other criteria are sometimes used, but not as often as net present value. Table 8.2 illustrates the present value of $10 at the end of specified years for several discount rates. The low range of present values at higher discount rates (10–15%) and for longer periods of time (25 years and over) demonstrates why analysts are wary of discounting the distant future heavily, especially for so-called "second generation" impacts, and seldom use discount rates beyond 50 years.

Table 8.2   Present Value of $10 at the End of Year (*t*) under Selected Discount Rates (*d*)

| | Discount rates (*d*) | | | | |
Year (*t*)	5%	7%	10%	12%	15%
1	9.52	9.35	9.09	8.93	8.70
5	7.81	7.14	6.21	5.68	4.98
10	6.13	5.08	3.86	3.23	2.47
15	4.81	3.62	2.39	1.83	1.23
20	3.77	2.58	1.49	1.07	.61
25	2.95	1.84	.92	.59	.30
30	2.31	1.31	.57	.33	.15
40	1.42	.67	.22	.11	.04
50	.87	.34	.09	.03	.009

Internal Rate of Return

The internal rate of return is determined by increasing the discount rate until benefits are equal to costs. The discount rate that equalizes benefits and costs is called the **internal rate of return** (IRR). The IRR was used extensively until recently. It is now criticized primarily because of difficulties in interpreting the information it provides. The manager should undertake only those projects that have an IRR greater than the established discount rate. The logic is that it pays to invest public funds in a project that earns returns at a higher rate than that at which the government could borrow funds. If a comparison is being made among several alternatives, the decision maker would look for the project that yields the highest IRR. The IRR criterion, however, is best applied only to projects that require a one-time critical investment with returns or benefits flowing over a period of time. Critics point out that calculating an IRR would not be as appropriate as calculating the *NPV* in instances when the project's discount rate changes in midstream, when costs are spread throughout the life of the project, or when the budget is constrained in some manner.

Cutoff Period and Payback Period

A *cutoff period* is often used in private industries that take calculated risks but do not wish to overextend their commitments. Establishing a cutoff period of ten years, for example, would mean that no benefits or costs (usually just benefits) that accrue after ten years will be counted. Cutoff periods are not often used in the public sector because government seldom needs to worry about such risks and time constraints. The cutoff criterion also favors projects yielding quick returns on investments and discriminates against programs whose benefits occur farther down the line. The *payback period* is the length of time it takes for a project's benefits to equal its costs. This criterion suggests that a project that recovers its initial costs in the shortest period of time is the most desirable project. It favors projects with immediate payoffs and discriminates against those with large but long-term benefits.

Benefit/Cost Ratio

The **benefit/cost ratio** results from dividing the net discounted benefits by the net discounted costs. It has been popular in the past, especially for demonstrating the benefits of water projects throughout the United States. This may seem to be a simple criterion. However, the major flaw in using this ratio as a sole decision rule is that a project having the highest benefit/cost ratio may actually have the lowest total net benefits of all the projects under consideration. People may want to spend more money proportionately in order to gain the higher net benefits provided by one of the other projects. As a general rule, the benefit/cost ratio is most useful in situations where the amount of money to be invested in a project or group of projects is limited.

Equity

The last decision criterion, **equity**, is not always considered in cost-benefit analysis because no effective way of incorporating equity in the mathematical models of the economists has been suggested. The proposed cross-town freeway mentioned earlier must condemn homes and businesses in its path. Using strictly cost-benefit figures would cause planners to recommend placing the freeway through the poorest neighborhoods. However, the value of home ownership of a $100,000 house, to its owner, is as great as that of a $400,000 house to its owner. Realistically, the owner of the $400,000 house is more likely to be able to locate replacement housing at the same price than is the low-end homeowner. Straight cost-benefit analysis would ignore the equity issues surrounding housing displacement.

The inclusion of equity as a separate factor in some cost-benefit analyses has resulted from pressure brought by interest groups and evaluators who recognize the need to include democratic principles and normative values in project assessment. The general approach at this time is to supplement the cost-benefit analysis with a report pointing to the special burdens or benefits adhering to a group. Critics still claim that even special reports on equity considerations do not guarantee full consideration of equity because of the difficulty of including it in the decision calculus.

Sensitivity Analysis

Managers often need to refine their assessments beyond net benefit data that are often based on calculations in which the manager has little faith. Sensitivity analysis allows this, simply by varying the value of one effect (say, the discount rate) until net benefits are equal to zero. Any discount rate below the final rate determined by the sensitivity analysis would result in positive net benefits. In this way, sensitivity analysis allows the manager to determine how crucial some of the assumptions and values are to the final results.

Making Choices Based on Cost-Benefit Analysis

The major contribution of cost-benefit analysis is its systematic approach to planning and evaluation. The cost-benefit specialist should remember that the technique is designed to organize information for the decision makers. The analyst's task is to see that the information is of the best quality, given operating constraints on the evaluation. Evaluators must also explicitly state any valuing used in the course of the evaluation.

Tips for Conducting a Successful Cost-Benefit Study

1. Identifying and Describing the Problem. The manager commissioning the evaluation should have primary responsibility for defining the problem or project to be evaluated. The manager is well served by consulting closely with the analyst and the program staff to focus the evaluation on the appropriate problem or project. Every problem has unique features, which should be identified and described early in the planning stages. Tasks that must be undertaken include: (a) drawing up a description of the status quo—that is, what the effects of the current policy are or should be; (b) identifying potential constraints on the project (for example, budgetary or resource limits, legal obstacles, administrative or institutional limitations, political problems, social considerations, and technological constraints); and (c) choosing decision criteria, such as the discount rate, the relevant time period, and the variables to be investigated.

2. Setting up the Design. Ideally, the cost-benefit analysis would systematically cover all aspects of a problem, but constraints on time, resources, and staff mean that the design must focus more on some effects than on others. In addition, the measurement and analysis of data will have to be based on the expertise available.

3. Collecting and Analyzing the Data. The format for presenting the data analysis should be determined before data collection begins. Original data should be collected when feasible, and sources used should be recorded for later updating and documentation. Both quantitative and qualitative data have a role in cost-benefit analysis. The analysis and interpretation of each should be carefully planned, documented, and justified.

4. Presenting the Results. The rationale for performing a cost-benefit analysis is to improve public policy. If the cost-benefit analysis is well planned and executed, the manager will have been informed of the progress through preliminary work plans and summary reports. Because cost-benefit analysis is controversial, the assumptions made in the analysis must be made explicit for those who will be basing their decisions on the final report. And, where possible, the report should include a discussion of other points of view that were not incorporated in the analysis. In addition, the manager must be sure that the study is written in prose that laypeople can understand rather than in the equations of the economist.

Advantages and Disadvantages of Cost-Benefit Analysis

The potential of cost-benefit analysis as a tool for decision making on public policies and projects is more controversial now than in the past. Supporters give it high marks for the order it imposes on the problem-solving process, the way it opens the governmental process to public scrutiny, and the information it consolidates. Critics, however, point to the theoretical and technical difficulties in applying cost-benefit analysis in the public sector. They claim that because it ignores the political process, critical questions raised by democratic principles may go unanswered, even when such questions as equity or conflicting values are addressed. Cost-benefit analysis may also encourage decision makers to put too much weight on quantitative information. It seems to work best for estimating multi-year costs of capital projects such as highway construction and weapons systems development and procurement. It is of lesser value for social planning.

Considerable attention has been focused on the problem of substituting the judgment of "experts"—whether engineers, scientists, systems analysts, or economists—for the judgment of elected officials. As a result, some efforts are now being directed toward subordinating cost-benefit analysis to the political process through renewed emphasis on public participation, consensus building, and the peer review process. Regardless of the outcome of this dispute, the manager must always subordinate cost-benefit analysis to management needs.

The rules regarding when cost-benefit analysis is the best choice for studying policy alternatives are not hard and fast. In some situations, using costs and benefits to weigh alternatives may be easier to justify than in others. For example, if the manager requests a cost-benefit analysis, the choice is an easy one. If the alternatives have effects that can be handily expressed in monetary units or other equivalent units, using cost-benefit analysis would be appropriate. The most important consideration, however, is that the analyst has an opportunity to provide useful information. The creativity and care with which the information is gathered, synthesized, documented, and presented can make an enormous difference in the worth of the final product. Managers who choose to use cost-benefit analysis must therefore be willing to allocate sufficient resources to do it right.

Risk Benefit Analysis

Whether or not they choose to make programmatic decisions based on cost-benefit ratios, all public and private managers must plan. That is, they must make certain budgetary assumptions in order to manage their finances. When they consider major new undertakings, they must assess the risks and benefits of the undertaking even when they do not attempt to analyze costs and benefits in the same unit of analysis. Doing the job correctly is known as *due diligence*, a legal term that means paying attention to details in a transaction, anticipating consequences, and undertaking appropriate safeguards to offset anticipated negative results. Failure to engage in due diligence frequently results in litigation from unhappy investors and victims of the organization's failure to take preventive actions.[18]

Notes

[1] For the current California law enabling and defining redevelopment agencies, see *California Community Redevelopment Law* (http://www.calredevelop.org/legislation/california_community_redevelopment_law.aspx). For a critical discussion of redevelopment agencies, see "How redevelopment agencies work and why Gov. Brown wants to scrap them." http://www.scpr.org/news/2011/02/02/23655/how-redevelopment-agencies-work-and-why-gov-brown-/

[2] For a history of the San Jose's sports center, see "HP Pavilion at San Jose—A Win/Win for All." http://www.hppsj.com/building_information/history.asp

[3] See "Reelection Rates Over the Years." http://www.opensecrets.org/bigpicture/reelect.php

[4] For a more complete discussion, see Tevfik F. Nas, *Cost-Benefit Analysis* (Thousand Oaks, CA: Sage, 1996); see also Edward J. Mishan and Euston Quah, *Cost-Benefit Analysis: An Informal Introduction*, 5th ed. (New York: Routledge, 2007).

[5] David Osborne and Ted Gaebler, *Reinventing Government: How the Entrepreneurial Spirit is Transforming the Public Sector* (New York: Plume, 1993), pp. 76–107.

[6] Health-care cost factors will equalize in 2014 when the Affordable Care Act provisions for universal coverage come into effect. For a comprehensive discussion of the act including the complete text, see "Understanding the Affordable Care Act: About the Law." http://www.healthcare.gov/law/about/index.html

[7] See W. Edwards Deming, *Out of the Crisis* (Cambridge: Massachusetts Institute of Technology, Center for Advanced Engineering Study, 1986); or W. Edwards Deming, *Quality, Pro-*

ductivity and Competitive Position (Cambridge: Massachusetts Institute of Technology, Center for Advanced Engineering, 1982).

[8] Keynesians derive their name from the theories of John Maynard Keynes, *The General Theory of Employment Interest and Money* (New York: Classic Books American, 2009, originally published by Palgrave Macmillan UK, 1936).

[9] To learn more about the debt ceiling crisis see Holly Epstein Ojalvo, "Teaching and Learning About the U.S. Debt Crisis and Credit Downgrade." *The Learning Network* (August 8, 2011). http://learning.blogs.nytimes.com/2011/08/08/teaching-and-learning-about-the-u-s-debt-crisis-and-credit-downgrade/?scp=19&sq=2011%20debt%20ceiling%20crisis&st=cse

[10] See "Credit Default Swaps," *New York Times* (April 29, 2011). http://topics.nytimes.com/top/reference/timestopics/subjects/c/credit_default_swaps/index.html/

[11] See "The Cleveland Voucher Program." http://www.aft.org/research/reports/clev/Cost.htm

[12] See Arthur C. Pigou, *The Economics of Welfare* (New York: General Books, 2010, originally published by Macmillan and Co., 1920). For a critique of the approach, see Ian M. D. Little, *A Critique of Welfare Economics: A Retrospective Edition* (New York: Oxford, 2002).

[13] For a complete clarification see Larry N. Gerston and Terry Christensen, *California Politics and Government: A Practical Approach*, 11th ed. (Belmont, CA: Wadsworth, 2011).

[14] See "September 11th Victim Compensation Fund of 2001." http://www.usdoj.gov/victimcompensation/payments_deceased.html

[15] See Mark S. Thompson, *Benefit-Cost Analysis for Program Evaluation* (Beverly Hills, CA: Sage, 1982).

[16] For a discussion of the equity issues between rich and poor nations and the efforts to correct global warming, see "Working Group II of the Inter-governmental Panel on Climate Change, Second Assessment Report, Working Group III." http://www.umep.ch/ipcc/sumvg3.html

[17] Discount rates for 2011 can be found at Office of Management and Budget, "Circular A4," Office of Management and Budget. http://www.whitehouse.gov/search/site/cost-benefit%20analysis%20discount%20rates%202011/

[18] Richard Wilson and Edmond A. C. Crouch, *Risk-Benefit Analysis*, 2nd ed. (Cambridge, MA: Harvard University Press, 2001).

chapter nine

A Ten-Point Checklist for Program Evaluators

Chapters 1 through 8 introduced a variety of evaluation concepts, and approaches, and a series of "do's and don'ts." Here we review elements that we believe to be important in the formulation and execution of evaluation research.

1. Is the program experimental, or is it ongoing? Experimental programs seek to test one or another social organization theory. By definition, there are fundamental questions as to whether experimental programs are worthwhile. With these programs, the central questions are: Will this approach achieve the desired ends? Will it do so at an acceptable cost to the organization or to society?

The methodologies appropriate to experimental programs are rigorous, costly, and time consuming. As such, they should be undertaken only when fundamental questions exist. The findings of experiments cannot be automatically generalized to all other situations due to constraints of the research environment. In the case of social experiments such as welfare reform or health-care funding, findings should be replicated using larger samples and less rigid control conditions before applying them generally.

Ongoing programs normally enjoy substantial support among decision makers and program executives. The issues driving an evaluation therefore may be program planning and organization improvement, accountability to external funding sources, or some combination of the two. Only rarely is program continuation at issue. Legislatures and overhead funding agencies want to know if a program is operating in an appropriate fashion based on accepted principles and the intent of the legislature. Those commissioning the evaluation may also ask whether desired outcomes are being achieved and whether operations can be improved.

Timing constrains the methodologies appropriate to such evaluations. It is simply impossible to conduct an after-the-fact experiment. The existence of generic indicators, however, facilitates comparisons with similar programs. Substantial differences in outcomes should raise questions as to program operations. If program operations are substantially the same but outcomes are different, closer scrutiny may be appropriate (including experimentation with alternative approaches).

2. Who is the audience for this evaluation? Throughout this text we have expressed our predilection for evaluations targeted at the needs of program staff. This assumes that the staff are most likely to use the findings to improve the program. Design rigor is less important than decision relevance in such an orientation.

Even evaluations commissioned by the legislature and motivated by program critics can achieve positive results. By involving staff in the design and implementation of a program audit, for example, the evaluator can raise the level of staff cooperation with the evaluation and acceptance of the findings. If the staff are empowered through participation, they likely will initiate change based on the results of the evaluation—even an evaluation that is highly critical.

3. Are the designs, measures, and indicators appropriate for the needs of the audience? Is a program audit or an outcome evaluation of the program desired? This query should guide the discussions between the evaluator and those commissioning the evaluation. An audit implies that the audience wishes to know if the program is being conducted in a manner consistent with general principles in the agency's field. Professionals in the fields of health care, education welfare, and law enforcement all have established guidelines for program performance. Decision makers may also wish to know if the program is being operated as efficiently as possible and if program officials are complying with regulations regarding purchasing, contracting, and so forth.

Outcome evaluations, on the other hand, ask how well the agency is achieving its goals. Outcome indicators and measures as well as rigorous comparisons are appropriate in such circumstances.

4. Is an outcome evaluation or an impact evaluation desired? Outcome evaluations may be further refined in terms of the appropriateness of the outcomes. If a substantial consensus exists that an agency is targeting the appropriate service group, then checking levels of service and customer satisfaction may be all that is necessary. A more complex design strategy may be appropriate if decision makers question whether the intended audience is being reached or whether the return to society from the program is worth the investment. The answer to this question will largely determine the extent and cost of an outcome evaluation.

More and more frequently, political decision makers are most interested in impact analysis—that is, whether the program significantly addresses the problem as envisioned in the legislative authorization. Impacts are becoming the bottom line, regardless of program efficacy. Well-managed programs that meet the needs of the community as intended may not be enough in an age of cutbacks and reductions in the public debt. Even very worthy programs are not immune.

5. What is the purpose of the evaluation? Some evaluations are undertaken to check a compliance box for an overhead agency or legislature. Others seek information on how the program is doing relative to similar programs. The evaluator also may be asked whether the agency is meeting its own standards. Program administrators may commission in-house data gathering as a part of a planned change strategy. Such data can be assessed in the aggregate or it can be parsed to achieve interunit performance comparisons. While staff size and funding for various units may vary greatly, performance goals for individual units may be negotiated with unit leaders. Thus, units can be compared on their progress towards the stated goals.

Compliance evaluations are necessary to ensure licensing and funding continuation. Sophisticated administrators understand that licensing and funding renewal require only that agencies produce documentation that program functions are performed legally and in a manner consistent with established professional standards. In normal times, even legislative critics can be pacified with a formal report that addresses their questions, regardless of actual agency performance. All evaluations, however, exact a toll on organization resources and staff energies.

Compliance standards exist, in part, precisely because overhead accountability agencies recognize the value of integrating ongoing, program-relevant evaluations into an organization's management system. This text began with discussions of systems theory and planning. Effective systems engage in ongoing self-monitoring. Well-designed program plans and change strategies include an evaluation to assess the effectiveness of program adaptations and their impacts on agency clients.

6. Do we seek decision-oriented data, or are we building a theory about client population? Program evaluation is rooted in the methodologies of social science research. Social scientists are greatly interested in the development of a body of theoretical knowledge about human behavior and motivation in a variety of settings. In contrast, program managers are primarily interested in providing maximum service to clients, within the limits of available resources and within legislative guidelines.

When choosing an evaluator or developing a design, the service needs of program clients and the information needs of program staff should be put ahead of the theoretical needs of social science. This caveat includes the relative sophistication of the research design and the writing of the report in clear and concise language. The report should also include concrete suggestions for program improvement.

7. Will the information be used to decide whether or how much to cut program funding or how funding can best be allocated among various components of the program? In times of funding rollbacks, administrators are often handed cuts that are based on the legislature's need to balance the budget. At such times, legislators have demonstrated little interest in service impacts. Legislative committees assume that program administrators will make the appropriate cuts to minimize service impacts and political heat. Agencies that have previously established databases which can report service levels and cost by program office will be better able to weather budget cuts while minimizing program damage.

8. Realistically, can a design be developed that conforms to the standards of quality evaluations within the limits of available funding? A cynical professor of program evaluation once noted that her students could readily come up with a $10,000 design to evaluate a $3,000 program. Furthermore, there are always interesting queries about this or that aspect of the program. The trick for the evaluator is to develop a design that provides program-relevant, decision-oriented data within funding limits. In this decision-making process, the evaluator should ask:

9. Am I absolutely sure that what I propose to measure is central to the goals of the agency as determined by my discussions with the program staff?

10. What are we doing, how are we doing, and who will care if we tell them? This final caveat is overarching. It insists that evaluations be tied directly to program goals as developed in consultation with the program staff and weighed against the intent of the legislature. The question of how we are doing expresses the need to make comparisons to similar programs, professional standards, or the quality and performance standards that the agency sets for itself. Finally, evaluators who aspire to have an impact on policy will do well to tailor their evaluations for consumption by those who will implement the recommendations.

appendix

Case Studies

Note: Some of the case studies in this appendix require you to create a project calendar. Microsoft Project is the best software for this purpose. Alternatively, several free project-planning applications are available online, or a calendar can be developed using any spreadsheet application. A calendar also can be drawn by hand.

Exercises in Process Evaluation

Case 1. The Drug Court Alternative: An Exercise in the Techniques of Planning

San Carlos County, California, is an urbanized metropolitan area very near the famed Silicon Valley. The valley is so near, in fact, that San Carlos County's main industry is semiconductors and computer software.

Chief Superior Court Judge Sylvia Cardoso became angry when she read the report of a citizen task force on California prisons. The task force reported what the judge had long suspected: The prison system was in crisis, largely due to the state's hard-line policy on drug offenses. According to the report, California currently has more people in prison for parole violations involving drug possession than the other 49 states combined. Furthermore, during a recent lunch with a colleague, also a judge, she learned that in a single morning her colleague had sentenced more than 200 people to prison as a result of drug-related plea bargains. "I am no longer a judge, I am a plea bargain clerk who doesn't have time to read the reports. I only pronounce sentence," the colleague complained.

Judge Cardoso reasoned that the current system just was not working, especially with regard to ethnic fairness. First-time offenders with family

205

resources or insurance were often referred to rehabilitation programs. Minority individuals, in contrast, were more likely to have low incomes, to have no insurance, and to have engaged in selling drugs to support their habits. The judge instructed her clerk to research alternatives to prison for these drug offenders.

A month later the clerk reported that a number of jurisdictions were trying something different: drug courts. First-time offenders were taken before a specialized judge and given the choice between prison or drug rehabilitation services. The department of probation would recommend whether the person was suitable for inpatient or outpatient treatment. Furthermore, truly enlightened jurisdictions recognized that, unless poor people could gain job skills and move out of the drug-infested neighborhoods, drug rehabilitation services would be to no avail. Fortunately, the Americans with Disabilities Act classifies a person in recovery from drug and alcohol dependency as having a disability. As such, they are eligible to apply for government-sponsored vocational rehabilitation services.

Judge Cardoso raised the possibility for a drug court at the next judicial conference and received unanimous support to move forward with the creation of a task force to make the drug court a reality. Judge Cardoso, the chief clerk, and the district attorney formed a subcommittee to study methods of implementation. The clerk became the coordinator and was responsible for note taking and the formation of a plan to bring the program online in eight months (two months before the November election).

The following two elements were identified for inclusion in the planning process: (1) designing a program, and (2) developing a proposal to present to the board of supervisors, outlining the funding for the drug court and the rehabilitation programs. The rehabilitation programs could be covered largely by diverting funds from county jail incarcerations for first-time offenders to the less expensive treatment program. The committee also determined that sufficient programs existed to provide the services without the creation of another bureaucracy. The various clinics and other providers would have to be contacted and rates for inpatient and outpatient services negotiated. A liaison clerk could be assigned the responsibility of managing the process. The State Office of Vocational Rehabilitation would have to be contacted to provide services to those who complete treatment. Finally, the committee decided that the program would have to be evaluated with regard to its operation and the outcomes it achieves.

Group Exercise

Develop either a PERT chart or a project calendar to account for the various elements defined in the drug court program. Be sure that you adequately sequence events and activities where appropriate and that you account for all the elements.

Case 2. An Abrupt Change of Direction: A Leadership Management Dilemma

The Mojave Valley is a combined city/county government structure struggling to keep up with an exponential population growth rate. In the past fifteen years, Mojave Valley has grown from a population of one hundred fifty thousand to just under a million. There is no sign that the growth will slow for the foreseeable future.

An influx of technology companies fleeing the high cost and pollution of the Silicon Valley had fueled the growth rate. They brought with them hundreds of thousands of jobs and workers to fill them. Developers could not keep up with the demand for new subdivisions. The building permits department was overwhelmed. For its part, the government could not build new streets, sewers, and water lines to keep up with the demand.

The growth has been primarily outward, leaving the central city to decay. Residents moved to the new subdivisions, and businesses relocated to the shopping malls. The board of supervisors was determined to stop this erosion. So, ten years ago they created the Mojave Redevelopment Agency.

The agency was given its own revenue base by dedicating property tax proceeds from the highest industrial growth area to the redevelopment and revitalization of the downtown area. This amounted to $150 million annually. The agency was also given the authority to negotiate tax incentive with businesses and to issue bonds for construction. These latter two items were subject to final approval by the board of supervisors.

The agency was set as a semi-autonomous entity. The director reported to the board of supervisors, bypassing the county manager. Agency employees were hired outside of the civil service system. Because the agency was to be temporary, its employees do not enjoy civil service protections. Their salaries are individually negotiated. They also do not participate in the city/county retirement system. As compensation, the salary packages of these individuals run 35–40% higher than those of civil service employees with comparable responsibilities. Agency employees also receive bonuses for exceptional performance that may amount to as much as 25% of their salary. The agency director has the final authority on compensation and incentive awards.

The first director of the Redevelopment Agency, William "Red" Johnson, was recruited from the planning department of a large eastern city where he had developed a reputation for getting things done. During the first eight years of his tenure, Red enjoyed spectacular success in converting the downtown to a showplace of symphony orchestras, civic light opera companies, and repertory theatres. Where low-income housing once stood, there are pedestrian walkways, coffeehouses, movie theaters and upscale restaurants, in addition to high-rise office buildings that house the corporate headquarters of tech companies and some of the country's leading banks.

The agency's proudest achievement, however, was building a sports arena and event center that became the venue for a National Hockey League team as well as rock concerts, circuses, and so forth. Agency critics pointed to the arena as exhibit A in what was wrong with the agency. Slated to cost $105 million, it ended up costing more than $120 million. The board of supervisors learned of the cost overruns after the fact, and they were given little choice but to approve the sale of additional bonds to cover the cost.

Red's "can-do" attitude infected his staff, who saw themselves as development entrepreneurs. Many of them came to believe that they knew what was best for the city. The Agency's motto seemed to be: "It is easier to get forgiveness than permission."

A major technology company was persuaded to relocate to Mojave, not only with tax incentives but also with public bonds issued to cover its construction costs. Again, Red went to the board of supervisors after signing agreements with the company that effectively left the board no choice other than to go along.

Red's cowboy style, while annoying, did little real damage until two years ago when the economy took a major downturn. Funding for schools and basic public services fell short. Layoffs were necessary in various departments, including the police and fire departments. Supervisors turned to the only pot of money left in the valley, the agency's development fund.

Red resisted any suggestion that funds be diverted from the agency to other public purposes. Cogently, he argued that using money for other purposes would be against the law. The county attorney agreed. To make matters worse, Red continued to spring surprise after surprise on the board.

In a special election, the board took back its authority over the Redevelopment Agency and its tremendous taxing power. Members explained that they needed the flexibility to tap the funds in hard times. They also wanted more say in how the agency was run. The new agency charter made its director accountable to the county manager. Agency expenditures henceforth would have to be approved on an annual basis. The board took the additional step of creating from within its ranks a three-member subcommittee of its members to oversee the agency. The director would have to provide the subcommittee with progress reports on current projects, and prior approval by the subcommittee was necessary before undertaking negotiations on new projects. Red and all three of his deputy directors resigned in protest.

The county manager immediately appointed Margaret Walker as the interim director. As a forty-two-year-old African American, she was surprised and delighted to get the appointment to head a largely white male agency. For the past six years Walker has been a team leader in the agency's planning unit. Prior to that, she headed the planning department of a nearby city of fifty thousand. She left that position to join the agency because of the entrepreneurial opportunities it offered and the significant salary increase.

The manager met with Walker to offer her his unqualified support. He authorized her to immediately name two deputy directors. She was encouraged to get her own team on board and to hit the ground running. The manager then announced that the agency's budget for the upcoming year would be held to $110 million, despite the fact that revenues from the agency's traditional base were projected to be $158 million.

Walker returned to her office and reviewed Red's preliminary budget. Red had planned to spend $115 million on projects that were already authorized but not yet underway. He also had undertaken preliminary negotiations with three companies to move their headquarters to Mojave. The cost of these proposals would be $40 million over the next three years. Nevertheless, should all three companies relocate to Mojave it would bring added tax revenues of $6 million per year, starting two years from now.

As she sat pondering what to do first, Walker received a call from her best friend, Harold Smith, who led one of the agency's planning teams. Harold was the only other African American manager employed in the agency. He reported that he has made great progress towards building a new community center to serve the low-income neighborhoods that remain in central Mojave. Several high-tech corporations have committed to providing computers and the participation of their employees in an after-school tutoring program in math and science. The center will cost $15 million to build and is included in current budget projections.

Group Exercise

Assume that you are Walker. Make a list of your five highest priorities.

1. Define these priorities as specific project components.

2. Specify timetables and milestones for their achievement. Illustrate them with a project calendar.

3. Develop a responsibility matrix for carrying out the project.

4. Consider the matrix in the following context:

   • What steps should Margaret Walker take to become the manager/leader of the Redevelopment Agency in fact as well as name?

   • How should she involve subordinates in the development of the priorities? Include your thinking in the project calendar.

   • What actions should she take to bring her budget into line with board expectations?

Exercises in Monitoring and Improving Internal Processes

Case 3. How Are We Doing?

Chief Arnold Escobedo is a newly appointed 38-year-old police chief in a city of two million people in the upper Midwest. Escobedo's predecessor resigned under a cloud of controversy when a trio of police sergeants were indicted for taking bribes and covering up drug trafficking in their precinct. The previous chief was criticized for seeming to sweep the matter under the rug. Now Escobedo wants to take immediate steps to:

1. Determine the extent of the problem, and

2. Develop a program to prevent recurrence of corruption that

3. Involves first-line supervisors in the design and implementation of the program.

He assigns Lieutenant Michael Freeburg, his administrative support officer, to lead the initiatives. Freeburg consults his advisor in the local MPA program who suggests two potential ways of proceeding that are not mutually exclusive. First, the professor suggests that the department's fifteen hundred sworn officers could be anonymously surveyed on the extent of the corruption in the department. Of course, by randomly sampling from a list of officers, useful information could be gained at less expense. Alternatively, a consultant could be engaged to conduct focus groups with rank-and-file patrol officers and a separate focus group composed solely of sergeants. The professor also suggests, if the department is to take the latter track, that the groups should be representative of the officers and sergeants according to length of service, ethnicity, and gender as well as functional responsibilities (e.g., patrol, traffic, gang task force).

Lieutenant Freeburg decides to consult precinct captains, who indicate they want the department to do its own laundry. "If we don't clean this up, the city council and community groups (who don't like the police) will do it for us and we won't like the results," one wizened captain indicates. The others agree. Bolstered by the commanders' support, Freeburg seeks and is given free rein by the chief to gather information.

Group Exercise

As a member of Freeburg's working group, your task is to design a survey questionnaire to get at the corruption issue. Since Freeburg intends a separate focus group for sergeants, the questionnaire will go only to officers below the rank of sergeant. Structure the questions you will ask to identify the components of corruption (personal knowledge, personal participation, precincts in which corruption occurs). Be sure that the questionnaire includes demographic items (e.g., age, time of service, and current functional responsibilities of the respondent) and open-ended questions that allow the officers to add material the workgroup may have overlooked.

Develop an open-ended research instrument that can be used in the sergeants' focus group. Define any special topics that the focus group leaders should probe. Decide whether the sessions should be video recorded or whether documentation should be limited to a notetaker.

Case 4. Social Service Problems in Balkinwalk

Balkinwalk, a typical mid-Atlantic seaboard city of 750,000, is growing quickly as a result of the migration away from the Northeast. As with other large cities in the state, Balkinwalk is responsible for the administration of social service programs as well as municipal services; in smaller jurisdictions, social services are county functions.

The new city manager has been in Balkinwalk for less than a year, during which time she has received a majority of complaints about the social welfare department. Citizens complain that they are not treated well at the department. Insensitive clerical staff make them wait for long periods of time and then tell them to come back the next day. The city manager had been passing such complaints along to the administrator of social services, but now she feels that she must personally take steps to remedy the situation.

The current head of the social service agency has held her position for eighteen months. She was a supervisor for the previous five years and a practicing social worker in the Balkinwalk agency for eight years prior to that. The previous administrator of the social welfare department, like his predecessor, had been hired from outside the agency. The immediate predecessor stayed eleven months, then left for a better paying job. His predecessor had remained in the job for just under two years.

The head of social services is aware of the city manager's concerns. She too has sensed that something is wrong and that service could be better. From her perspective, the primary problem stems from the heads of various branches of social services, who seem bent on frustrating each other and her.

The service delivery operation is made up of three units. The eligibility unit employs twenty workers and one supervisor, all of whom are paraprofessionals whose job it is to determine benefit eligibility. These workers have acquired a good deal of knowledge regarding policies and procedures. The agency administrator is aware that workers in this unit resent the low wages and bare-bones benefits they receive. In addition, they have expressed scorn for social workers, whom the eligibility workers believe to be "a bunch of overpaid, smart-alecky college kids." Eligibility workers also resent the hiring of what they perceive to be underqualified minorities for positions in their unit. Recently these unhappy workers formed an employee association, even though there is no law in the state either permitting or forbidding collective bargaining.

The other two units are made up of social workers: The family counseling unit contains twelve workers, and the individual caseworkers' unit contains eighteen. Each unit is headed by a "working supervisor." Social workers resent the amount of paperwork they must do as well as the large caseloads they must manage. The caseloads preclude them from giving individualized counseling to even the most needy clients. They believe that routine clerical tasks could be delegated to eligibility workers. The discontent among social workers has resulted in a high turnover rate, which some attribute to excessively heavy caseloads and others to the attraction of higher-paying jobs in nearby agencies.

The personnel unit within the social welfare department is responsible for recruiting and training personnel for the department. In addition, it oversees and implements the social service component of the citywide affirmative action plan. The personnel director has held that post for less than nine months but has already incurred the anger and resentment of the program staff because she insists on vigorous enforcement of the affirmative action plan.

The accounting and payroll unit has two functions. The first entails preparing the necessary forms so that the regional office can make payments to aid recipients. Until recently the checks were dispensed locally, but the new regional procedure requires redesigning tasks and implementing a new technology in the form of computerized records. This changeover requires either training current personnel in new skills or recruiting new people from the outside. Accounting and payroll do not believe that the personnel department has been helpful in this regard.

The payroll division of the accounting and payroll department is also experiencing its share of employee anger and resentment. The agency lost a recent employee appeal to the Civil Service Commission. The appeal was filed by an African American female employee who had been fired for poor attendance and tardiness during her probationary period. The agency lost because it could not document the employee's failures. In reaction to this loss the department installed a time clock that has alienated all employees, including the social workers who frequently have to drive long distances to clock out at the appointed hour, causing further reductions in time spent in service to clients.

In consultation with the city manager, the agency head has decided to seek expert help to answer the following questions:

1. What is the level of service in our agency?
2. Are our organizational arrangements appropriate? For example, do we distribute the work evenly and have enough supervisory personnel?
3. How do we stack up against other comparable programs?
4. Is the turnover rate inordinately high among social workers?

5. Do all clients share the sentiments of those who are complaining to the manager?

6. What can the agency do to extricate itself from the dilemma?

Group Exercise

Assuming that the answers to questions 2, 4, and 5 turned out to be yes, design an evaluation project in the process mode to help the agency define and solve its problem. How would you proceed? From whom do you collect data? Do you merely interview staff, or should clientele also be surveyed? What can be done to help the agency get back on the right track? How can you find someone who cares about the evaluation toward whom you can direct the findings? (Hint: Begin by diagramming the structure of the agency to see who is reporting to whom. Then ask why it is the way it is. Is it logical, or is it what is known as "management by peculiarity?" How might it be improved?)

Exercises in Mixed Process and Outcome Evaluations

Case 5. Change of Command

The Third Battalion, Forty-Second Field Artillery, is a proud unit with a long and distinguished record of service to the nation in time of war. The peacetime mission of the unit is to engage in training in order to maintain the highest degree of readiness.

Organizationally, the battalion consists of three separate firing batteries, each of which is equipped with six 155-millimeter howitzers. In addition, the battalion has a headquarters unit and a service unit (which are also called batteries). At full strength, the battalion consists of 210 personnel, including a complement of 30 commissioned officers and 70 noncommissioned officers.

The operational mission of the battalion is the conventional and nuclear fire support of the First Brigade, Fifty-Second Mechanized Infantry Division. When engaged in support fire activities, each of the three batteries is assigned to support a specific maneuver battalion of the brigade. The artillery battalion is dispersed when in operation, making coordination difficult. Thus, effective command requires a high level of training, mutual loyalty among the officers, and effective lines of communication—both electronic and interpersonal. Maintaining the high level of training and loyalty is the responsibility of the headquarters and service batteries. Maintaining effective communication is a function of the commanding officer.

For four years, command of the battalion was in the hands of Lieutenant Colonel Rock Smirnoff, who made it known at the outset that his goals were a vigorous program of personal fitness, a smooth-running command, and an uneventful final tour before his retirement. It is not surprising that Lieutenant Colonel Smirnoff delegated many command responsibilities to his executive officer, Major Jackson Beauregard Daniels. Major Daniels proved to be more than competent, and the performance of the battalion on such things as its efficiency rating, Army Training and Education Program, and Inspector General (IG) reports was consistently superior.

Eighteen months ago, however, Major Daniels received a transfer and was replaced by a young major named N. C. Cureley, who did his best but lacked the personal assertiveness of Major Daniels. Major Cureley refused to take responsibility for making command-level decisions, and both morale and performance declined until the retirement of Lieutenant Colonel Smirnoff three months ago.

Smirnoff's replacement was an upwardly mobile academy graduate with stars in his stars, Lieutenant Colonel I. M. Acomer, who immediately assumed command of everything and accepted responsibility for decisions down to the battery level and below. Discipline problems at the squad level were not beneath his concern. His organizational goal (as stated at the first officer's call) was "to build the best battalion in the army." An inspector-general's report just received, however, indicated no improvement in either morale or overall battalion performance. In fact, reported incidents of disciplinary problems were increasing. Realizing that something was seriously wrong, Lieutenant Colonel Acomer approached the base's quality improvement effectiveness officer to get help in diagnosing and solving the unit's problems. The officer took the commander and senior officers on a weekend retreat, during which they arrived at a set of definable problems and a set of solutions. The problems identified included:

1. Ineffective communication
2. Failure to delegate authority
3. Low morale
4. Discipline cases involving alcohol and drug abuse
5. Declining reenlistments
6. Decline in overall combat readiness
7. Equipment problems traceable to failure to accomplish scheduled maintenance

The officers agreed to set up a program to correct the differences, including improved lines of communication, a more cooperative mode of management involving delegation and trust, a stepped-up program of training, an agreement to go by the book on scheduled maintenance and dealing with subordinates, as well as a commitment among themselves to assertive leadership by example and an overall commitment to the organization.

Lieutenant Colonel Acomer has agreed to this program, but he wants the proposed changes to be monitored to see whether the desired effects are achieved. To his delight, the commander learns that three of his officers (two captains and a lieutenant) are enrolled in a masters of public administration program at a nearby university. Acomer orders them to institute a task-force approach to correct the unit's problems.

Group Exercise

You are the officer in charge of the task force.

1. How will you proceed?

2. Develop an evaluation strategy that will provide hard data on the battalion's progress and outline who is in charge of each component.

3. Develop a project calendar and responsibility matrix to achieve the desired changes.

Case 6. Troop B

Troop B of the Shiprock Highway Patrol is responsible for law enforcement on the highways in and around Gotham City. Although not the state capital, Gotham City and its environs account for 40% of the state's population and a preponderance of commuter traffic. Troop B's commander, a twenty-year veteran of the roads, has a strong sense of duty and even stronger feelings about what constitutes an appropriate service level to the citizens of Shiprock. For the first five years of his command, Troop B led the state in enforcement performance levels.

However, a recent report from the department's central office indicates that the performance of Troop B has dropped dramatically over the past 18 months. For example, traffic collisions involving personal injuries and property damage are up 43% from the previous year. A disproportionate percentage of such accidents involve drivers under the influence of alcohol (DUI). The accident trend is particularly disturbing to the commander, who believes that the solution to the problem is vigorous enforcement of DUI statutes.

The commander is equally disturbed by an increased number of citizen complaints against the members of Troop B. Some 95% of these complaints involve verbal abuse of citizens by officers. A review of personnel files indicates that in the previous 18 months, disciplinary actions involving suspension without pay have amounted to in excess of 100 days of suspension for the troop of thirty officers. These suspensions have occurred over such issues as neglect of duty, rule infractions, and insubordination.

Morale in Troop B is low. The officers are disgruntled over a recent statewide study that recommended pay increases of 15% for supervisors and only 5% for troopers. Other morale and discipline issues stem from an increased tendency to transfer "problem" troopers in other parts of the state to Troop B. The commander feels that this trend was somewhat offset in the past by a tendency of those whose careers are on the fast track to seek assignment to Troop B.

In addition, a review of logs shows that some troopers take as much as two hours per shift for meals and breaks, which in itself would account for much of the decline in enforcement efficiency. Some troopers also take an inordinate amount of sick leave. State regulations allow employees to accumulate up to 10 hours of sick leave per month; leave not used within 45 days is lost. The troopers who exhaust all their available leave each month make it necessary to pay other troopers overtime to cover the zone. Finally, bickering has occurred among troopers and dispatchers over call assignments.

The troop commander has resolved to take immediate steps to remedy the situation, but he sees that the problems may be beyond the expertise available in the department. He decides to retain an outside consultant.

Group Exercise

Assume you are that consultant. What would you recommend to the commander? Specifically:

1. In what sort of problem identification activities would you engage?
2. What are the problems?
3. Assuming that your list of problems is substantially the same as the commander's, what solutions would you recommend?
4. What sort of implementation strategy do you recommend?
5. How do you propose to tell whether your solutions worked?

Exercises in Conducting an Outcome Evaluation

Case 7. Are Drug Courts Worth the Costs? Design for the Drug Court Alternative

Assume that the drug court experiment you defined in the first case, pp. 205–206, has been ongoing for two years. Design an outcome evaluation to determine if the court has reached its intended goal of reducing drug dependency through a program to divert first-time offenders into treatment rather than sending them to jail.

Group Exercise

1. Develop a set of appropriate indicators and measures to assess the program.
2. Be sure your methodology examines the ability to stay clean and sober and compares recidivism rates between drug-court diverted offenders and those sent to prison.
3. Your evaluation design should further examine the relative success rates of both (a) inpatient programs and (b) outpatient programs.

4. You should also compare the success rates and relative cost levels of public programs, not-for-profit private agencies, and for-profit private treatment programs.

Case 8. A Public Health Program Assessment

Budget cuts at all levels of government greatly impact the variety of services it can provide. Often, delivery mode of an essential service is modified to provide the best possible services with reduced staffs. The Santa Bernicia County Health Department Tuberculosis Prevention and Control Program is no exception. In 2007, budget cuts led the Health Department to adapt its service delivery system to provide the highest-quality service possible to both treat and contain TB in the county with substantially fewer resources.

In 2008 the program moved from a specialist to a generalist approach, in which operational practices and monitoring functions took on a very different format. The change permitted the layoff of a number of public health nurses. The shift was a bold change for a county with the third highest TB infection rate in the nation's most populated state. Under the new program, generalist public health nurses would visit TB patients, providing in-home treatment and referral services to inpatient facilities as necessary. These services were to be in addition to their other duties.

Specialists within the department argued that there simply were not sufficient resources to do everything well and that reduction in services to TB patients put the entire population at a greater risk of infection. The warnings went unheeded in the face of shrinking resources.

In 2011 a new director was appointed from outside the agency. The skeptics wasted no time in appealing their position to him. The new director listened to their concerns as well as the warnings from his financial section regarding the cost impacts of returning to the specialist modality. Caught in the middle of two seemingly reasonable arguments, the director decided to make a decision based upon data rather than staff conjecture. He has ordered his evaluation staff to compare the two approaches. He requires that the findings be on his desk in time to incorporate them into his 2012 budget, which is due in six months.

Group Exercise

Assume that your group is assigned the task of conducting the study. No funds, however, are available to retain external consultants. A small budget is approved for a survey of the staff members who currently provide services to TB patients. All other information must come from existing data.

1. Generate a list of indicators that will allow for a meaningful comparison of the two-year generalist program with its specialist predecessor.

   a. Decide how you will measure quality of care as well as impacts.

   b. How many years of data prior to 2009 will be necessary?

2. Devise a survey for distribution to current generalist staff, asking them to qualitatively assess current services.

a. Incorporate structured opinion questions, using a scale such as the one below:

The current visitation schedule is sufficient to track patient treatment progress.

5 Strongly agree
4 Agree somewhat
3 Disagree somewhat
2 Strongly disagree
1 Unable to say or no opinion

b. Devise open-ended questions that ask staff to make concrete suggestions for improvements in the program and in the department generally.

Case 9. Victim/Witness Service Center

Suppose that you are a member of a team of program evaluators from the State University who are asked to assess the victim/witness service program presented in chapter 3.

Group Exercise

Local officials would like answers to the following question:

1. How successfully does the victim/witness center carry out its functions of (a) service to victims and witnesses and (b) provision of effective liaison services between prosecutors, defense attorneys, and sitting judges?

2. Determine whether or not the project has enhanced the trial process in terms of (a) length of time of trial and (b) length of sentences meted out to those found to be career criminals.

3. Officials also wish to know the effectiveness of the police training program.

4. For his part, the chief of police wants impact information that links the success of the program to various categories of crime in the jurisdiction. He does not want to spend a lot of money, so limit your design (or this aspect of it) to generic indicators.

Case 10. Program Experimentation: Welfare Reform

In the late 1970s the state of Wisconsin sought and received Department of Labor funds to experiment with a new job placement program for welfare recipients that cost more than their current program but held a promise of more meaningful work, which in turn might lead to longer-term job retention. The new program involved work-readiness training for welfare recipients with the goal of enabling them to compete for available jobs.

In the 1990s, data indicated that job-readiness training was most effective for persons who had been on welfare a relatively short time but had little impact on long-term welfare recipients. California state officials sought and received permission from federal officials to experiment with an alternative approach. In Alameda County (in the Bay Area) the training program was continued. In Riverside County (east of Los Angeles) a program involving placement in work as a condition of receiving benefits was implemented. Recipients had to accept employment to receive other benefits, such as housing subsidies, Medicaid payments, food stamps, and so forth. The intended special impact of the Riverside program was to get long-term welfare recipients successfully into the workforce.

Group Exercise

The Bureau of Government Research at Ivory Tower University contracted to perform an evaluation of the two programs. Assume that you are an employee of the bureau. Develop an evaluation design to test the effectiveness of the programs in meeting their goals.

1. Begin by using the evaluation model presented in chapter 5 to define the theoretical intent, program goals, program functions, proximate indicators, and measures.

2. How will you go about selecting program participants to ensure that there is a minimum of bias built into the evaluation design?

3. What kinds of measures are available for testing the impact(s) of the culture of poverty on the participants? Is there a difference between people on welfare and the general population with regard to their attitudes about the value of hard work?

4. How will you determine whether the work requirement, work readiness training, or some combination of the two is most effective in getting welfare recipients into the workforce and off welfare rolls?

5. What kinds of indicators will you use to see whether there is a difference between the experimental program and regular programs in terms of placement in meaningful work?

6. How and when will you know if the program was a success?

Case 11. Evaluating a Training Process (NASA–ASEE)

Each year the National Aeronautics and Space Administration (NASA) cosponsors a training program for college professors with the American Society for Engineering Education (ASEE). One stated goal of the program is to acquaint an interdisciplinary research team of engineering and social science professors with skills in systems design. The hope is that these professors will return to the classroom and teach their students systems design techniques. By so doing, NASA and the ASEE hope to broaden the pool of persons in society with these skills, thereby benefiting the engineering profession, NASA, and society as a whole.

A second goal of each annual project is to solve a problem that is of interest to NASA. Teams may work on such problems as designing an offshore airport, the applications of aerospace technology to agriculture, or the design of transportation accesses to international airports. The idea is to tap the existing skills of the professors as well as to equip them with new skills. Assume that you are the project director and that for the last three years the process has gone as follows: Twenty professors are brought to one center for ten weeks. There they are briefed on the resources available—for instance, computer access and library resources. After the one- or two-day orientation, the team settles into its ten-week work assignment.

The team is divided into small groups of five members from a variety of disciplines. Each group is to work independently of the others and define the elements in the systematic resolution of the current year's problem, a phase that takes about two weeks. Then the groups report their recommendations to the larger group, and a consensus on direction is reached, with the entire design team working as a single unit. This portion of the deliberations may take from one to two weeks, depending on the diversity of the various groups' recommendations. Once consensus is reached, the professors are divided into smaller work units, which take responsibility for various phases of the design project. The remainder of the project involves independent work on the part of the professors and small groups. An editorial board is responsible for synthesizing the productivity of the subgroups in a final report, which is presented to the NASA officials.

Group Exercise

Assume that you as project director wish to answer the following questions along with your staff:

1. How effectively has the process taught systems design to the professors?

2. How effectively has the design-team experience utilized the skills of the various participants?

3. What phases of the process could be done differently, and how might these differences affect the professors' perceptions of project success?

4. How might you determine if current or former participants have incorporated their systems training into the curricula of their home institutions?

Assume that you are drawing near the end of a design-team project. You want to experiment with changing the design-team experience in order to use the ten-week period more efficiently and to reduce the amount of anger experienced by some participants who do not believe that their small-group outputs were treated fairly by the larger group.

1. What changes will you make in the processes the next design team will undergo?

2. In order to develop baseline data on which to assess the merits of the changes you are making, answer the following questions:

   a. What outcome measures will you use?

   b. What elements in the process will you assess?

   c. How will you assess the current year's process now that it is nearly complete?

Case 12. Migrant Workers

Each year there are a number of accidental pesticide poisonings of migrant farm workers. The actual number of cases is difficult to determine because the symptoms (headaches, nausea, vomiting, and so on) are common to other ailments, such as flu. As a result, people may or may not know that their illness is pesticide related. The number of documented cases, however, is sufficiently large to warrant governmental countermeasures. Officials of the Environmental Protection Agency (EPA) and the Department of Agriculture (DOA) are convinced that the poisonings are mostly accidental and stem from improper handling of pesticide materials by workers. For example, workers may not be aware of the need to wash their hands after handling pesticides before eating and after using the restroom, or to change work clothes each day when handling pesticides. Other poisonings are the result of workers' storing unused pesticides in milk cartons or other improperly marked containers.

The EPA and the DOA will cosponsor a program to educate migrant workers about the hazards of pesticides. The EPA has agreed to provide $100,000 for a pilot program to administer the grant. The actual training will be provided by the Florida Department of Labor and be overseen by the Florida Department of Agriculture.

The grant specifies that the Florida Department of Labor will develop and pilot-test education modules aimed at preventing accidental pesticide poisoning. The program, which is to be developed in both English and Spanish, will initially involve two hundred migrant workers. Program development will be particularly difficult, given the low levels of literacy among migrant workers. The evaluation, to be conducted by the Florida Department of Agriculture, is to assess the impacts of the program and should include: (1) a method for assessing the quality of the education modules developed in the program; (2) a method for assessing the actual delivery of the training; and (3) a method for measuring the success of the program in improving the knowledge of the participants regarding the correct use of pesticides and potential dangers of mishandling them.

Group Exercise

1. Specify goals, elements, indicators, and measures that are appropriate.

2. Develop an appropriate design strategy using *X*s and *O*s (see chapter 7) to illustrate how you will proceed.

3. Discuss the limitations that influence the evaluations. What kinds of general program application inferences will you be able to make on the basis of this evaluation?

4. Remember that the label *migrant worker* indicates a class of workers who do not stay long in one location, making follow-up evaluations impractical. Remember also that the goal is to develop a program that minimally educated supervisors can use in the future.

Case 13. Teachers' Aides

The city of Sorghum is a community of 20,000 located in northwestern Arkansas near the Oklahoma and Missouri borders. For the last fifty years the population of Sorghum has been engaged primarily in agriculture or in servicing the agricultural community. Five years ago, the major utility company finished construction of a nuclear power plant that serves the needs of cities in three states. The plant now accounts for 54% of the jobs in Sorghum. Seventy percent of those employed at the plant are recent arrivals who have no roots in the local community. This population influx resulted in rapid construction of two new grammar schools (grades one through six) and one new middle school (grades seven and eight). The next anticipated pressure will be on the high school, which must expand its facilities to accommodate the maturing newcomers.

The district now has four grammar schools, two middle schools, and one high school. Some 24% of the students in the district are bused in from farms surrounding Sorghum. A pilot program for busing city residents also has been underway for two years as a result of threatened lawsuits by the local African American and Native American communities, who feel that the current racial composition of the schools is inequitable. Generally, the minority communities are made up of long-term residents.

The racial composition of the schools causes community unrest. The high school is fully integrated. Problems at that level center on student assignments to the new and old facilities when the new facility becomes operational. The middle schools also are relatively balanced. Johnson Middle School is 75% white, 20% African American, and 5% Native American; Kennedy Middle School is 34% African American, 12% Native American, and 54% white. The actual racial composition of all school-age children in Sorghum is 60% white, 31% African American, and 9% Native American.

The principal problems of racial harmony stem from student distribution in the grammar schools of Sorghum. Jefferson School is located in a predominantly white part of the city. The student composition at Jefferson is

95% white; as a result of the pilot busing program the remainder of the student population there is 3% African American and 2% Native American. Lincoln School is located in the black section of the city, and its student composition is 84% African American, 11% Native American, and 5% white. The white students are bused to Lincoln School. The two newer schools (Carver and Roosevelt) have operated for three years and are located in areas accessible to all three communities. The composition of the student body at Carver School is 65% white and 35% African American. Roosevelt School is 40% African American, 40% white, and 20% Native American. Minority parents are as much concerned about the overcrowded conditions at the Lincoln and Roosevelt schools as they are about racial balance.

The Sorghum school board is made up of seven members elected at large. The membership includes five men and two women. To date, no African American or Native American has secured a seat on the board, although African American and Native American candidates have made strong showings in the last three elections. The occupational status of the board members reflects the community they serve. The president of the board is a farmer in his ninth term. Two other rural residents also hold seats on the board: One, in her eighth term, is a retired teacher and the wife of a farmer; the other, in his third term, is a medical doctor who raises horses near town. The remaining board members are a grocer, now in his second term; a housewife, now in her first term; an executive at the power plant, also in his first term; and a service station operator, who has been on the board for 30 years and is in his last term.

The membership of the board is deeply divided on the question of busing; the newer members see a need for the program, and the senior members strongly oppose such innovations. The swing vote on such issues rests with the doctor, who voted for the busing program in the interest of community peace. The board is also skeptical about ethnic studies programs and special programs for persons with learning disabilities, even though the presence of the power plant has considerably increased district revenues. The conservative members of the board would rather return excess tax revenues to taxpayers than sink them into high-cost, low-return programs for the educationally challenged. They want the curriculum to consist of reading, writing, and arithmetic. The vast majority of teachers in the district are Sorghum natives who attended one of the two state-supported universities for four years and returned home to teach. Most recently, however, an increasing number of the teaching positions are being filled by newcomers who are affiliated in one way or another with the power plant. Most notable among the new hirees are four African American teachers who are not Sorghum natives, bringing the total number of African American teachers in the district to twelve. The remaining eight African American educators are longtime Sorghum residents, one of whom is principal of Lincoln School.

The school system is headed by a 35-year-old superintendent, now serving his second year, who has a doctorate in education from a university in a neighboring state. He has spent the last 18 months getting acquainted with the district and establishing himself with the board, the staff, and the community. He has acquired a reputation as an innovative, level-headed person, but there is some resentment about his appointment stemming from his being selected over two local candidates—one the African American principal of Lincoln School, the other the high school principal.

The superintendent has two assistants and a clerical staff of four to run the entire district. The void is filled somewhat by school principals, who assume more duties than are required by the normal course of school operations. This strategy has worked fairly well, but the superintendent is preparing to push for additional central office personnel in the upcoming budget year.

Two months ago, a notice from the State Department of Education arrived at the superintendent's office specifying that an evaluation of the teachers' aide program (which had been funded for a five-year period) was overdue. If the district wished to apply for continued funding of the program, it would have to demonstrate that the goals of the program had been met. The last sixty days have been spent reviewing the original grant proposal and examining how the program was set up and operated. A central office review of the program indicated that the former superintendent had indeed secured a grant for a teachers' aide program. Because Jefferson and Lincoln were the only two grammar schools at the time the grant was secured, all the aides had been placed in those schools, where they remained. The office staff vaguely remembered that the former superintendent, now deceased, had two motivations: first to preserve racial harmony in the district, and second to run "some sort of experiment."

The Department of Education wants to know how well the program is achieving its stated goals. The program calls for an aide in the classroom so that (1) the teacher can spend less time on administrative duties and more on teaching, (2) classroom discipline can be improved by the addition of another adult, and (3) students can receive more individualized attention in math and reading. All this was supposed to improve the educational experience and provide maximum educational benefits for the dollars spent.

The present superintendent has called a meeting of the two central office professionals and the principals of the four Sorghum grammar schools. The purpose of the meeting is to determine how to proceed in light of the following facts:

1. The district intends to reapply for the funding.

2. The superintendent wants to know whether there is a better way to distribute the aides.

3. There is a $10,000 in a contingency fund that could be expended on the evaluation, but the superintendent would prefer to spend the funds on books for the library.

4. It is hoped that the evaluation will demonstrate program success, which will support the request for additional funds from the board in the upcoming budget year.

Group Exercise

Using the background provided in this case:

1. Define the audience of the evaluation.
2. Determine whether the evaluation should be internal or external.
3. Specify the goals of the program.
4. Devise an appropriate evaluation design.
5. Identify the indicators you will use to determine program success.
6. Specify the control mechanisms you will employ as necessary.
7. Rough out an appropriate design using *X*s and *O*s (see chapter 7), and tell why this strategy is preferable to others.

Be prepared to defend your recommendations to the superintendent.

Case 14. Continuity and Change

The San Clarisimo Unified School District serves an affluent suburb in northern Los Angeles County. Over the years, the district has vigorously resisted being annexed into larger districts and participation in any busing or other programs that might dilute its student base of high-performing, middle-class, native-English speakers. District performance on the state-wide Stanford Achievement test has consistently ranked in the 98th (the top) percentile for all elementary grades. District performance is so good that skeptics accuse its teachers of "teaching to the test" rather than teaching overall academic skills. Similarly, 80% of San Clarisimo high school students taking the Scholastic Achievement Test (SAT) score in the top 25% nationwide. These scores make San Clarisimo students competitive for admission to elite colleges and universities.

The majority of residents are registered Republicans who voted for John McCain in 2008 by a margin of 68%, despite the fact that Barack Obama carried California. Residents were enthusiastic when former President Bush announced his No Child Left Behind initiative. Mostly, they thought it was a good idea for other people. After all, San Clarisimo students did not need improvement or a change of testing standards. The five-member school board, however, included three politically ambitious Republicans who thought that rich districts like theirs must show their support for the initiative, even though the district was unlikely to reap much in the way of supplemental federal funding to "bring up their scores."

The board has decided that San Clarisimo will participate, but they want assurances that student performance under the new testing system will not slip from its current top level. They instruct district administrators to continue giving the Stanford test for an additional two years while the new system comes online. They further instructed officials to report the findings on the new test in a manner that will allow them to make meaningful comparisons with the Stanford results over time. Ideally, they want the data integrated into a common reporting system so they could track results overtime. Design a system to achieve this end.

The Obama administration altered a rigid application of the standards of the No Child Left Behind Act. The decision was a disappointment to the board because the district's student testing indicated that San Clarisimo had consistently met the goal of 100% proficiency in reading and math since before the inception of No Child Left Behind. Now the board wants to become eligible for "Race to the Top" funding grants from the federal government.

Group Exercise

Your task is to:

1. Draft a memo to the board that tactfully explains the district's ineligibility based on past performance.

2. Word the memo in the most diplomatic terms possible, praising the board's leadership and initiative.

3. Take this opportunity to propose dropping the double testing program.

Case 15. Cutback Management

Porno Valley, California, is a community of 300,000 persons located thirty-five miles southeast of Los Angeles. The city boasts a major steel manufacturing plant and several smaller manufacturing enterprises and acts as a bedroom community to a number of other industrial centers in southern California.

Porno Valley has a council-manager form of government. The city manager, who has occupied the position for fifteen years, enjoys adequate working relations with the council despite several major disagreements over funding for nonessential services. (A nonessential service, from the point of view of council hardliners, is anything not having to do directly with police, fire, garbage, sewer and water, or city maintenance services.)

One program that has come under particular scrutiny as a nonessential service is the fifteen-year-old tuition assistance program that helps city employees take courses applicable to their jobs. The courses may be vocational, managerial, or professional, and the program will pay for any expense that can be applied to an employee's job, whether or not the employee applies the course toward an academic degree. A cursory check of the records revealed that less than 40% of the city's employees participated in the program over its fifteen-year existence.

This program has come under direct attack by council militants as a giant bureaucratic boondoggle that does not serve the needs of the community. They claim to have proof that tuition assistance has resulted in a building full of public employees who cheat the city out of a full day's work. Public employees, especially managers, are said to waste their days preparing for courses and cheat the city by using city clerical services for preparing term papers. The militants have called for the firing of any employee so abusing the program.

The city manager likes the tuition assistance program. He believes that the benefits of the program far outweigh any minor instances of program abuse. He is convinced that the program is useful and rewarding for employees and the city, and he favors this program for nostalgic reasons: Tuition assistance was his first managerial innovation when he came to Porno Valley.

The tuition assistance program has some council support. Two members of the council are strong supporters of the manager. One, a dentist, was instrumental in the initial hiring of the manager. The other is a progressive business manager of a large electronics assembly plant. Two other members of the council generally tend to vote in support of the manager. Both have privately expressed their willingness to go along with anything the manager thinks necessary to sustain current service levels and balance the budget, insofar as possible. Publicly, however, they are reluctant to enter into open confrontation with the three militants.

The manager does not wish to spend a lot of money to evaluate a program that costs only $25,000 per year. He contacts the local university, where a public administration professor agrees to make the evaluation of the program a project for his methods class.

Group Exercise

Develop an evaluation strategy to address the above issues. What kinds of data are available that would facilitate an evaluation? What kinds of additional data must be generated in order to evaluate the program? What evaluation design could facilitate realistic comparison between program participants and nonparticipants? Who is the probable audience for the data? What format will best serve the needs of the evaluation audience?

The evaluation team must determine whether the charges of the council militants are true. It must also determine whether there are appreciable benefits from the program to the city which can be used to justify the program's continuation. If employees had to choose, how would the tuition assistance program stack up against other benefits such as parking, health care, and the payment of professional memberships? Are there any differences between employees who have currently or formerly participated in the program and employees who have not participated? Is it worthwhile surveying supervisors on the relative performance of participants and nonparticipants? Begin your efforts by applying an outcome evaluation to the ongoing program.

Exercises in Budgeting and Program Planning

Case 16. Roads, Rails, Trams, and Trains: An Exercise in Cost-Benefit Analysis

California voters have long exercised their collective will through the initiative and referendum processes. An initiative is placed on the ballot by grassroots petitions. Interest groups solicit signatures from registered voters in shopping malls and other public places. Once passed, these propositions are binding on elected officials unless opponents can mount successful constitutional challenges to the content. A referendum, on the other hand, is a process whereby the legislature seeks voter approval for public policy initiatives. Referenda may be required by law, such as when officials wish to issue bonds or raise taxes.

The most famous initiative was the 1978 Proposition 13 that strictly limited possible increases in residential property taxes. This limitation dismantled the ability of local elected officials to fund government activities from roads to schools. Funding for public schools shifted primarily to the state, because local revenues simply could not keep pace with demand. In 1988, school supporters used the initiative process to fix the percentage of state funding that must go to public schools (kindergarten through the community-college level). Legislators may grant schools a larger percentage but may not fund them at less than 40%. Proposition 13 contained another troubling provision that required a two-thirds majority vote of the people for any new tax. Ironically, Proposition 13, which passed by less than 60%, cannot be repealed by less than 66.6%.

The state's vaunted freeway system and other road construction projects have been particularly impacted by all these limitations on public spending. Competition for road construction funds is intense. Resentment is particularly high in the state's rural counties that simply lack the legislative clout to compete with the delegations from Los Angeles and the Bay Area. All road repairs and construction in rural Placer County, for example, could be accomplished for the price of one mile of freeway construction in Los Angeles County.

Local leaders are at liberty to fund new road construction from their own existing resources. They are also at liberty to put their own political careers at risk by trying to persuade voters to raise local property or sales taxes to fund new construction. Wise politicians do so only for critical needs or projects that benefit a sufficient number of voters to warrant a get-out-the-vote effort. Such levies work best when tax increases are for a limited duration and for very specific projects. Projects also stand a better chance of passing if they can be sold as cost effective.

Normally, public works projects are initiated before taxes are collected to pay for them. Local governments borrow the funds by issuing bonds that are sold to investors at a favorable rate of interest. Even though these rates are normally lower than what corporations must pay, the security of government issues and their status as exempt from federal taxes make them attractive investments. Exactly how much interest must be paid is driven by the market. The amount of debt carried by a government entity also influences the rate it must pay, much the way individuals' creditworthiness impacts the amount they must pay for credit. These realities of the credit market further inhibit decision makers from undertaking projects lightly.

A combination of shrinking state resources and exploding populations in San Clemenza County brought the board of supervisors face to face with the risky necessity of seeking voter approval for locally funded transportation construction. In the previous ten years, the population had grown by 30%. The computer revolution had brought the county dynamic new industries and jobs. The resulting prosperity brought about increasing demand for new single-family homes. The new industries spread across the county because cities were hungry to attract new industries and the jobs they create. Industrial property values, moreover, are exempt from Proposition 13 tax limitations.

The new housing occurred primarily in the southern end of the county where open space made construction possible. The county is primarily situated in a valley, which inhibits expansion of housing. Environmentalists, moreover, successfully passed an initiative limiting new construction on the hillsides of the eastern part of the county. Expansion northward is impossible due to county lines and existing urban sprawl. To the west are the coastal mountains that are prohibitively steep for large construction.

The southern end of the county is bisected by a low range of hills that has caused development in the western and eastern quadrants to be largely independent. In the 1980s, the first surge of housing construction occurred in the southwestern quadrant. Traffic moved at a snail's pace as residents used limited roadways to get from their homes to northern-county jobs.

The Board of Supervisors responded to the traffic problem with a ballot proposition known as Measure A that called for a temporary tax to build an expressway that intersected the county from southwest to northeast. The expressway also passed through the center of the county's largest city. Measure A also called for funding a light rail system that linked the southwest quadrant to the northeast and northwest quadrants, again passing through the civic center of the largest city. Frustrated commuters and other growth advocates gave the supervisors the two-thirds majority mandate to build the expressway and light rail line.

By raising the local funds, the county became eligible for state and federal matching funds that covered approximately 50% of the costs. The expressway quickly filled, and slow-and-go traffic conditions returned. The light rail never reached its hoped-for potential because many commuters refused to give up the convenience of their personal cars. A follow-up citizen survey cited convenience as the principal reason for not using public transportation. Respondents also noted the difficulty of getting from the station to the actual work site or home, and they complained of a lack of parking at the light rail stations.

Matters were further complicated by recent industry migration into the southeastern quadrant of the county. Thus, traffic jammed in both directions as northern and central county residents began working in the southeastern county. Of course, all these problems could be solved if workers would live where they work. However, the unwillingness to do so is more pronounced among freeway-oriented Californians than elsewhere in the nation.

In 2010 the supervisors decided that transportation slowdowns must be addressed despite the fact that the budget had to be cut in the previous three years due to downturns in the economy. In 2011 the economy began to recover ahead of the rest of the country although the new revenues would do little more than restore previous cuts. Supervisors reasoned that, if sales tax revenues were on the upswing and unemployment was down, voters might again authorize a transportation bond issue. The supervisors have instructed the representatives of their staffs to work closely with employees of the transportation agency to come up with a formula that will solve the transportation problem and be acceptable to two-thirds of the voters.

The problems of the transportation planners are further complicated by a newly emerging political coalition primarily made up of Latino residents of the east-central quadrant of the county. Currently there is no light rail service to this area, despite the high probability that these low-income residents would use the service more than do the more affluent residents of the suburbs. This relatively cheap five-mile extension proposed by the coalition is advocated as a matter of equity. Extending the service will realistically link these neighborhoods to high-paying jobs located throughout the county. Critics note, however, that the voting rate in this area is about 16%, while citizens in the northern and southwestern quadrants vote at a rate of above 80%. Despite all these negatives the board decides to press ahead with a "shovel ready" project eligible for federal infrastructure grants. The proposals are as follows:

1. Build an eighteen-mile freeway from the northwest quadrant to the southeast quadrant.

2. Build a ten-mile light rail extension into the southeast quadrant from the central linkage point.

3. Build an additional twelve-mile extension of the light rail into the northeast quadrant to connect with other rail transportation systems of neighboring counties.

4. Convert the current twelve-mile expressway from the southwest quadrant into a full-blown freeway and extend it to twelve miles into the northeast quadrant.

5. Build a five-mile light rail extension from the central linkage point into the east-central neighborhoods. The per-mile costs of the various components are:

   a. Cost of light rail per mile, including station construction—$28 million

b. Cost of new freeway construction with on ramps—$30 to $50 million per mile, depending on whether the freeway is located in open spaces or urban areas (Because the areas to be traversed are 70% urban, the cost per mile is $44 million.)

c. Cost of converting existing expressway—$18 million per mile

Roughly 50% of all the above costs can be shifted to the state and federal government through matching transportation grants. The phase-one changes contained in Measure A cost county taxpayers $450 million. Increased property values, inflation, and construction costs have since driven up the costs. If all the proposals are included, the amount the county will have to raise is $990 million. The chairperson of the board indicates that a two-thirds majority vote will not be realistic for a proposal that costs more than $750 million.

_____

Group Exercise

1. Come up with a transportation proposal totaling no more than $750 million including funds raised in the bond issue and the matching 50% federal and state funds.

2. Decide what costs can be included in the proposal and what should be left to future decision makers. Be prepared to justify your figures economically, politically, and in terms of equity.

3. Be sure that your assessment reflects realistic probabilities that commuters will use the services you propose.

4. Be prepared to justify the deferments you recommend.

Case 17. Developing Assumptions and Placing One's Bets

Much of higher education funding in the Midwestern state of Bliss is produced from a well-head tax on oil production—that is, producers are taxed on each barrel of oil they produce. Because the costs are largely passed on to consumers in other states, the well-head tax is very popular within the state. The president of the Bliss State University is told by her crackerjack staff that there is a direct correlation between the price of West Texas Light Sweet Crude (the type produced in the state of Bliss) and the university budget.

- A $1.00 change in the price per barrel results in a 2% change in state funding for the university. This figure was arrived at by tracking funding for the last 15 years. The analysts assure the president that they are 90% confident in this number.

- Current state funding from the well-head tax is $56 million, or 58% of the budget. Another $40 million, or 42% of the current budget, comes from student fees and research grants for a total of $96 million in the current year.

- The current state-level certification is for $98 per barrel.
- As of today, the price per barrel is $101.
- Social uprisings in several Middle East petroleum-producing countries suggest an upward movement in price. How much is anyone's guess.

The president has several projects she would like to advance, should extra funding become available. One is in the College of Petroleum Engineering that would provide consulting services to the oil industry on a per fee basis. Another in the College of Humanities would create a series of university-funded literary meetings that would bring noted scholars on various literary figures to the university during the summer to conduct seminars and workshops. A third project would create an Institute for the Study of Politics and the Media in the Journalism School. Each of the projects would create endowed professorial chairs to lead the efforts. Filling these chairs with leading scholars would greatly enhance the university's prestige. The sooner the projects are undertaken, the sooner the university will begin to reap the ensuing rewards. The table below illustrates the impacts of the various budget options listed in the left-hand column under several possible prices (the unknown factor).

Group Exercise

1. Study the chart and make a recommendation to the president on what sort of funding to plan for.
2. Discuss the benefits of guessing right and the pitfalls of guessing wrong.
3. Based on the numbers, how confident should you as an analyst be in your recommendations?
4. Remember that unspent surpluses will likely be recaptured by the state legislature and are therefore as potentially damaging as the deficits that would come from choosing incorrectly.

Table A-1   Impact of Various Budget Options under Several Price Options

	Price Option		
Budget Option	**$98 per barrel**	**$101 per barrel**	**$105 per barrel**
No change in budget	0	$3.36 surplus	$7.84 surplus
Budget 5% increase	$2.8 deficit	$.56 surplus	$5.04 surplus
Budget 8% increase	$4.48 deficit	$1.12 deficit	$3.36 surplus

All impacts in millions

Glossary

accreditation   Certification from a professional association that the program in question meets the standards for program quality and operational procedures. Very often, accreditation is required for a program or agency to be eligible for payments from third-party payers such as insurance companies or government agencies.

advocacy planning   A type of planning that presupposes the value of a single policy outcome (e.g., service to a specific neighborhood) as opposed to approaching problems from a neutral perspective that does not champion any particular policy option or group.

audit   An examination of a program or project to verify that its implementation meets stated objectives and rules or regulations.

benefit-cost ratio   The ratio of benefits to costs, which provides decision makers with information on whether a program is economically viable.

business goodwill   An intangible asset that cannot be calculated like hard assets such as property, cash on hand, etc. In part it reflects the synergy among the various components of an enterprise that adds overall value. It may incorporate positive relations with customers and suppliers as well as a general positive reputation.

causal modeling   Constructing a theoretical process that "explains" events by identifying the direction of the change one phenomenon has on another and that can be tested with empirical data.

Congressional Budget Office   Created by the U.S. Congress in 1974 as part of an effort to improve its budget actions, the CBO provides staff support and computer-based analysis for the House and Senate members to help them anticipate and monitor the broad economic impacts of specific legislation.

control group   A group used as a point of reference for purposes of comparing the impact of the experimental condition on the experimental subjects. In experimental research the experimental and control groups may be identical through random assignment by the researcher to both groups. In nonexperimental studies, control groups are roughly equivalent to the study subjects (e.g., a similar city or a nearby school). Alternatively, the research findings are

233

compared to state or national data reports on findings of similar studies, especially when generic indicators are used.

correlation analysis   Systematic examination of certain phenomena usually expressed as data, to determine whether the phenomena are related or associated in the sense that when one phenomenon occurs the other also occurs.

cost-benefit analysis   An analytical framework for evaluating a program or project through a comprehensive assessment of both the advantages (profits) and disadvantages (costs) that would occur if the program were implemented. Applications range from a broad, conceptual evaluation to a quantitatively oriented comparison of specific projects.

cost-effectiveness analysis   A type of cost-benefit analysis in which the costs of the programs are assessed against the level of service rendered rather than economic benefits. Alternatively, if the benefits of the programs are identical, only the costs need to be compared.

Critical path method (CPM)   See PERT/CPM.

Delphi technique   Developed at the RAND Corporation, the Delphi technique attempts to improve the judgments of a group of experts by providing them with anonymity while they are asked questions about problems and issues. The group is then supplied with a summary of the results and asked to reconsider their original answers and justify or explain them if they do not move toward the consensus position that emerges. The process is repeated until a consensus is achieved.

discounting   The devaluing of benefit-to-cost ratio of a project to adjust for opportunity costs lost by selecting the project. The rate is normally determined by the cost of borrowing money at the time the program is initiated.

entropy   The second law of thermodynamics (entropy law) states that matter and energy can be changed only in one direction—from usable to unusable, or from order to disorder, or from available to unavailable, or from structure to chaos.

equity   A desirable distribution of goods and services to all members of a society through a just allocation of costs and benefits.

experimental design   A research model that utilizes random selection from the population of interest, control over the experimental variable or event, and a control group for comparing the performance or results with the experimental group.

experimental mortality   The loss of subjects from an experiment due to such factors as illness, lack of interest, or refusal to participate, which affects the comparability of results between the experimental and control groups.

externalities   The unintended and often unrecognized costs and benefits of a project which accrue to those outside the scope of a cost-benefit analysis. These costs and benefits are typically difficult to value in monetary units.

external validity   The extent to which measurements obtained in a particular situation or context can be generalized accurately to other situations or populations of interest.

Federal Register   Since 1936, the government has published a public record of every regulation and related amendments having legal effect that have been issued by federal agencies with congressional or presidential authority. The regulations and amendments for the preceding year are codified every January 1 into the *Code of Federal Regulations*.

genius forecasting   In contrast to highly computerized forecasting models, using experts to "brainstorm" how future events will occur in order to take advantage of the experts' knowledge, creativity, and intuition.

goal reification   Defining the goals of an ongoing program specifically for the purposes of designing an evaluation. The danger of goal reification is that the definitions can become so abstract that they make the subsequent findings of the evaluation meaningless to program officials.

Gross National Product (GNP)   A measure of the goods and services produced by the United States, aggregating personal consumption expenditures, gross private domestic investment, net exports of goods and services, and government purchases of goods and services.

history   Extraneous events, outside the control of a study but occurring between the first measurements and subsequent measures, which may have affected the results of the study.

impact analysis   A study that seeks to measure the effects of the program on the intended group or social problem defined by the legislature.

incommensurables   Costs and benefits stemming from completion of a project which appear to fall outside the typical measures used in the analysis, although they may be measurable in another context.

instrumentation   A loss in the effectiveness or consistency of the measuring instrument—for example, from change in the springs of a scale or changes in the observers or methods of scoring.

intangible effects   A term used in cost-benefit analysis to designate consequences that appear to be beyond quantitative or economic expression.

interaction effect   The effect of a combination of the threats to validity, which may be more significant than the individual threats.

interactive managerial audit   A review of actual and prescribed agency policies and procedures using reciprocal, cooperative relationships with program staff. Staff have ownership of prescribed changes and willingly implement adaptations flowing from the audit.

internal rate of return   The discount rate that would reduce the present value of a project under consideration to zero.

internal validity   The extent to which an indicator or set of indicators accurately measures the concept or variable in the situation or population of interest in a particular study.

market pricing   Pricing or valuation based on the interaction of buyers and sellers as they exchange goods without artificial or arbitrary restrictions.

matched-pairs designs   Designs in which individuals or units under study are assigned in pairs to control and experimental groups according to characteristics that they hold in common. For example, one might match fourth-grade boys on the basis of reading scores.

maturation   Any natural change in subjects during a study period, such as aging or learning, which was not caused by the study itself but may have affected the results.

multiple regression technique   A quantitative approach used to determine how well two or more events together seem to predict the occurrence of another event, either singly through use of statistical controls or together.

multiple treatment interference   The effect of applying multiple treatments to the same respondents, thus precluding an assessment of the impact of any one treatment.

mutual-control designs   Research designs in which subjects of one experiment are used as the control group of another experiment, and vice versa. The experimental conditions must be different and the evaluator must be sensitive to the elapsed time between phases of the experiments to avoid the threat of maturation.

net present value   A number representing the current value of a potential project after the stream of costs and benefits expected to occur over the project life are discounted and aggregated.

nonequivalent control group design   When random assignment to groups is not possible, individuals or groups with characteristics similar to those of the participants in the program or experiment are used as controls.

nonexperimental designs   Research designs that do not account for or control for alternative explanations for the change that may occur, for example, before-and-after studies of a program or an after-only study. These are particularly useful for descriptive purposes and for obtaining insights about ongoing programs.

nongovernmental organizations   Private, not-for-profit organizations that provide important public services. National examples include the American Red Cross and the March of Dimes. International examples include Doctors without Boarders, OXFAM, and C.A.R.E. On a much smaller scale, locally operated programs like Meals on Wheels (which provides home food deliveries to the elderly) receive their funding from local government grants as well as private donations. The example in this book, the Pacific Rim Foundation, receives funds from private contributors, The US Agency for International Development (USAID), and other charitable groups.

Office of Management and Budget   Formerly the Bureau of the Budget, the OMB is the division of the Executive Office of the President with primary responsibility for preparing the executive budget presented to Congress.

outcome evaluation   Sometimes referred to as summative evaluation, this type of evaluation measures the degree to which a program has succeeded in achieving the goals prescribed in its legislative mandate or mission statement. This includes measures of outcomes, whether the program accomplished what it promised, and impact analyses that ask whether the program affected the target population in the manner intended.

participant-observer approach   An evaluation method in which observers take an active part in the situation under study in order to record events with more insight.

process evaluation   Sometimes known as formative evaluation, this type of evaluation examines program forms of organizations, policies, and procedures to determine whether they are consistent with standards prescribed by accrediting agencies or overhead administrative offices. The latter could include whether the agency adheres to prescribed procurement and contracting procedures.

process intervention   This diagnostic and prescriptive approach is an outgrowth of the field known as organizational development. Interventions may be organization wide or limited to a single program component or operating unit. This involves planned change to improve productivity or operations quality.

pecuniary benefits and costs   Terms used in cost-benefit analysis to distinguish external and financially related effects stemming from completion of a particular project, such as an increase or decrease in the cost of goods or services that depends on the project output.

program validity   An evaluation design that has program validity utilizes indicators to test program outputs and statistical manipulations that are understandable to program officials. The reports of such evaluations should provide information that is useful in upgrading program performance.

PERT/CPM   Program evaluation review technique/critical path method is a planning device for managing time and resource allocations to complete projects on time and within budgets. It is linear and sequential. All events in a PERT/CPM chart that precede an activity on a line must be completed before the activity can commence.

project calendar   A device used to plot the time frame in which various components of a project are to be complete. It may also illustrate the points at which various expenditures must be met.

proximate indicators   Used as surrogates for the actual completion of a program goal, they measure progress toward goals rather than the goals themselves. For example, customer satisfaction is a proximate indicator of service quality.

queuing theory/flowcharts   A variety of systems applications used to diagram the flow of work or decisions through the organization. This allows managers to assess organization procedures for appropriateness and efficiency.

random selection   A sampling process through which individuals in the population of interest have an equal chance of being chosen and in which the choice of one individual has no effect on the choice of any other individual.

responsibility matrix   A management control tool whereby the duties of specific individuals in carrying out planned changes are juxtaposed against the various components of the change strategy.

risk-benefit analysis   A type of cost-benefit analysis in which the negative consequences of a project or program are measured in terms of the types and magnitude of risks to individuals or to communities instead of in monetary units.

selection bias   Occurs when random sampling or matching for ensuring comparable experimental and control groups is not feasible and subjects are chosen in a manner that might affect the results.

sensitivity analysis   A slight varying of the values of parameters or variables in a model in order to see the effect of such changes on the outcome, particularly useful when there is uncertainty about the accuracy of the data used for the analysis.

shadow pricing   Approximate valuations of true values for goods and services used by analysts when there is no market for the good or service, a situation which exists for many public projects. Shadow pricing is accomplished by substituting the value of a similar good for the actual good being considered—for example, substituting the cost of renting an hour's use of a private tennis court for the value of an hour's use of a court in a public park.

solomon four-group design   An experimental design that addresses the problem of external validity by controlling for both testing effects and for interaction effects between testing and treatment. This design uses the pretest-posttest with and without treatment and the posttest only with and without treatment.

standards   The objective criteria against which program performance will be judged. Standards may be generated by licensing agencies, engineered by program staff, or imposed by third-party payers as a condition of payment.

statistical regression   If study subjects are initially selected because of extreme scores, their scores on the subsequent measures can be expected to move inward toward the mean score. This is known at statistical regression.

structural functionalism   Talcott Parsons' theoretical framework for approaching problem solving, which suggests that structures (hierarchies, social classes, departmentalization) can best be understood and explained by looking at the functions they serve in the broader context.

suboptimization   Utilization or management of resources in a less than optimum or less than efficient way.

subsystems   The operational components of a system, characterized by specific structures that are initiated to carry out particular functions.

suprasystems   The larger, interrelated entity of which a system is a part. For example, an academic department is a subsystem of the university college suprasystem; the suprasystem for the college is the university.

tangible effects   A term used in cost-benefit analysis to designate consequences that can be identified and measured in some fashion.

testing effects   The effects that the initial act of testing or measuring a subject's performance can have on subsequent tests or measures.

time-series design   The extension of the basic pretest-posttest design to repeated measures of a particular set of variables or individuals, usually characterized by a specific time interval.

trend extrapolation   A common mathematical method of forecasting the future, assuming that the future will repeat the past—that the variables that have caused changes in the past will continue to cause changes in the future; if a trend can be identified (e.g., the cost of providing a service over time), planners can project future costs.

welfare economics   A branch of economics concerned with providing a method of evaluating the social gain or loss stemming from economic changes. Theories of welfare economics have been constructed using individual preferences and social preferences.

Index